THE

NEW PRACTICE OF

SUPERVISION AND

STAFF DEVELOPMENT

THE
NEW PRACTICE
OF
SUPERVISION
AND
STAFF
DEVELOPMENT

A SYNERGISTIC

APPROACH

Paul Abels

ASSOCIATION PRESS   NEW YORK

International Standard Book Number: 0–8096–1919–9
Library of Congress Catalog Card Number: 76–56176

Library of Congress Cataloging in Publication

Abels, Paul, 1928–
The new practice of supervision and staff development.

Includes bibliographical references and index.
1. Supervision of social workers.   I.   Title.
HV41.A25   658.3′02   76–56176
ISBN 0–8096–1919–9

Printed in the United States of America
Designed by The Etheredges

To those who know me best
and know how to help me:

My wife Sonia Leib Abels
and daughters
Barbara, Abigail and Beth

CONTENTS

PREFACE

Although this is a book which encompasses the supervisory relationship, its primary concern is social practice. From the beginnings of our identifiable social work profession as "overseers of the poor" to our most recent steps toward an ecological and transactional paradigm, supervision has followed the practice themes. It has progressed from supervisor as *overseer* to supervisor as *counselor*, to supervisor and supervisee in a reciprocal transaction within an agency system amid a broader environment.

It is natural for innovation in practice to come from the practitioner. The front-line people are always exposed to the stress of practice and to the need of finding ways to alter paradigms toward greater effectiveness. The practitioners are likewise most likely to be in touch with new trends in the field as they review their colleagues' work. Does this mean, however, that supervision must always follow the lead of the practitioner? that it must be reactive rather than proactive? The purpose of supervision is to enable the worker to grasp a more holistic view of the situation, i.e., to see that he, the client and the agency are involved in a drama that must be played out; but the drama can be altered only if all parties can examine their parts in the drama. A tragic ending is avoidable if a change in one role is sympathetic to the modifications which will have to be made in the rest of the script.

This book suggests that there is an important role for supervision and staff development beyond the traditional administrative support system—the role of supervisor as synergist, one who helps unite divergent views, and who helps locate new knowledge so that it can be synthesized with the old into a greater whole. He explores and synergizes internal conflicts for workers related to their values, their confusions and conflicts with clients, with other professions, and with the goals or policies of the agency. There are uncertainties which keep people from learning and doing, and thus from growing, but also certainly can likewise inhibit effectiveness. A narrow approach or a rigid model can create a rejecting environment for those whose ideas may differ.

The changing models of supervision reflect our changing understandings of what the nature of the relationships among people needs to be. The models change not because they are better, but because the times demand the new approach. It is natural to assume that when the person was seen as a machine that breaks down, supervision would reflect that model. We are now entering the ecological and holistic periods of our profession's development, and supervisory roles need to reflect these more synergistic concepts. One uses what is effective for the times. Models from earlier periods will still be valuable, but will not be as effective as the new, for the new models recognize the interdependence and interrelationship of people with each other and their environment in a way which has not been generally conceptualized since earlier periods of human development. Primitive cultures, alchemists, native Americans—and now systems analysts and ecologists—are just a few of the groups which have recognized the close relationship of humans with all elements in the environment. This book is concerned with those approaches which help people see their relationships with one another, and help them understand the importance of mutual aid in the accomplishment of learning. Synergistic approaches move people to unity and minimize the statuses and differences that separate them. It is these approaches upon which this book builds its inquiry along with its hopes for the future of our profession and the people it serves.

THE
NEW PRACTICE OF
SUPERVISION AND
STAFF DEVELOPMENT

CHAPTER 1

SUPERVISION:

A CHANGING PROCESS

We must go very, very carefully at first. The great serpent to destroy is the will to Power: the desire for one man to have some dominion over his fellow-men. Let us have no personal influence, if possible—no personal magnetism, as they used to call it, nor persuasion—no "Follow me"—but only "behold."

D. H. LAWRENCE

INTRODUCTION

Throughout this country, in virtually every profession, there is a growing concern with the educational preparation, continuing education, supervision, and overall effectiveness of its members and practitioners.

The future of any profession depends not only on its ability to transmit its knowledge and values to new members but also on its being open to new ideas and new knowledge. Supervision has recently come to be viewed as a necessary evil—at best a source of idea testing, at worst a block to creativity and a bottleneck to autonomous practice.

My view is that in social work supervision is part of the life stream of our profession, a source of wealth to a worker—under the right conditions. We have taken the easy way out: we have maintained supervision as we learned it fifty, thirty, or ten years ago. Supervisors have not only failed to reconstruct our profession but also they have been content to be accepted by staff as a fixed entity, not a source of dynamic learning.

Human service practice has benefited from exposure to new approaches to helping: gestalt psychology, transactional analysis, encounter groups, yoga, Zen, behavior modification, and reality therapy. Have these modified supervisory practice or merely met supervisor acceptance?

There are changing techniques of supervising, administrating, and teaching, and there are new views: some brand-new, like learning contracts and values clarification, some ancient, like the tao, or the Sufi teaching stories. We shall examine new approaches in supervision and staff development to assess and integrate some of them into a direction that supervisors can accept as a project for the future.

In preparing this book, I attempted to maintain a balance between theoretical concerns and practical application. I felt that it would make sense for there to be a book on staff development and supervision which could be used by students who might in the next few years find themselves in supervisory positions, as well as by those who were currently practicing supervision and might want some fresh views on supervisory practice. Both the theory and the practice, however, are oriented toward a style of supervision which we will refer to as synergistic-normative. If we could create the best of all possible practice worlds, what would we want of the supervisory relationship? What would we expect of the administrator? How would we go about improving our practice?

These are the themes that will appear repeatedly throughout. I hope the melody will become so familiar that you may feel that you wrote the lyrics. In fact, you did. The ideas have come from countless discussions with workers, students, and supervisors who have worried over what they were doing to others as well as how they themselves were being treated. Many had had good experiences, but most felt that supervision was at best a necessary evil which was too much a part of the human service profession. No doubt what they say is partially true. You can be assured that as you read this passage, somewhere people are meeting to discuss ways in which a probation officer, social worker, aide, nurse, street worker, job counselor, teacher, psychologist, or (you fill in your specialty) might be more effective in their practice.

The odds are also high that the people involved in the transactions are eager to come up with helpful approaches. And many will: some by chance, some because they have the training and experience in supervision which can help them do their job effectively. The purpose of this book is not to furnish solutions to supervisory problems, but to examine the processes of reaching "good" solutions.

A great deal of the literature on supervision has been of two types: (1) How to supervise, and (2) What's wrong with supervision. Although these have frequently offered important insights into supervisory practice, too often they have skimmed over some other very important considerations. For example, supervision for what? Why bother with the superstructure in the first place? Why become involved in a process that by most reports leaves people unfulfilled, uncertain, and often dependent? Very few current articles on supervision have spoken of its glories. Current modes of supervision do not seem satisfying. The reasons may be that we have lost sight of why we supervise, or perhaps we may be holding on to practices that no longer fit current life-styles. These dilemmas will be dealt with in this volume not as theoretical concepts to be meditated on, but as concepts to be thought about and acted upon. We are suggesting that underlying the supervisory purpose should be a social goal. Indeed the supervisor can play an important role in restructuring our profession.

Following establishment of our vision of the field of supervision and staff development, we will examine some of the historical developments leading to current supervisory practice. This will be followed by consideration of the normative-synergistic approach to engaging individuals and groups in the supervisory process. One chapter is devoted to staff development techniques as separate from supervision, and the conclusion pulls together synergistic approaches to innovative learning in the agency.

The recognition of its accountability to the community for quality service has led to a culture of supervision and staff development within the human service agencies, reaching back to the attempts of the charity organization societies to influence practice and of the agencies to be more scientific in their delivery of services.

One of the major tasks facing any of the mental health–human service agencies is the delivery of services to people in an effective, comprehensive, and competent manner. In order to provide these community services, the agencies require varied cadres of staff, with a wide range of skills, experience, and education.

The training of social workers is probably one of the more important internal problems in social welfare today. It is directly tied to the ability of social work to deliver service to the community. At the heart of all supervision and staff development programs is the idea of innovation: people being helped to learn new ways and use new ideas to help people or to change agency practice. Supervision is innovation.

Social welfare requires a trained group of workers available to offer services to the client. But over 75 percent of the social welfare workers in the United States will have no initial training in social work beyond what they get on the job. Staff development programs play a significant role in agency service and consume precious resources. For example, the state of New York estimates that it costs $5,000 to train a new worker in the welfare department.[1] If the person is not helped to do the job properly or leaves because of conflict with supervisor or administrator, not only is there a financial cost to the agency but also a psychological and social cost to all parties as well.

STAFF DEVELOPMENT: A SYSTEMS VIEW

Staff development is the total planned process by which the staff member is helped to understand the agency, carry out his function, and improve the agency's capacity to serve the client.

> It is an over-all program related to the development of the practices of all staff—social service, clerical, and ancillary personnel—that directly or indirectly affect services to individuals, groups, or the community. Broadly defined, staff development may aim toward improving the attitudes of staff, encouraging them to think and make sound judgments, and supporting their desire to learn.[2]

The mechanisms which an agency develops as a means of orienting its staff, providing help in delivering services, and helping the worker learn how to maximize his work with the clients, no matter how simple or complex the mechanisms may be, are all subsumed under the general concept of staff development. The growing impact of systems theory has helped us see the interrelatedness of all parts of the system and the impact of any part on the whole. It helps us recognize that the interactions of staff at all levels, along with clients and board, will determine the type of staff development program that an agency can maintain. Furthermore, the impact of the staff development program on the staff will be related to the degree of interaction and involvement of all levels of staff in both the planning and execution of the program.

What do we mean by *system?* Simply, we suggest, that system is a set of bounded interacting parts coordinated for the accomplishment of a goal. An open social system is a grouping of people who are within conceptual or actual boundaries (community, classroom, profession) and whose interventions on each other matter.

Almost all systems writers will agree that a system is a set of parts coordinated to accomplish a set of goals.[3] Social systems are always open. They can be affected by environmental forces.

They can change. Among the major characteristics of open systems itemized by Katz and Kahn are:

1. *Boundaries,* which define the system from nonsystem.
2. *Importation of energy:* the inputs (staff, funds, clients).
3. The *throughput:* transformation of this energy into a product (the work, or process).
4. The *output:* the service results.
5. Information *input, negative feedback,* and the *coding process:* systems obtain information such as negative feedback and this can be used by the system to adjust itself (an evaluation from the client that he doesn't feel he is getting help is negative feedback).
6. The *steady* state and *dynamic homeostasis:* the tendency to maintain some balance or equilibrium within the system while the system modifies itself.
7. *Entropy:* the imperative of all systems to run down. (Negative entropy is the attempt to maintain the system.)[4]

Ludwig von Bertalanffy, the generally accepted "father" of modern general system theory, acknowledges his development of system principles from the context of biological theory and its subsequent use in other fields including social work:

> The present writer has stated a number of "system principles," partly in the context of biological theory . . . However, . . . the main principles offered, such as wholeness, sum, centralization, differentiation, leading part, closed and open system, finality, equi-finality, growth in time, relative growth, competition, have been used in manifold ways (e.g., general definition of system types of growth; systems engineering; social work).[5]

Herein lies one of the cautions to be used in thinking about system theory: superimposing concepts from other mechanical and natural systems onto thinking people and thinking social systems can be problematic.[6] A person, as an open system, can alter goals and control his system inputs and outputs in ways impossible to other systems. Another problem relates to the location of the boundaries of the social system, both for analysis and practice. For example, each of the following can be considered an open system:

A SYSTEM | client-worker |

A SYSTEM | worker-supervisor |

A SYSTEM | client-worker-supervisor |

A SYSTEM | client-worker
supervisor-administrator |

A SYSTEM | clients-workers
supervisors-administrator
other staff |

OR

| clients-worker |

OR

| worker |

A SYSTEM
| Community |

A SYSTEM
| Agency as those things within the walls |

We can view each component as a link to the next component. Thus the administrator can serve as the system's link with the board, or with staff. The client is often a link to the community.

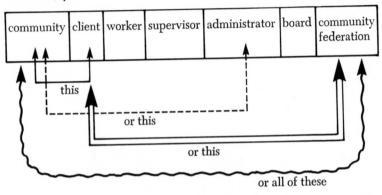

In addition, as a leading systems analyst states, "Systems are made up of sets of components that work together for the overall objective of the whole." [7] But do they always?

There is another way to look at system thinking.

Imagine the following scene. It takes place in New York City outside a welfare office. The time is 7:00 A.M., and although the office does not open until 8:30, the line started forming at 6:30. Since this has been occurring each day for the past few weeks and the neighbors have been complaining about the noise, there are now two or three police officers attempting to keep the line quiet. Their presence makes those waiting edgy. By 8:30, there are almost a hundred people shoving to enter as the doors open. About three hours later, a woman denied service, angered over a new regulation and having gone through a four-hour wait, demands to see a supervisor. She starts to yell and wants to hit the worker, but is fortunately held back by a friend. The woman is taken off to jail; the worker is distraught and is consoled by her supervisor and another worker. Other clients stand by and watch. The work continues, and a railing is installed to keep the clients three feet from the workers. The next day the welfare rights group pickets the agency.

Who or what is the system here? The client and worker? The policy makers and the staff? The community and the agency, the neighbors? Should the woman in prison still be counted as part of the system? Does the welfare department have any responsibility to her? Will the judge be concerned with her family? Figure 1 provides an overview of these interacting systems.

As Garrett Hardin has pointed out, it is impossible to do only one thing,[8] and in fact we should always be alert to the repercussions any action—however routine it may appear to us—might have. In the example above, a single change in a regulation had impact on the staff, the client, the community, the police, etc., etc. By attempting to anticipate these developments we can take full advantage of the insights of systems thinking.

Usually the boundaries of the action system are more closely defined: the worker and the client, the worker and his supervisor, and significant rules or procedures in the agency. Where people within the system are working for a common goal, there is clarity of effort, and the operation has a chance of success. Where the goals are not common, we have a nonsystem situation.

We know that in some systems in which we work, people like prisoners and guards, probationers and probation officers, and clients and workers do not have the same objectives. We can only use systems theory as a tool for understanding; we cannot expect to use it as we might use a piece of apparatus in the natural sciences.

THE SERVICE SYSTEM

In order to orient ourselves to staff development as an interrelated part of the total agency system we must place the staff development program in the context of the agency service system.

Staff development is a *planned approach to helping people* (elements of the agency system) *learn how to be of maximum service to the client system.* It assumes a number of intervention points in which innovations can occur. This may be in areas

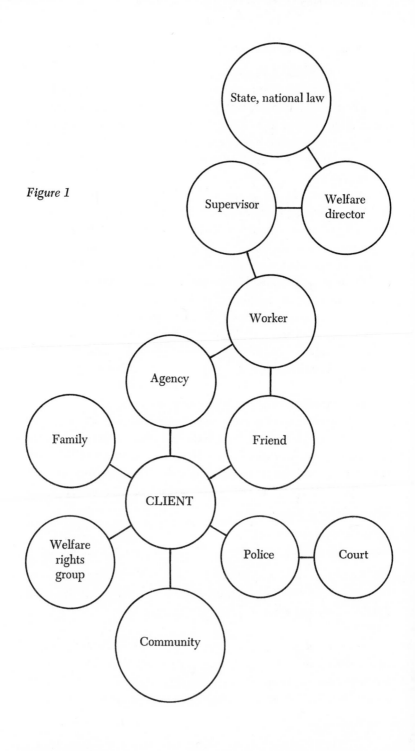

Figure 1

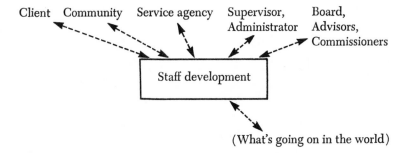

Client Community Service agency Supervisor, Board,
                                   Administrator Advisors,
                                                  Commissioners

Staff development

(What's going on in the world)

interfacing the service agent and client, the supervisor and service agent, the administrator and supervisor, or by and with the board. At all levels innovative thinking can change the agency service and better the community.[9]

THE ELEMENTS OF THE SYSTEM

The client. This element of the system generally refers to the person, group, or community segment which is seen as the target of help or change. Until recently, the importance of recognizing that the client was an important portion of the agency system was neglected. Requirements for client participation in programs and confrontations between agency and client have altered the entire approach to service planning and delivery.[10]

The community. The client does not exist in a vacuum. He is influenced to a great extent by the community. This element's views of the agency can have strong repercussions on whether or not a client will be willing to accept help from that particular agency. Often the staff development program will call for interpretation of community life and needs to other staff. Resources will be used from the community to help teach, and often community people will be employed as staff. These people will bring their biases and know-how, and will be vital sources of information to the agency.

The service agent, the worker. This term will refer to the person who works directly with the client, whether caseworker, group worker, community worker, generalist, indigenous, or untrained worker.

The staff development person or supervisor. The person given the responsibility for helping a worker perform his job more constructively. This may be through training programs or direct supervision. The person may be employed within the agency or hired as a consultant.

The program head or director. Primarily an administrative functionary who may or may not be a supervisor, branch director, or even the director of the agency.

The board or planning body. The responsible agents for the overall functioning of the agency, who generally delegate this work to a paid director.

These are the people who in addition to office and maintenance staff and miscellaneous other staff (business managers, publicity men) and the physical plant make up the organization or agency.

The agency. An organization can be viewed as an interrelated group of people bound by certain common goals and in communication with each other. The agency is a complex organization which may employ a number of people, many with specialized skills, who are there to carry out the major goal of the agency's existence—the provision of effective service.

In order to ready itself for service, a complex organization generally sets up chains of command and control, defines areas of responsibility, and attempts to assess its effectiveness. The structural chains are usually set up as bureaucratic hierarchies. Such a bureaucratic structure often becomes a self-perpetuating, reified entity in itself, and may actually interfere with adequate service. But bureaucratic structures are not bad in and of themselves, and in fact help the work of the agency get done effectively and with a minimum of red tape.

If the agency is to be successful, conditions must support staff development; and when we speak of agency support we run squarely into the area of agency administration. A good staff development program depends on sound administrative procedures being adhered to. Some of the important supports are:

Clear lines of authority, responsibility, and accountability, as well as *clear and open* channels of communication.

Adequate job descriptions and publicized personnel policies.

Clear production expectations and performance standards.

Salary scales adequate and equitable so that people who learn and acquire new skills can be rewarded.

Clarity of agency purpose, policies, and scope; clarity of units within the agency and interrelations.

Mechanics to influence the policies.

Provisions for staff development and supervision.

Climate which promotes independence and autonomy; desire to seek knowledge.

Means of staff participation in agency planning.

Most of this in writing.

We would hope, as well, that the agency would behave in a moral manner to the staff and to the clients. Abuse, neglect, or "cooling out" of the clients can only have a destructive, corrosive influence on the staff.[11]

The authority of supervisors and administrators falls into Weber's category of legal authority. According to Weber, obedience is not owed to anyone personally but to enacted rules and regulations which specify to whom and to what rule people owe obedience.[12] The person in authority, too, obeys a rule when giving an order—namely, "the law" or "rules and regulations," which represent both abstract norms and concrete policies.

In the social agency, the enacted rules and regulations are a set of standards drawn up by administrators to achieve optimum client service. One problem for administrators who are also professionals is related to differences in professional and administrative norms. Etzioni discusses this difference:

> The ultimate justification for a professional act is that it is, to the best of the professional's knowledge, the right act. He might consult his colleagues before he acts, but the decision is his. If he errs, he still will be defended by his peers. The ultimate justification of an administrative act, however, is that it is in line with the organization's rules and regulations, and that it has been approved—directly or by implication—by a superior rank.[13]

Not only is there a difference in the nature of authority, but there are differences between the administrative and professional cultures. Vinter neatly summarizes this point:

> The profession values skill rather than procedure, and service rather than routines. The agency, in contrast, interposes a variety of requirements relevant to the operation of a complex organization.[14]

Thus the social worker is caught between conflicting claims to his values and his loyalty and has to make some kind of adjustment.

For Wilensky and Lebeaux, the social worker suffers role conflict not only in terms of differing demands of the profession and the agency, but also in the clash between humanitarian values and agency and professional norms, and in terms of the discrepancies between agency and professional roles:

> The person caught in the cross-fire of competing claims typically makes some kind of adjustment: he tries to reshape the role or roles to make the demands compatible; he quits the role; he adapts to the role by playing up one set of obligations, playing down another, and so on.[15]

These same dilemmas confront the social work administrators, who are faced with major responsibilities for the functioning of the agency. Often they are given more power than they want, need, or should have because the staff would prefer to give up its administrative responsibilities. Nevertheless, the administrator should perceive his major function as that of facilitating the work of the agency, of making it possible for the staff to do the job they were hired for. In a sense he builds a hierarchy around a supervisory system to perform this function.

THE GOALS OF THE SYSTEM

The goals of the agency need to be related to the historic mandate of our profession: the building of a just society. The specific tasks of each agency will differ according to its own area of practice, but in general they would be (1) helping people arrive at sound judgments regarding what ought to be, all things considered; and (2) securing social arrangements and individual effectiveness in conformity with such judgments.

THE SUPERVISORY BASE

Although there will be a number of sections dealing with staff development tools and training, our major emphasis in this book will be on the supervisory process. Supervision has been the traditional tool within staff development for the ongoing day-to-day learning of the worker. Through focusing on supervisory transactions we will have grounded material for use in consideration of staff development approaches. In addition, the supervisory process may be one of the most important aspects of staff development, because:

1. All agencies—large and small, wealthy or poor, professional or novice—have some supervisory procedures.
2. A great deal of staff time is spent on that process.
3. The supervisor (aside from the client) is often a key figure in the work life of the worker.
4. The quality of service is linked to the ongoing ability of the agency to monitor its service. The supervisor and the worker are the direct agents of quality control. They are close to the service.
5. It permits an individualized approach to the learning needs of the worker.

Supervision has become such a natural part of the social work scene that schools of social work offer courses in supervision, staff development, consultation, and training. Continuing education programs attempt to upgrade the teaching and practice skills of all levels of practice, and the professional organizations provide guidelines—and in fact demand certain levels of practice.

Although agencies vary, staff expectations often demand that the span of control for the supervisor-supervisee relationship remain about one to five. Students graduating from schools of social work seek good supervision as one of the requirements for accepting a position. These expectations for supervision are socialized into the student during professional education.

Supervision is part and parcel of the helping profession. It would be natural to assume, therefore, that any interactive process demanding such a degree of time and energy would entail carefully thought-out processes and procedures on the part of the agency as well as special training in order to assure that the energies, funds, and time devoted to the improvement of agency practice are well spent. Toward that purpose there have been a number of attempts to bring together the content and procedures that would make for a sound approach to the teaching of the supervisory processes. Some of the classic texts still remain very helpful, but they are dated, not incorporating the different expectations that the young worker of today brings to the job. Work alienation has become a national concern and certainly must be avoided in our profession. New demands for autonomy and a critical stance toward authority have become ways of life among the youth of the sixties and seventies. Obviously the youth of the sixties are the supervisees of the seventies. Supervision, along with other elements of social work practice, needs to change as the style of human negotiation changes.

New texts must examine the new supervisory knowledge and evolving effective transactional styles. They must take into account the demands for "humanistic" and "status reduction" approaches in the workplace. This certainly is the purpose of this book. But in addition to exploring some of the range of style in supervision, we will focus on some of the modern trends which seem to be developing in maximizing the transactions that take place between people in any learning, teaching, or helping process. Although there may not be entirely unique differences in the supervisory processes in human services, schools, business, or industry, the least one might expect is that the processes in the human services arena bear allegiance to, and utilize some of the finest material available in, the interpersonal/human relations fields. We might add that since they are the leaders in the quest for human understanding and change, theirs might be the profession that brings an innovative approach to the battered vision of supervision.

THE ESSENCE OF SUPERVISION

Supervision is the process by which people assist each other in learning the skills, attitudes, and knowledge which they will need to perform their function in the agency in an effective and satisfying manner. In essence supervision is a consciousness-raising process, in which the awareness of all parties in the transaction is increased on behalf of effective practice.

Although traditionally we have assumed that supervision is a tutorial process in which a person with more experience or higher status assists the novice with his learning tasks, this is not necessarily the case. As we shall see, supervision may take place among a team of equals, or among those with different technical skills. And often new workers with fresh ideas and knowledge can offer the latest ideas, and the "open" experienced practitioner can also be "supervised."

Often a staff development specialist in a large agency will have less actual helping experience than many of the staff. What this person can offer in the supervisory process may be skill in helping people learn, techniques for "opening groups," or knowledge of new techniques. Admittedly the usual case will be that the more experienced, senior members of the staff will end up in the supervisory positions; but this need not be the only model, and in some cases may not be the most efficient model. It may rob the agency of its best practitioners, and at times may lead to serious problems for the supervisor, particularly if he is misfit in the role of supervisor.

The importance of supervision is not who does it but whether it is achieving the purpose for which it was developed. The purpose of supervision was and is to insure quality control by helping people learn the tasks they need to know in order to serve the client effectively. This is the basic task which should be the foundation of the supervisor-supervisee contract.

Supervision should provide the following aids to the worker:

1. An opportunity to learn the skills necessary to carry out his function.
2. Opportunities to explore the frame of mind for helping— the values, attitudes, and ethics of the helping person.
3. The support of a person with an "objective" or more disciplined, or more experienced, or "different view."
4. An opportunity to learn the theory and a knowledge base to support the skills and practice.
5. A buffer against which to test out ideas and to be tested in return.
6. A link in the agency through which accountability flows.
7. A link in the agency for both client advocacy and agency change.
8. A source for "quality control" in dealing with the demands for effective practice.
9. A milieu in which scientific thinking is the life-style.
10. An opportunity to quest (as part of a moral community) for "what ought to be."

Vital—certainly to the new worker, but to the old as well— is the knowledge that he is not alone, that there is someone to go to when help is needed, someone with whom to share ideas, concerns, and visions for his clients, the agency, and the profession.

THE PREVALENCE OF SUPERVISION

Supervision is a ubiquitous process in the total human services field as well as within the individual agencies. Although it may run slow at times, it often supports the life blood of the agency, pushing here, pulling there, attempting to maintain some level of practice in keeping with the "ideals" of the agency and the profession. The "commonness" of supervision, however, is one of the major reasons it is neglected, done poorly, taken for granted, and in the end does not accomplish its task of enhancing effective practice.

Since supervision is everywhere around us, it may suffer by not being seen as something requiring exceptional skills or in fact exceptional people. Almost anyone who lives long enough becomes a supervisor if he so desires. Ask the administrator to define the criteria for a good supervisor, and the most prevalent response (often the only one) is that the person should be "a good practitioner." This is vital, but it is also important that the supervisor be a good teacher. Good supervision cannot be founded on poor practice, but one must also have skill in transmitting what one has learned in order to qualify for the label "good supervisor."

SUPERVISION AS A LIFE EXPERIENCE

Some of the traditional problems related to the supervisory experience are in fact similar to the human interactional problems of everyday life, being rooted in experiences with more or less powerful "others." They are reflected in our orientation to people, in our views of what is morally correct, in our search for the good life, and in our quest for security by hoping to make people over in our image. By attempting to formulate some image of the world—what others are like or need—we hope to ensure satisfactory experience. But views of the world of power relationships differ, as Douglas McGregor, a behavioral scientist, shows in his concept of the X and Y managers.

Do we believe that people need to be controlled in order to do their jobs, or do we believe that people will do their jobs without tight control? Do we see people as good, or bad? It was McGregor's contention that in the long run, treating people as honest, motivated, sincere workers was important as a human process and would "pay off." A summary of some of his X-Y dichotomy appears in Figure 2.

FIGURE 2
TWO SETS OF ASSUMPTIONS ABOUT PEOPLE

TRADITIONAL (X)	POTENTIAL (Y)
People are naturally lazy; they prefer to do nothing.	People are naturally active; they set goals and enjoy striving.
People work mostly for money and status rewards.	People seek many satisfactions in work: pride in achievement; enjoyment of process; sense of contribution; pleasure in association; stimulation of new challenges, etc.
The main force keeping people productive in their work is fear of being demoted or fired.	The main force keeping people productive in their work is desire to achieve their personal and social goals.
People remain children grown larger; they are naturally dependent on leaders.	People normally mature beyond childhood; they aspire to independence, self-fulfillment, responsibility.
People expect and depend on direction from above; they do not want to think for themselves.	People who understand and care about what they are doing can devise and improve their own methods of doing work.
People need supervisors who will watch them closely enough to be able to praise good work and reprimand errors.	People need a sense that they are respected as capable of assuming responsibility and self-correction.

SOURCE: Douglas McGregor, *The Human Side of Enterprise* (New York: McGraw-Hill, 1961) pp. 33, and Lecture by Goodwin Watson in Reports of National Training Laboratories Key Executive Conference, 1961.

If we feel we would like our agency/community to foster people more like the Y's, we are in fact committing ourselves to work for "what ought to be," and in fact that is one commitment of this book.

A SPECIAL VIEW OF LIFE IN SUPERVISION

In the human services we start with the assumption that most workers in social welfare want to do a good job. It becomes the function of the supervisor to help them to do that job, no matter how the job is described.* Some workers do the job well and feel good about what they have done. But some do the job poorly, and they generally feel bad about that—until doing the job badly becomes a way of life and they begin to accept that way of working.

In social work, we know that everything we do has two aspects, the doing and the feeling. For some people the doing is giving help—or supervising. For some people the doing is asking for help—or getting supervision.

It is important to note that people have feelings about going for or taking help from other people. It is not easy to seek help from people, nor is it easy to seek help from people who are in a position of authority. There are certain costs involved to the person. When the help is given freely—without strings, and in a manner we can use—the costs to people are slight and the rewards can be high. For some people, the costs of asking for help may be too high: the supervisor is haughty, or brags, or puts a person down. In those cases the supervisee seeks help only in emergencies, if at all. In general, *behavior is motivated by concepts of costs and rewards*.[16] A person balances these in his mind, seeking actions which will provide the rewards he wants at the least cost to himself.

It is important, however, that these concepts of rewards

---

* We recognize that at times the job to be done is a "bad" job, in that it does not aim to help people, but rather to "cool out" or manipulate for the benefit of others. We would hope acceptance of the normative approach to social work and supervision would eliminate that job description.

and costs as motivators of behavior be taken out of the realm of cut-and-dried "business," or the traditional understanding of "economic man." [17] Rewards are love, status, significance, and a feeling of worth. Many of these needs are intrinsic and relate to the quest for self-actualization and autonomy. Indeed, Maslow's hierarchy of needs on a personal level may well have relevance for our understanding of reward systems.[18] In fact we might transpose the concept of costs and rewards to a more humanistic understanding, which suggests that man will select the activities and relationships that enhance his self-image and avoid those that negate his individuality, growth, and quest for identity and autonomy.

Autonomy is the ability to make decisions that affect one's life and to know there is some possibility that these decisions can reach fruition; in essence, it is the ability to control both one's inputs and outputs so that one gets the rewards in life one wants. The ultimate goal in a just society would be a community in which people help each other because it is the right thing to do.

CHANGE AND LEARNING

Naturally most people are neither X's nor Y's; they are themselves, combinations of both. And we naturally view people as whole people, quite complex. The important question is whether people can learn to be either one. The answer is yes. Behavior is learned, and where the motivation is high enough, and self-image enhanced, learning will influence behavior.

We see learning as a process that leads to change, new ideas, values, knowledge, and understanding that can help people act differently. When a supervisee examines different ways of working with a client in a supervisory conference and then attempts to deal with a client in a new way, he has changed his behavior. Learning which leads to different ways of working with people is a change-oriented process, and should be basic to the supervisory goal.

THE PURPOSE OF SUPERVISION

Part of the responsibility of the supervisor is to help make the supervisory relationship a rewarding one for the supervisee; certainly it should be rewarding to the supervisor as well, since this will make the supervisory transaction a growth experience. Some of the rewards will be out of the direct control of the supervisor. These may include salary, personnel practices, etc.; but rewards such as a positive working climate, increased knowledge, skills, and appreciation are within the supervisor's authority.

Studies of job satisfaction have shown that beyond the basic financial rewards, the items which provide the greatest worker satisfaction are what Herzberg calls "hygienic factors," a feeling of being worthwhile, wanted, doing useful work, etc.[19] Rewarding supervisory experiences will be those in which the supervisee feels he has learned, has been treated as an adult, and has been able to maintain his integrity. Malcolm Knowles's concept of andragogy suggests the need to approach adult learners in an individualized manner.[20] In essence, where the costs of learning are kept low, self-esteem rewards are high.

Supervision is in part a learning-teaching transaction. We are in fact seeking of the supervisee that he learn some new ways of understanding and acting, that he change his behavior. In the process the supervisor—also a thinking, acting, learning person—should change as well.

Learning is change, and the supervisory process is a change process, with the major agent of change being the supervisor. But is the current pattern of hierarchical supervision adequate for our current professional needs? Can a supervisor meet the challenge of the new consciousness? He too will have to learn new ways of helping and teaching, or else he teaches, unknowingly perhaps, to maintain the status quo. Or worse yet, he thinks he is teaching while in fact the dependence and anger created by hierarchical organizational frustrations prevent significant learning for change from taking place.

THE SEARCH FOR SYNERGISTIC SUPERVISION:
BEYOND SUPERVISION

One of the strengths of our profession has been that we have consistently borrowed relevant ideas from other professions and disciplines, modified them, and used them on behalf of people. We have been fortunate enough, because of this lack of a unified and rigid body of knowledge, to adapt our techniques to the changing needs of people and to deal with problems on many levels. We have, however, been remiss in seeding our ideas and in harvesting for ourselves the unique insights of our own discipline.

We have been what Robert Lifton terms "Protean Man" (named after the Greek god Proteus, who was able to change into anything he wished): Protean Man is open psychologically, an experimenter, the opposite of "constricted man." [21] In supervision we want to help develop the open mind—open to new ideas and self-appraisal. We have, in fact, become experts in moving people through conflict, whether internal or external, through competition, to mediation and synergy. "Synergy," says Charles Hampden-Turner, "consists of an affective and intellectual synthesis which is *more* than the sum of its parts, so that each party to the interaction can win a "return on investment" that is greater than the competence risked." [22]

Ruth Benedict, analyzing what she considered rather successful, productive, creative, and friendly cultures, noted that what seemed to encompass and differentiate these communities from others was the ability of the various parts of the community to work together for mutual benefit. She referred to this phenomenon as synergy (which comes from the Greek word *synergia,* "working together," from *syn,* "with," and *ergon,* "work.") To Benedict, it represented that quality "in which the individual by the same act and at the same time serves his own advantage and that of the group." [23] This seems to me to be what social work might be about, now and in the future.

The concept is certainly not new to social work. It has been tangentially available through the work of Mary Follett, who in the twenties wrote *Constructive Conflict* and suggested the concept of "integration." "When two desires are integrated, that means that a solution has been found in which both desires have found a place, that neither side has had to sacrifice anything." [24] She was discussing conflict between groups; Abraham Maslow notes that "synergy applies not only to the relationships between people and groups, but that synergy within the person promotes a synergy between persons and vice versa." [25]

When elements of our profession have refused to accept supervision as similar to casework or as purely a control or administrative process, the subsequent dialectic exchange led to a synergistic result of an enlightened membership and strengthened profession. It offers us a balance, *or* what Buber has called "a unity of contraries." [26]

The synergistic approach has valuable contributions for the supervisory relationship as well as other helping processes. Can something greater emerge when two people or a supervisor and a group attempt to go past their individual ideas to a better way of helping the client? Can each put aside his own biases and favorite approach in order to look at something new? We think there is pay dirt here, and we will focus on synergistic transactions as a cornerstone for the supervisory interactive patterns.

As mentioned earlier it is the author's hope to move up from the concept of supervision, which as a concept has vestiges of dependency and controls. What we suggest is that supervision was an idea that grew out of our cultural heritage and that filled a need when our profession was young and needed to exert strong controls in order to establish its identity, boundaries, and accountability. Now that these are established and we realize the secondary results of continuing dependency and continued hierarchical agencies, we must move up and set the standards for higher forms of learning and for demonstrating performance validity on the job. This new form, a mutual seeking for the truth among involved persons, leads to a synergistic approach, to synteraction rather than to supervision.

In the next chapter we shall look at the roots of supervision and the evolution of the synergy idea. How does it look in practice, and what are the theoretical underpinnings which suggest that this could become a major style of mutual helping —synteraction among people?

CHAPTER 2

HISTORICAL

PERSPECTIVES,

EMERGING TRENDS, AND

CURRENT PRACTICE

The basis of all social work is the deficiency of every legal organization.

PAUL TILLICH

Since American social work had its roots in the casework orientation of the charity organization movement, it seems natural that the supervisory approaches in the field would have been modeled after that movement's attempts to come up with a codification of "correct," "scientific" approaches to problem solving, as well as a one-to-one orientation to the supervisory transactions.

THE BEGINNINGS OF SOCIAL WORK SUPERVISION *

One of the first social workers to deal with supervision in social work was Zilphia Drew Smith, of the Boston Associated

* A great deal of this early historical material was excerpted and adapted from Sidney S. Eisenberg, *Supervision in the Changing Field of Social Work* (Jewish Family Service of Philadelphia, 1956). That important work contains significant historical interpretations.

Charities. In 1885 she addressed the National Conference of Charities and Corrections and described the functioning of her Boston agency, one of the most progressive in the country at that time. In her paper she described the district as being in charge of an executive committee "composed of the most experienced visitors and persons having special administrative ability." [1] A paid staff person, or agent, made an initial investigation at the client's home and outside inquiries to learn what problems existed, to verify the need, and to ascertain the moral character of the applicant. This was then reported to a more experienced district committee. The committee then chose "the visitor needed to form a permanent and helpful relationship with the family." [2] The teaching role was emphasized, and authoritarian approaches were minimized. Correspondence between agent and visitor was one of the methods of record keeping, and the agent's responsibility was to see that progress was reported regularly.

In 1892 Miss Smith noted that the new visitor needed the steady hand of another to guide him through experiences so new and strange "that he cannot judge them rightly." [3] She discusses how to help the visitor make his own relationship to a new family, encourages him to trust his own feelings and thoughts, and helps him to see whatever he is overlooking in their situation. Eisenberg suggests that Miss Smith was not merely conveying content, but seemed even more concerned with the development of the visitor into a mature practitioner. The intention here was to develop independent visitors. She seemed quite aware that supervision was a helping process. In an address given at a national conference she stated:

> In order to make friendly visiting succeed the committee and agents must care to really help the visitor,—not merely to give what the visitor asks, but, with tact and patience, what he needs, and to go at it simply and informally. You see I am saying much the same thing about helping visitors as we say to visitors who would help poor families, for visitors are just as human as the poor people. The agent and committees must learn patiently to know and understand the new visitor . . . Thought must be given

to his problems and both direct and indirect means used to help him help himself in working them out with the poor family.[4]

Just before the turn of the century, Octavia Hill of the London Charity Organization Society "stressed the need for organizing the visitors, for training and oversight and advice along the way so that these efforts might be strengthened and directed and inevitable periods of discouragement overcome." [5]

We see that in the historical development of social work, there was always an emphasis on providing the highest level of practice possible. This was reflected in agencies through supervision and by setting up training programs like the New York City Charity Organization Society's development of a summer training class in philanthropy. In 1904, this became a one-year course under the banner of "New York School of Philanthropy." Within the next four years, four other such schools began programs.[6]

Thus we see that agency supervision and training programs were the forerunners of our schools of social work.

Eisenberg suggests that nothing more basic was formulated about supervision for the next thirty years. But this neglects the role of the Red Cross, which during World War I trained many volunteers to work with families of soldiers. In fact the Red Cross was a catalyst for training programs throughout the United States in many schools of social work. In 1920 another significant step was taken to develop supervisory practice by Virginia Robinson, bringing a sound understanding of timing in education and the importance of relationship.[7] In 1927 Grace Marcus enunciated a strong plea to emphasize the helping-counseling role in the supervisory relationship.[8]

But the days of the amateur were numbered. Miller points out that "the overshadowing of the administrative function by the teaching function was influenced significantly by the development of the university-based graduate training for practice." [9] In social work the way was open for a change in emphasis and direction. The growing interest in mental hygiene, in its psychiatric and psychological aspects, began slowly at first, but was very definitely reflected in education for the practice of social work and, presently, in supervision. From this point on, American social work began to develop primarily as a psychologically oriented body of knowledge and method.

SUPERVISION AND THE NEW PSYCHOLOGY

During the 1920s, it was recognized that supervisors strongly influenced the quality of casework practice, and recognition was given to supervision as a vital function in the agency. At the same time, Freud and his disciples were having an increasing influence on counseling. Grace Marcus, for example, regarded supervision as the most strategic position in the field of casework and one of its "most dynamic functions." [10] She advocated full-scale casework treatment of the caseworker, just as the worker "investigates and treats . . . the client." [11] Eisenberg suggests that "while this was extreme, Miss Marcus was at work on a basic problem which had been troubling supervisors for a long time." [12]

The practice of supervision was moving in a different direction from the fundamentally authoritative and manipulative method which had so long characterized it. There was now the expression of concern for the development of the worker. This is emphatically borne out in both of the articles which Miss Marcus wrote on supervision in 1927.

> The supervisor who defines casework as an art and philosophy formulates as her function something more than the full communication to the student of the technique of investigation and treatment . . . She wants to develop in the student the capacity for thinking, feeling and living a casework that she need not scruple to employ on herself. It cannot come through learning rules of procedure; it rests on understanding and personal development which furnish the real resources for that casework growth toward which we are all struggling.[13]

She develops two main lines of thought. One is a helping process to enable the worker to see what she has missed in the case and to understand what she sees. The other is to help the worker with her personal problems as reflected by her practice.

In another paper which she presented at the National Conference of Social Work in 1927, Miss Marcus asked, "Is it better for the supervisor to deal with every personal issue as a matter for executive action or to broaden her concept of casework to include those personal issues and so subject her handling of them to conscious analysis and control?" [14]

Articles on supervision began to appear with increasing regularity in the professional journal *The Family* and in the *Proceedings* of the National Conference of Social Work.

Most caseworkers and supervisors in the twenties were products of the apprentice system.[15] Agency training leaned heavily on Mary Richmond's "social diagnosis." The work was now being done largely by full-time, paid employees. John Dewey's learning theory was adapted and refined in the light of Freud's psychoanalytic theory and led to a perception of the supervisory relationship in therapeutic terms.[16]

Group work, having many of its roots in the education-recreation movement, was similarly influenced by the concept of "inspection of the teacher by the supervisor." [17] The relationship between teacher and supervisor was that of subordinate to superior. The method of supervision was authoritative, not autocratic.

The idea of the expert-apprentice relationship as the supervisory model is supported in group work by Margaret Williamson, who, in speaking of the supervisor-supervisee relationship, says:

> In this relationship, one person, the supervisor, by virtue of special preparation and experience in a particular field of work assumes by assignment, responsibility for helping another person with relatively less equipment and experience in the particular field to develop his abilities in it so he can do a more effective job, derive greater satisfaction from such doing, and grow continuously as a person.[18]

This is just an echo of her casework sister Virginia Robinson, who in 1936 had defined supervision as "an education process in which a person with a certain equipment of knowledge and skill takes responsibility for training a person with less equipment." [19] Bertha Reynolds called for a drastic change in that authoritive approach.

> For a long time social work has been turning away from an authoritative practice comparable to the teaching of arithmetic by means of an answer book in the teacher's hand, and has been seeking answers from the facts about the relationships of living forces in a changing society. When science was not supposed to have anything to offer in the realm of human behavior, there was a tendency to set up procedures which were thought to be the good or right ways of dealing with various kinds of problems, and these constituted the body of knowledge of social work. For instance, there were accepted ways of dealing with unmarried mothers, giving relief to widows, making foster home placements. Workers who have asked the insistent question, "What shall I do?" were given from the experience of older workers what was supposed to be good principles of practice. It was an advance over "doing good" because one felt inclined to be able to say: Never give relief without investigation. Always place children of the same family in the same foster home if possible. Nevertheless, these set procedures were predicated upon a belief that situations could be treated as more or less standardized. The variations shown by the people *in* the situations were noted more often as interferences with carrying out what the worker thought should be done than as indications of the need for a more flexible practice.[20]

Further evidence of the different views of the supervisory process which were being developed in the thirties is indicated by one teacher of supervision, who wrote:

> Indeed, the word "supervision" has unfortunate association with the dictatorial and the martial. It is often assumed that to supervise is to control and to coerce. This book is an intelligent and lucid exposition of supervision of a very different sort. Its aim is not to force leaders to a preconceived pattern of conformity, but rather to help them to find and to develop their own particular gifts through quickened insight into the meaning of social situations, broadened knowledge, and the sure skill that comes of practice under guidance.
> It is soundly based on a sincere regard for the experience, the ideas, and the convictions of the leaders under supervision

and, back of them, for the integrity of the groups they have been assigned to lead.[21]

Lindenberg, the author of the first book on group work supervision, pointed out:

> Along with this change in objectives, progressive group work organizations are changing their whole idea of supervision of activities and workers in agencies. Heretofore, supervision was almost purely an administrative technique. Supervisors conferred with workers on the basis of activities that were in the program or might be added. They acted as "supreme disciplinarians" when the teacher in charge couldn't "bounce" some individuals out of activities . . . Individual needs or group needs were mere words to most supervisors, who planned programs only on the basis of what they thought would be good for the agency's clientele.
>
> Now, this rather sordid picture of supervision is taking on a somewhat brighter hue in the more progressive group work agencies.[22]

If casework influenced supervision style in group work and community organization, it is interesting to note that as these two disciplines obtained status and acceptance in the total profession they had an important impact on changing supervisory styles in the profession.

One significant stimulus to the development of supervision was the nationwide economic depression. The massive job which needed to be done in social work, particularly by the public relief agencies and by untrained workers, required new tasks for supervisors. One of the chief jobs of the supervisor heretofore had been record analysis. However, it was no longer possible for the supervisor to take responsibility for the casework activity in any total sense by reading all the records of all the workers. There were too many, and the needs of the clients were too pressing for such activity.

The depression taxed the ability of the workers to deal with the vast numbers of cases, and agencies were not nearly able to meet the financial needs of people. For the first time, the federal government moved forward with vast welfare programs, work relief, social security, and welfare. This led to a government-prepared manual for the training of social work staff and an extremely influential philosophical approach to working with people and to supervision. Charlotte Towle, who prepared the document, states:

> Insight into basic motivations in human behavior and common human needs has great significance for supervision of public assistance staff . . . Supervision in public assistance programs has been defined as an administrative process which has as one of its purposes to contribute to staff development. Every staff member in a position of responsibility for the work of other staff members has an obligation to give leadership which develops the abilities of the staff under his immediate direction in the useful application of knowledge and skills on the job. It has been emphasized that "the adequacy of agency function in terms of service to people in need occurs in direct relation to the growth of individual staff members in their capacity to render these services. Accordingly, supervision, in addition to having the derivative meaning, 'to have a general oversight of,' must focus upon the development of knowledge, the use of that knowledge, and the application of skills by staff in their day-to-day activities on the job." Supervision in public assistance, therefore, has been envisaged as a teaching-learning situation, that is, as an educational rather than as a purely administrative process.[23]

EMERGING TRENDS

Miller reports that the 1950s introduced some new and rediscovered themes into the professional literature which influenced supervisory practice. Three of these were:

1. An interest in the agency system itself, the relevance of organizing theory for the way supervisory role and function might be conceptualized and the impact of organizational processes upon supervision.

2. A concern with the strains and conflicts inherent in a supervisory role when it combines both an administrative and teaching function. Consequently, proposals and efforts have been made to separate these functions by vesting them in different

positions. This is intended to mitigate such inherent strains and conflicts and facilitate the independent functioning and professional growth of the practitioner.

3. Growing interest in and experimentation with the use of consultation, peer group supervision, team supervision, and various group methods in supervision, to supplement or substitute for the traditional and primary technique of the individual conference.[24]

Some of the changes were directly related to the changing nature of practice. Use of groups, family counseling, accountability to government funding sources, community organization, social action, and community involvement. Miller elaborates on some of these changes:

> In the usual casework situation, there is little or no visibility except as the practitioner makes the information available, as well as considerable power and ability on his part to control the terms of the helping process.
>
> These factors, among others, may account for the more intensive attention paid to supervision in casework as compared with group work or community organization. The typical group service situation is in these respects somewhat different. What goes on in the group is not only experienced by many people but often becomes visible to others in the organization as well . . . It is possible to suggest, therefore, that the group record serves the additional purpose of "protecting" the worker. It places the worker's definition of what happened on the record along with competing definitions of others. Related to this is that, in ways not apparent in casework, groups have considerable countervailing power regarding the worker. In order to carry out the service, the worker has to accommodate, adapt, and come to terms with the demands and definitions of the group, much more so and in much more direct ways than is the case in the comparable one-to-one helping situation . . .
>
> In community organization work there is usually a high degree of visibility about practice and a different distribution of power between the worker and the client than obtains in other helping relationships. There is some variation depending upon whether the persons with whom the worker is engaged are the direct beneficiaries of the service or are being persuaded to work on behalf of others. In either case, but most apparent in the

latter, the worker is in a work situation in which the other person (i.e., the client) asks him, "What can I do for you?" This surely influences the patterns and preoccupations in supervision of community organization practice.[25]

The development of social welfare services, particularly the growth of the mental health movement following World War II, opened up new demands for mental health consultation. Shortages of staff and experienced mental health administrators forced the use of the limited manpower into consultative and teaching roles.

Availability of funds from the federal government seemed to increase the use of consultation and made this process, which had been around for years, recognized and in some cases expected. In 1942, Bartlett defined consultation as a "process of shared thinking that brings enlarged insight and increased ability to deal with the problem but leaves responsibility for decision and action with the persons seeking consultation." [26]

Mary Gilmore traces some of the historical roots of consultation:

Originally, the professional consideration of consultation arose from two different fields of practice: the field of public welfare and the practice of medical social work.

Large public welfare organizations, and related state and federal agencies, needed intra-agency reinforcement of professional skills, and provision for control of the activity of partially educated or professionally untrained workers in a burgeoning service. Thus social work consultation in public welfare had the dual objective of administrative accountability plus in-service training.

Some of the special practice needs of social workers in host settings (primarily medical social workers in the beginning, but now including psychiatric group workers in institution, school social workers, and community organization personnel in urban renewal) involved collaborative activity on an interdisciplinary basis. Thus, the purpose of medical social work consultation was defined, in part at least, in terms of achieving maximum interdisciplinary collaboration through a consultative form of teaching.[27]

Under the leadership of Dr. Gerald Caplan and his associates at the Harvard School of Public Health, a formulation has evolved that utilizes problem-solving techniques with educational and therapeutic components for the purpose of increasing the consultee's awareness of, and ability to manage, the mental health aspects of his work. Caplan's typology of mental health consultation is fourfold: client-centered case consultation, consultee-centered case consultation, program-centered administrative consultation, and consultee-centered administrative consultation.[28]

These latter influences in mental health consultation helped modify the traditional status relationships between supervisee and supervisor and offered an alternative model. They did not serve to minimize hierarchical relationships but provided an expert among experts. One value was that the consultant, often as an outsider, had to search with others for common information. This search served as a mutual learning situation.

Changes in supervisory practice were influenced by a number of changes related to "good" mental health. (1) in the forefront of these influences was the development of mental health consultation, which made heavy use of social workers as consultants to schools, mental health centers, and the like. The work of Caplan and Rappoport is notable in this area. (2) The growth of human relations in management with the work of McGregor, Argyris, and Maslow began to filter into all fields of supervision. Problems related to status and bureaucratic hierarchies were explored and became concerns of laymen as well as professional and business groups. (3) The growth of sensitivity, encounter, or self-awareness groups helped open communications across all status lines and modified supervisee-supervisor relationships. (4) The use of agency-trained, indigenous workers also set new supervisory and practice expectations. (5) Dissatisfaction with the effectiveness of the clinical model in practice suggested the possibility that a similar model in supervision might also have shortcomings.

Generally the supervisory styles followed broad societal changes, shifts in social science thinking, and the changing demand of the practitioner.

Some of these developments are typified by the research and concerns related to (1) motivation and job satisfaction, (2) the changing nature of organizations, and (3) the concepts of "social justice"—including civil rights and the women's liberation movement and, most recently, the concerns related to our political leadership.

WORKER MOTIVATION: HUMAN NEEDS

There have been numerous studies concerned with worker motivation, satisfaction, and productivity. These studies have produced some findings which were contrary to earlier beliefs that a worker's satisfaction with his employment was related primarily to his salary.

Blauner found that there are marked differences in work attitudes and expectations from one occupational level to another, and that the "principal source of job satisfaction is autonomy and independence on the job." [29] Herzberg found that "the principal sources of satisfaction were achievement, recognition, the work itself, responsibility or advancement." [30] He also reported that the amount of salary itself is not a source of job satisfaction but that "low salaries, or those considered unfair, *are* a source of job dissatisfaction." [31] In a survey of job attitudes compiled from sixteen studies with a combined sample of over 11,000 workers, Herzberg (1957) summarized factors which were important to the worker. [32] The highest-ranked items were security, interest, and opportunity for advancement.

Most other studies report similar findings—in essence, wages, which are generally ranked by administrators as one of the major factors in job satisfaction, are rarely rated among the top three "satisfiers" by staff. People seem to want to work where they have some opportunity to control their work situation and where they have some degree of independence. They seem also to seek achievement, recognition, responsibility, and the opportunity for advancement. These might be considered as the mental-health, or ego-building aspects of the job. Herzberg points to two sets of factors which are important to job satisfaction. The first group he labels "hygienic"; these only tend to prevent dissatisfaction and poor job performance.[33] The secondary factors, the "motivators," lead to "self-actualization" or "self-realization." The most important of these motivators, those mentioned most often, are achievement, recognition, the work itself, responsibility, and advancement.

In social work the nature of the job itself can often provide satisfaction in the areas defined as motivators; responses from social workers have often indicated that there is a great deal of satisfaction in helping people, and that the work itself is rewarding. We have to examine more closely, however, whether such rewards as achievement, recognition, and advancement are distributed to the agency-trained worker on the same basis as they are distributed to the professional.[34]

The job must offer the worker a certain amount of stimulation and opportunity if he is to try himself in new activities and with new tasks.[35]

Lack of interest in the content of the worker assignment has been a source of dissatisfaction in social work as well, and in one study proved to be the major reason given for leaving a staff position.[36]

WORKER SATISFACTION

The concern with worker satisfaction as an important factor in worker morale, job attitudes, and worker turnover has been studied by a number of investigators.[37] Pearlin, in discussing organizations, states: "In order to retain its staff and to maintain itself as an on-going institution, [an organization] must gear itself not only for the attainment of the ends for which it was established, but also for the satisfaction of the diverse aspirations and opportunities sought by its members." [38] Collins and Guetzkow point out that there are a number of terms which have been used interchangeably with satisfaction: "A highly satisfied person has high morale and the satisfied worker has job satisfaction or favorable job attitudes . . . Most researchers define satisfaction as a judgment of a subjective state of feeling or evaluation." [39]

Management studies such as the Hawthorne research began to alert psychologists to the realization that people respond to other than financial rewards. One of the major influences in our current recognition that man does not live by bread alone came from the work of Abraham Maslow, whose development of the concept "hierarchy of needs" has led to what is known as the "new" movement in understanding human behavior.

Maslow holds that "the human being is motivated by a number of basic needs which are species-wide, apparently unchanging and genetic or instinctual in origin." [40] As Figure 3 shows, these needs, beginning with physiological states, proceed to a quest for self-actualization.

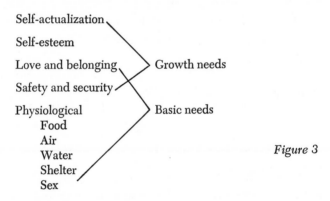

Figure 3

In fact, it was Maslow who called attention to Ruth Benedict's writings on synergy. He notes that "synergy applies not only to the relationships between people and groups [and] that synergy *within* the person promotes a synergy *between* persons and vice versa." [41]

THE CHANGING ORGANIZATION: A TEMPORARY COMMUNITY?

The more mechanized our society becomes, the more important people will become to each other as sources of warmth and human concern. People will seek engagement in new ways and in new places. Increasingly man has begun to demand that his workplace offer some of the benefits of the traditional community. He objects to being seen as an interchangeable piece of machinery, and his protests against assembly-line methods have increased both in this country (as evidenced by Lordstown) and in more welfare-oriented societies such as Sweden, where the workers at the Volvo plant likewise objected to assembly-line methods. Concepts of "self-management" are being discussed and attempted with varying degrees of success.

Even the workplace, however, is undergoing dynamic changes. Bennis and Slater foresee the organization as becoming a "temporary society" in which "there will be adaptive, rapidly changing temporary systems. These will be task forces composed of groups of relative strangers with diverse professional backgrounds and skills organized around problems to be solved." [42] No doubt these temporary arrangements will call for new techniques which will permit "strangers" to work together and bypass the "fear of the stranger" which often leads to hostility and avoidance.

The types of temporary communities with which we deal are not those fleeting contacts of task forces made up of chance strangers, but the communities provided by the geographic limits of a workplace in which people often spend up to 50 percent of their day and in which they have continued contact with many of the same people on a routine basis.

The modern organization is certainly taking on a great many nonwork oriented obligations that have generally been seen as community functions. These include medical care, marriage counseling, counseling for alcoholism, executive counseling, softball leagues, etc. Berkley estimates that "one third of all educational programs in the country are now being carried on by work organizations . . . Especially noteworthy is the growing evidence that work organizations are able to provide such community-like services in a highly effective manner . . . The success rate of such programs was 55 to 70 percent higher than those operated by hospitals and clinics." [43] It may be that the motivation to "improve" in order to maintain a position, or the fact that others in the community are sharing the experience with the client, aids in the rate of improvement. In summing up, Berkley, who also sees the organization as a community, states:

> The modern organization, it is true, does not provide its members with the 24 hour-a-day association which has characterized residential communities in the past . . . But . . . the modern work organization as it is evolving seems to be the institution most capable of providing what modern man most desperately needs: shelter without walls.[44]

THE NONMECHANICAL ORGANIZATION

Hierarchical status is one of the most pronounced features of organizational life; yet when it comes to the consideration of strife, injustice, and conflict in organizations, the reigning tendency is to ignore the basic structure of the organization and to regard these problems simply as "accidental malfunctions" which can be remedied by peripheral reforms and interpersonal adjustments.

Still, those committed to human relations approaches and so-called participatory decision making have been uneasy with the straight factory model of job specialization and vertical authority. To a large degree, alternative solutions have produced some partial solutions to the tensions arising from status differentials—partial because there has been powerful resistance to even imagining organizations without these differentials. One of these partial solutions has been the artifact of the "therapeutic team" which would supposedly democratize staff relationships, free communication, ensure the flow of ideas, and create numerous coordinates for decision making. Our contemporary mental health organizations have come a long way from the straight "line authority" model of organizations. Social work, as a profession rooted deeply in agencies, modified the traditional bureaucratic functioning of its organization by superimposing professional values and styles on traditional structures. It therefore was a leader in developing what we now call the human relations management approach, or therapeutic management and milieu.

The nature of organizational change, therefore, is still another factor which helped alter the traditional supervisory relationship. But perhaps most important has been the pressure from staff itself for more autonomy.

THE QUEST FOR SOCIAL JUSTICE

During the past decade, continuing examination of the nature of relationships between people, focusing on status, class, and manipulation of minority groups, has brought a new awareness and urgency in the quest for social justice. It would be strange indeed if efforts on behalf of equal treatment for minority groups, students, and women would not influence the nature of relationships in agencies as well.

Long before Watergate, concerns on the part of staff to find ways to alter harmful agency practice came face to face with demands for agency loyalties. Major questioning of obedience and following mandates of powerful others were raised. Profession practice was reported at odds with agency policy, and the differences between professional and agency-oriented staff were being explored.[45] The search for justice was mangled in the tangles of red tape and hierarchical agency decision-making regulations.

In the name of social justice, decisions need to be made on the basis of a moral stance which sees equality and participation as well as evidence as the bases of the vitality of agency decision making. Fired by the desire to overcome the discrepancies of the past, many workers have become wary of agency environments in which minorities, "the lower classes and women occupy positions in the lower echelons while many executives and boards are overly represented by the upper classes." This certainly became a crucial factor in the War on Poverty during the sixties, with the emphasis on maximum feasible participation.

Although the War on Poverty and many of its ethical mandates have faded, the facts and the early rhetoric influenced our understanding of the hierarchical structure of our society and its dangers. These lessons have called forth a demand for more democratic structuring in our agencies, which together with a younger, more radically oriented staff has in many cases resulted in a more open structure. This structure has used colleagual, team, and peer decision-making processes, or at least made some attempts to modify the traditional chain of command, which indeed "chained" people to fixed boxes, authority, and relationships. Supervision has been modified in these more open agencies through use of group decision making, recourse for appeals, and increased use of peer supervision.

The concept of supervision in social work began with the charity organization movement as the desire to become scientific and control worker actions was paramount.

> The need to teach others how to work became the second task for the supervisor as volunteers and professionals moved into the growing welfare institutions.
> A third thread—treatment, counseling, enabling developments—came as the profession emerged and began to understand more of the dynamics of human interaction, including concepts such as "resistance" and "blocking." The emphasis was on the enabling of the worker to function more efficiently, the helping aspect of supervision.[46]

During the development of supervision, the relative importance of these factors has been argued, but the tasks are still generally seen as the tasks of the supervisor.

Supervisory techniques and styles have varied as (1) social demands (such as wars and depressions) created manpower demands, (2) knowledge has become available (Freud, andragogy), (3) human services have changed (mental health movement, community involvement, paraprofessionals), (4) institutions have changed (human relations in management, work-management relations), (5) social interaction has been modified (encounters, self-actualization movements), (6) demands of minority groups for social justice have increased, and

(7) the profession itself has matured and made new demands (ACSW, professional levels, and specialization).

Many factors, have converged in the direction of a more humanistic synergistic approach to human interaction. A movement from status to contract, from hierarchical relationships to teams, colleagues, and community, based on social justice and "what ought to be," founded on a scientific search for truth. With this statement one might think we could draw a circle around supervisory practice and look at the impact of these new ideas as reflected by more effective workers or more autonomous-satisfied staff. But as we shall see, supervisory practice has not improved in the past ten years, nor does there seem to be a greater worker satisfaction with the agency-administrative-supervisory complex.

At the same time that management concepts have begun to feel the influence of more humanistic personnel approaches and pressures from workers to move from a machine model to a human model of the worker, the human services have begun to adapt some of the dehumanizing management approaches and imposed them on welfare services.[47] The reasons vary, but one factor has been the effort to become more efficient and effective in the services offered, and as a response to attacks that social workers were "too easy." Part of the reason, however, is that our profession continues to search for answers outside our own practice, from the research of social science management.

CURRENT PRACTICE

SUPERVISION FOR WHAT?

The basic task of supervision is to guide and build practice so that people can overcome the problems which immobilize, create suffering, and perpetuate alienation. This can be done by individual change and learning and by working to develop a society which is ennobling to people. As we shall come to describe supervision in this book, it will lead us away from the concepts of control which reduce the person to someone who needs overseeing. Our profession is leaving that form for "good practice" in a "good community." Since we feel it is impossible to separate ends from means, we will begin this section with a vision of good supervisory practice and then analyze its elements. If our vision seem utopian, so much the better, since it is our belief that having created current realities, we can also create future realities.

Supervisory practice is an environment, context, pattern of skills, process, a unity for providing an opportunity to find the "good way," the best moral way, of helping people achieve a productive life. It is a search for knowledge and technique that can help people fulfill their healthy functioning in a healthy society. It is a guarantee to the community that committed workers with training and skill are using the best available methods of inquiry to find the best solutions.

THE HUMAN VISION

The ultimate goal of supervision and staff development transcends the purpose of good agency practice. One must always ask, Practice for what? And the answer ultimately must be, For a better society. There are five elements in our vision.

1. *A better world.* Surely the focus, the heart, the crux of all service is the provision of a better life for people. It is our struggle to make a better world for whatever client system we are dealing with. This is the major force which provides us with the power to perform. In the long view we are certainly not working to enhance our egos or the agency's reputation, but to increase the opportunities for a more worthwhile existence for our clients. We are working for a free and open society, searching for a just community.

2. *The staff.* A group of creative, interdependent workers who not only work well together, but use each other on behalf of and with the client to increase their knowledge and ability to function as competent professionals. The accountability of the staff is to each other, client, and society in general, rather than to a professional supervisor or a hierarchical structure.

3. A responsive, proactive organization. A social agency made of open interactive components, constantly focusing on the job to be done and on improving its ability to work for the good life for all. It is an organization for status reduction and synergistic problem solving.

4. Knowledge. Generated through scientific exploration for the good and the true, openly shared and utilized for the benefit of all. Such knowledge is sought not only by staff, but by the client and the community in common cause. It is knowledge grounded in the context of practice experience as modified by unifying concepts from other disciplines.

5. A moral community. A working group of client-workers, administrators, or community people who see themselves as part of the problem to be solved, not separate from it. They are unified by the concepts of relevant moral interactions and the dignified use of human beings.

In summary, then, the vision is of workers, clients, and communities working together, using scientific procedures to find the best moral ways of dealing with a particular problem, united as agency, workers, and clients, open and continually building, engaging each other and confronting change for "what ought to be," a better life.

The vision presents a challenge to any profession—certainly to agencies, which are often beholden to outside groups, elected officials, and political sycophants for legal and physical existence. Not accepting the challenge, at least in part, condemns the human service professional to either seek this vision through private practice, to subjugate his vision to daydreams, or to repress them except for occasional outbursts. It is this vision which is the root that developed into the concept of normative supervision. It is an approach to supervision grounded in "normative practice," the practice of "what ought to be," a new paradigm for the helping profession.[48]

How does current social work practice measure up to this vision? There have been numerous reports suggesting that indeed we have not been effective in providing the skills and knowledge necessary to change. If this is so, then supervision itself must share some of the blame for a poor showing. The leaders in the field are the administrators, supervisors, and teachers. If they persist in maintaining supervisory paradigms which continue to support noneffective practice they can only lead the human services into stagnation.

Supervision is meant to raise the level of practice. One of the difficulties, however, is that the concept of primacy often operates.[49] The way you were first supervised will probably be the way you in turn will supervise. There is a flowing continuation of humanistic but often noneffective practice.

One of the major shortcomings in the profession is a lack of knowledge coming out of our own practice. Our professional practice has fashioned itself on the clinical model and seems to be moving to a learning model. It has not, however, changed its supervisory model in the same way, but instead has attempted to emulate management control models.

CONTEMPORARY MODELS OF SUPERVISION: A CRITICAL VIEW

Four models of supervision are described by Laura Epstein as representing current supervisory practice.[50] She notes that these models set forth ideals, but none offers help in guiding specific actions. Three of her four models will be summarized briefly, but since we feel that one of them, group supervision, does not really reflect a unique model, but rather a technique which could fit into all supervisory approaches, we will not include it here. Naturally, these are rough characterizations of complex human interactions, and some overlap is to be found in all the models.

1. The growth model. In this traditional approach, supervision is a process of helping, teaching, and administrating. The supervisor helps the supervisee gain self-awareness about his job. His aims are to enhance the practitioner's use of self, and a strong degree of control is maintained through regularly scheduled individual conferences. Education seems to be the highest priority. There seems to be some confusion between the concept of student and worker, which can become dysfunctional.

2. *The quasi-autonomous model.* Here, "helping" as a concept is dropped, and in some cases the teaching and administrative functions are carried by different people. The worker may choose experts to help him rather than any one regular supervisor. The object is to facilitate cooperative staff work. Professional development is seen as the practitioner's responsibility. Group learning may replace individual conferences. Communication—what is going on—becomes a problem.

3. *The autonomous practice model.* This last model of supervisory practice "means exercising the right and power to practice without outside controls, within the context of appropriate social sanctions." [51] The physician is used as the model here. Epstein sees this model developing in social work as we mature and as licensing of social work becomes more extensive. Some practitioners are currently following this model when they are cut off from traditional bureaucratic structures like traditional agencies, perhaps working under the disciplines. Some become field instructors, or are "unsupervisable" because of their length of experience, or are in private practice.

There is an attempt to emulate the university in colleagual decision making and relative freedom. The model is also used a great deal in settings demanding interdisciplinary teamwork. But successful practitioner operation requires ample "feedback" experience and does not resolve the dilemmas of the less-experienced or new workers.

Generally speaking, these three models (including use of groups) seem to cover the range of current supervisory practice. And similarly, they seem to reflect some of the difficulties of modern day supervision in the human service as well. Some of the major shortcomings are:

1. Hierarchical arrangements are institutionalized in the agency. Even in group supervision the supervisor is seen as "leader-administrator." [52]

2. The concepts of professional status hierarchy and rivalry are promoted, as "when a psychiatrist is in charge of the team and wields the power of his status." [53]

3. There is a reliance on the expertise of specialists rather than a mutual search: ego orientation rather than community orientation. "Experienced practitioners, to some extent, have also found ways of carving autonomous niches for themselves . . ." [54]

4. Concern becomes centered on teaching, or helping, or administration, rather than on a mutual search for ways to help.

5. There is a separation of client from agency—the client is someone you do something to.

6. The search for open community is lost. "A controlled degree of intimacy between practitioners and supervisor is also sought." [55]

Professor Epstein sees some answers to the problems in the increased demands for the autonomous practice models. She believes autonomous practice is possible if agencies publish results, monitor, appraise, etc., but admits these will depend on two changes:

1. decentralization of bureaucratic authority and responsibility, and

2. abandonment of the obligatory teaching-learning posture as the major means of controlling professional behavior. [56]

We concur with these qualifiers, but would suggest that we need to increase our attention to the larger moral concerns: Autonomy for what? Supervision for what? Concerns with sources of knowledge and with accountability are more urgent than she would admit, as is a broader commitment to community and social change. Without a commitment to social goals and a moral community, the autonomous practice model lacks knowledge and an ethical base and is a hollow image of the medical-professional model, cut off from its social work knowledge and roots. We happily accept her more modest vision, but see the concept of autonomous practice as a fragmented solution. Autonomy in the sense of "capability" is a worthy goal, but autonomy simply as "independence" can alienate and separate the practitioner from the profession's broad social goals. One concern of those who oppose the licensing of social work is the feeling that this would alienate workers from the social goal to a private practice orientation. What we will be faced with is increased numbers of self-sufficient, private practitioners or autonomous workers trying to do "good" as they see it in agencies set up in self-defeating structures. Perhaps a look at some current agency practice might help clarify these points.

In many institutions the frictions generated by hierarchical systems cannot be contained, and consequently they erupt in outright competitiveness, dissatisfaction, and struggle over territory —which affects the quality of care.[57] Consider the relationships between two disciplines (nurses and child care workers) in a children's psychiatric hospital.[58]

The division of responsibility is roughly as follows: the nurses have the immediate responsibility for the management and administration of wards. Some of the nurses' tasks are delegated to "psych-aides," child care workers who are certified to dispense medications by virtue of their successful completion of a psychiatric aide program taught by the nursing department.

The child care worker and the nurse together have day-in-day-out responsibility for the children. Both work the ward, which is "home" for the children, and both are involved in the "life-management" of the children: waking them up, getting them off to school and to recreation programs, dealing with behavioral problems, arranging ward programs, putting the children to bed, getting their meals, readying them for home visits, and attending to the other innumerable details of daily life.

The nurse's role is that of the superior and supervisor; the child care worker has responsibility for ward housekeeping and carries out some ward management functions delegated by the nurses.

This relationship between the nurses and the child care workers carries within it the seeds of domain conflict. First of all, status and power differentials almost always provoke resentment. In this case the resentment is magnified because the child care worker is an important therapeutic agent. Although his role is one of the most critical in carrying out the mission of the hospital, he is paradoxically the most disvalued in terms of organizational status and prestige. This contradiction between formal status and actual importance is an important source of conflict.

The administrative authority which the nurse has over the ward carries with it hegemony over the child care worker down to the question of what the child care worker may or may not do with the children. For example:

> On one occasion a child care worker had planned to take his ward group off the grounds to a basketball game and had managed to obtain free tickets. The group had planned the trip for about a week, but one of the children misbehaved in class and the nurse said that he could not go on the trip. The child care worker felt that the nurse had no right to make this decision, that it would be harmful to the child and that it interfered with his jurisdiction. The child care worker pointed out that he would also bear the brunt of the hostility and problems that would follow. The nurse said it was her decision to make, not his.

The principle of "justice by status" gives the nurse legitimacy, authority, and expertise. In short, it is the nurse's decision to make, and not the child care worker's. A smoother operating nurse might "cool out" the underling by more subtle use of process, but in the final analysis the decision is based on status and formality.

Increased hierarchy of authority typically produces worker alienation [59] and such correlates as work dissatisfactions, slowdowns, simmering resentments, and explosive reactions; in a psychiatric hospital these may mean missed medication, interdepartmental feuding, poor service, and often countertherapeutic transactions with children. The child care workers treat the children the way they themselves have been treated. Feeling on the low end of the status hierarchy, and seeing themselves as being "had," many child care workers seek someone over whom they can be "one-up." So if the children either challenge or confront the power of the child care worker, as many of these children are prone to do, a fairly typical response from the child care worker is, "You are not going to be the boss," or "You're not going to do that as long as I am the boss on the ward." Confronted with the thrown gauntlet, a well-adjusted child would probably make the proper "passivity signals" and back down, but these children unfortunately do not know the rules. In effect, the child care worker looks for the vulnerability in the child and communicates, "Now I've got you"—a repetition of what the child care worker feels is his treatment at the hands of the nurse.

After-the-fact justification for the child care worker consists of "These kids are sick. They need discipline. You can't let them get away with this. They have to learn how to act with adults when they get out . . ." Justification for the nurses is "The child care workers are untrained. They are untrained transients. They need structure . . ." Both the child care workers and the nurses feel guilty about their action afterwards, but the damage is done. Both would like to work together, but the status hierarchy closes them out from each other.

Is this the way it should be? Most of us as supervisors would recognize that these are "heavy" problems, not about to disappear, and in fact likely to repeat themselves. It is a bad situation.

If a problem of this nature were to be dealt with through the traditional supervisory processes, what might it look like? Could a solution arise out of the relationship in which the nurse is supervisor and the child care worker is supervisee? A more probable model would be the head of nursing or the doctor/ psychiatrist attempting to confront the problem. The process might normally incur a conference with the nurse, then the child care worker, perhaps a meeting with both, perhaps a staff meeting to open up and discuss the conflicts. At best the meetings would be a search for information and solutions in a hierarchical system in which those in power might be asked to relinquish some. At worst the conferences might be a reaffirmation that the nurse is the boss: "Shape up or ship out."

Sensitive handling would avoid the latter, but the options would be limited. Even within this extremely hierarchical system, however, a new vitality might be achieved by an insistence by the supervisor that "we search together for evidence and proofs of a better way of working together." Then, of course, there must be a commitment to implement these new findings. The traditional method in supervision, as we saw in examining the historical perspectives, is a one-to-one tutorial hierarchical approach.

The notion of the autonomous professionals is of little help when we are faced with a situation of many professional groups fighting for their own autonomy at the cost of the other profession's dignity and the client's welfare.

We have some ideas of what ought to be done in this situation. With a lot of skill we might be able to help our staff come closer to the ideal. But why not make the ideal part of the ongoing contract—the life-style of the agency? Paying lip service to worker concerns or meeting with the staff as a group, or even being sympathetic to the worker's difficulties with client or with other staff, is not enough to overcome some of the alienation felt by staff. In reasons given for leaving their jobs, William Tollen found "dissatisfaction with supervision" was listed third in frequency after "to accept a better job" and "moved from community." [60]

Alienation, it is suggested, is often caused by the individual's feeling of separation, hopelessness, and estrangement from himself or from others. [61] Workers in an agency can feel apart from others when the structure of the agency separates them from the planning, from decision making that affects them, from their co-workers, or when work with the client itself becomes partialized. We have come to recognize the negative impact on clients who are seen by many different workers and must relate their problems over and over again, or who are shifted from office to office, or seen by one human service worker for one thing, and by another worker for something else.

We see, in the following fictional excerpt, some of the consequences to the social worker of this fractionalized approach to working with people. In order to maintain some semblance of continued competent action the worker must insulate himself from the terrors of the client, but this walling off of himself can only lead to alienation of any person with a desire to be helpful to his fellow man.

At the beginning of my career, I thought: It's like swallowing fistfuls of mud; I can neither digest it nor vomit it up. In the last ten years I must have said, "Have a seat, please," thirty thousand times. Apart from colleagues, witnesses, informers, prying newspapermen, and a few inoffensive mental cases it was distress that drove most of them to my desk. In most instances their anguish was massive, tentacular, and incurable; it weighed on me in this room where people cry, "Believe me, it hurts," "I can't go on," and "It's killing me," as easily as they would scream on a roller coaster. On the whole, my interrogations make me think of a surgeon who sews up his incision without removing the tumor.

Every institution makes for a specific state of mind. At the circus my client laughs, at the public baths he day-dreams, on the streetcar he stares into space, at a boxing match he is aggressive, in the cemetery subdued, and so on. To this room he brings a few samples of his sufferings and of frustrations that he has handed on to his sons and daughters. Quite possibly the image I get—the barest tip of the fragile molehill of his life—is deceptive. Yesterday he was kicked, today he gets apologies and tomorrow he may even come in for a caress or two, but all I see is his past. Nevertheless, I trust the momentary image, though with some caution. I may not know the man himself, but I know his circumstances. A diagram of his blunders, superimposed on those of other people, brings out what is specific to him, showing that what is unpredictable in him is infinitesimal compared to what is predictable. His circumstances are, let us say, straitened. In my official capacity I am informed of his job, habits, and previous blunders; this allows me to estimate how much freedom of action he has. Of course, what I see isn't the man himself, but only the envelope in which he moves about. Yet, reluctantly, I identify my client with all these odds and ends, and feel sorry for him because so many obstacles have impeded his development. It would be commendable if his relations with his environment were somewhat more complex, if the rules he chose to live by were a little less conventional. But his system is depressingly lacking in complexity, his income wretched, his physical surroundings dreary, his vision blurred, his burden heavy. His freedom of action is below average, his drives, which are without direction, conflict and sometimes collide head on. When this happens, the traffic jams up and official intervention is needed to start it moving again. Since my job is to protect children and safeguard the interests of the state, the most I can do is reconcile him with his circumstances and oppose his propensity for suffering. I do what the law and my fumbling judgment permit; then I look on, mesmerized, as the system crushes him.[62]

Whenever people feel separated from others, or from seeing or controlling the results of their work, there is potential alienation. This has been fairly well substantiated in assembly line jobs and in other forms of mechanized structuring of work. Only recently have we come to understand that alienation is a more generalized, pervasive phenomenon in our society. It touches the upper class as well as the lower class. It seems to be the nature of the "anxiety of our times."

This same hopeless, alienated feeling of the caseworker engulfs the worker who is departmentalized, touched by a client, and not able to deal with the suffering he sees because there is another more qualified worker who can step in and negate the work being done. This need not be a supervisor, as we shall see in the following record; it can be a colleague.

EXAMPLE: PUBLIC WELFARE AIDES

Here we see how a lack of integration and sense of community in the agency frames demands for angry reciprocity. Not only are hierarchical concerns evident, but fears related to "domain," "turf," and intra-agency competition abound. The degree of anxiety created by these negative forces combined with a destructive agency structure makes finding solutions complicatingly difficult.

SUPERVISOR: As I entered the office at 2:00 P.M., I was confronted by the clerk saying that there was an emergency situation. Immediately after that, Aide A came into my office in an upset mood (which is unusual for this aide).

AIDE A: "Sup, here is a case where the case worker is refusing to grant this client her full budget." (She went on to explain the case and her feeling that the budget had been figured incorrectly.)

SUPERVISOR: "Has the caseworker been contacted?"

AIDE A: "No, that's why I brought the case to you. The client has tried to get the caseworker to change the budget but the worker told her that she wouldn't do it until she had seen her." (The aide is now very excited and angry and continued saying) . . . "You always said that right was right, and the worker is wrong so what are you going to do?"

SUPERVISOR: (I felt pressed at this point as Aide B and Aide C were present and were in agreement with Aide A.) "Wait a minute Aide A, we ought to get the worker's side of it."

AIDE A: "She is wrong, that's all."

AIDES B AND C: (Nodding in approval.) "That's right."

SUPERVISOR: I felt that the question was whether or not I would back the client or the worker and that for me to back the worker would be intolerable to the staff. (The worker has her own opinion.) "Often, workers don't have all the information they need to make a decision; she may be working on it."

AIDE A: "This is no reason to punish the client."

SUPERVISOR: "You're right, but it's obvious to me that there is something personal going on between the client and the worker that is not coming out. She is considered a very good worker."

AIDE A: "She is still wrong."

In this situation we see how the supervisor has attempted to deal with the problem. It seems to get nowhere, and the fighting continues. Basic to the problem is the sense of alienation the aides might be feeling. They huddle together as a group but feel apart from the real decision making and outcomes.

The task for the supervisor in the future will be to build a sense of community, of common purpose, within her own agency and to mend some fences with the other office.

But there are some important issues related to moral behavior in this record. They center around attacks on colleague performance, disparaging a worker, and confidentiality. Part of the normative stance would be searching for ways to raise the staff (including the supervisor's) level of morality. The group is a natural context for such an endeavor, and at least one method which claims to be effective has been enumerated by Kohlberg, in his work on levels of moral development. This is discussed at greater length in Chapter 7.

Moral concerns have been raised in relation to current supervisory practice by a number of practitioners, both student and expert. They range from the lightly provocative "Games People Play in Supervision" [63] to the more serious appraisals made by students related to supervisory power,[64] and the highly philosophical dictates of Charles S. Levy.[65] The moral concerns seem to center around:

1. The power relationships of the supervisor "over" the supervisee both on and beyond the job.
2. The supervisor's stance of possessing superior knowledge (even when he doesn't).
3. The pressure on the supervisee to reveal himself.
4. The supervisor as a representative of management.
5. Role conflict for the supervisor.
6. The creation of dependency and need for approval.
7. Subtle forms of behavior control.
8. Unsupportiveness and aloofness.

These pressures on supervisors and supervisees take their toll on individual worker growth and creativity. They muddle the ability of the agency to assess "honest" responses and may subvert good practice. It leads to some supervisees conveying "the impression of compliance or willingness to comply." [66] Says one student in an article dealing with problems of supervision:

> I tried to cope by "playing the game." This took the form of pretending that everything was going well and answering all questions according to what I thought she [the supervisor] wanted to hear.[67]

Is this just the concern of one or more unusual and isolated student? Should we assume that it is only a student concern brought on by the stress of student life? I think not. Practical experience and continued contact with the written and spoken testimonies of many workers would suggest that this response to supervisory teaching is more prevalent than we would wish it to be. What it means is that for whatever reason, people are not risking, sharing their concerns, looking to the supervisor for help, or in fact raising their practice competence through the traditional supervisory channels.

Blau spoke to this point somewhat in his work on formal organizations.[68] He pointed out that there was a cost involved in seeking help from others. Some charged too much for the help they gave, or gave none. The workers sought help from those who were able to deliver, and who charged a fair price.

To put things in the terms of costs may seem crass, and indeed it may in fact be an oversimplification. But we must admit that there is a cost to the profession when students and workers feel they must cope by telling their supervisors what they think the supervisors want to hear. On an obvious level the cost is to the client. We would hope that as new models of supervisory practice develop, such costs will be minimized. In fact that was one of the purposes for analyzing our current approaches to supervision: to point out that although there were strengths and some promise in the direction of autonomy, there were costs, and that improved practice must cope with these costs. We are saying that a higher level of supervisory practice would provide more opportunities for moral decision making. It would structure the arrangements among workers and supervisors in a way which would lead to a healthy coping, rather than a self-defeating defensiveness. In the next chapter we shall start to formulate a more normative value-oriented supervision.*

---

* It would be helpful if it were possible from this point forward to substitute another word for *supervisor*. The word itself has connotations which are negative in many people's minds. Perhaps the word *synergist* would suffice. Unfortunately the title *supervisor* is so pervasive I feel it would be a herculean task to introduce a new word. One is reminded of the movie *The Wizard of Oz*. The film is in black-and-white until Dorothy reaches Oz, then everything is in color. I would like that to happen in the reader's eye from this point on.

CHAPTER 3

THE NORMATIVE STANCE:
TOWARD A SYNERGY
MODEL OF SUPERVISION

*We are driven to seek meaning, and find it by discovering a
necessary relation between our lives and some larger purpose.*
ALLEN WHEELIS, THE MORALIST

Any statement which suggests a particular approach or specific
guidance in trying to solve problems is a normative statement.[1]
When we seek to solicit the profession to support a normative model, what is it we have in mind? We are suggesting that a
particular model of supervision, a model which holds out the
ideals of "what ought to be," is most likely to produce a superior
supervisory practice. We admit to a bias, but we think that any
model, even one presented as being value-free, must by the mere
fact of making choices reflect some priorities on the part of the
author. In essence then, our suggested problem-solving approach
is a normative model, a model, that is, derived from a sense of
what ought to be, not a statistical "norm."

WHAT SHOULD SUPERVISION LOOK LIKE?

If we were given the opportunity to initiate our ideal of supervisory practice, what might it look like? What would be its basic model? What would be the core which would set the atmosphere for practice? First, the approach would have to be in keeping with the essence of the human service profession. It could not be alien to the professional life-style of those involved at working for the profession nor to its historical heritage. In essence it would have to be a natural approach, natural in the sense that it could not be alien to our culture if it was to be nurtured and survive. It would have to grow out of our own practice experience, have to be grounded in human service practice, not medicine, or management, or public administration. And it will assume that there are ways in which problems that arise in supervision "ought to be handled." This would include the free expression of ideas, treatment of each other with respect, and a way of gathering evidence for sound solutions.

With this in mind let us attempt to rewrite the scenario of one of our earlier recorded examples. Let us imagine that we have returned once more to the children's hospital and are involved in the staff conference that is about to take place. What would you hope to see? Let us refresh your memory by reviewing the episode.

> On one occasion a child care worker had planned to take his ward group off the grounds to a basketball game and had managed to obtain free tickets. The group had planned the trip for about a week, but one of the children misbehaved in class and the nurse said that he could not go on the trip. The child care worker felt that the nurse had no right to make this decision, that it would be harmful to the child and that it interfered with his jurisdiction. The child care worker pointed out that he would also bear the brunt of the hostility and problems that would follow. The nurse said it was her decision to make, not his.

Now, of course, there are aspects to this situation which are no doubt out of the range of direct supervisory responsibility and direction. Some of the problems in the interrelationships are created by the structure of the agency as well as the nature of the problems which the children present. But still, within the range of supervisor influence, how might you go about handling the problem? We have previously reviewed some of the approaches that might be taken by the usual supervisory processes. Now let us see what a synergist would try to do in this situation. Think about the approach for a moment. Here are some possibilities.

First, he would try to frame the problem and raise the awareness of the members of the "set," or system, involved in the situation. Then he would explore various ways of handling the situation, listing the alternatives, without commenting on the pros and cons, of each suggestion. Then he might focus on those which seem acceptable, searching out the available evidence for a particular viewpoint.

All efforts of the staff would be directed at creative problem solving, not avoiding conflict, but turning the conflict into substantive suggestions for action. But of course this could only take place in a situation supportive of and committed to this type of shared problem solving. A synergistic approach has to be learned, lived, practiced, and rewarded.

Let us assume that you are a new supervisor, faced with this as a problem as you begin a new job. You are in the position of ward director and thus in an administrative position where teachers, nurse, and child care worker are responsible to your office. A first task would be to raise the awareness level of yourself and the staff.

AN AWARENESS OF WHAT OUGHT TO BE

A guiding principle is "what ought to be"—what would be good in this situation. This would seem to us to be a natural way to start.

THE GOAL: What would be best in this situation? That too seems like a natural concern.

THE CHILD: It would be good for the child if he could participate in the project his group was working on. It is an opportunity to get out of the institution, be with his group, have fun. At the same time, it might be good if he didn't feel he had "won out" if the decision were changed (we obviously need more data here).

THE NURSE: It would be good if she did not lose face, could be more thoughtful in decisions, less punishing and more ready to involve the child care worker in decisions.

THE CHILD CARE WORKER: It would be good if he didn't have to bear the brunt of hostility, didn't feel he had lost his authority.

THE SUPERVISOR: It would be good if a solution was reached that did not harm any of the parties, gave people new understandings of their behavior, and made for a closer community.

We could spell these out further, or do a similar projection for other people involved in this scenario or set.

The role of the supervisor (recognizing that we are for the time being accepting the structure of the agency) is to engage all of the parties in a search for a solution which will be a good one. This is a commitment which must come from all the staff. This search requires a mutual respect for the members in the community and a search for evidence.

For example: Under what conditions is it good for children to be punished? Do we have an experience indicating that the children are helped to function on a more adequate level if these types of programs are withheld? Do the feelings of the other group members become expressive? Is this good or bad? How would we find out?

Do nurses feel guilty afterward about the way they handled the situation? Are relations with child care workers better or worse? Is this good or bad for the community? What problems are presented to the child care workers when these decisions are made? Is there any evidence of this? We have raised a large number of questions. By selecting some to examine, the staff can begin to partialize the problem and search for some evidence to support action.

What other ways of handling these problems have been tried? Which one works better than others? Do all children respond the same way to this type of discipline? What about this child? What are his special needs? Only when this type of search is engaged in can all the parties begin to look at the evidence and begin to contemplate creative ways to deal with situations. Otherwise, the responses are based on habit and idiosyncratic feelings of the moment. As the evidence accumulates over time, through exploration of many cases, these decisions may become more automatic. But they will grow out of actual practice experience, not out of hypothetical constructions.

Cases which seem contrary to accepted practice or to our accumulated evidence need to be reviewed carefully, for clues to understanding that they may offer.

Through working with all parties—including the child, whenever possible—this mutual search becomes a peak learning experience, a community endeavor, a community problem, not the child's problem or the nurse's problem, etc.

We need to look at supervision as ethical practice. In that light we need evidence as to what ought to be the best way to work with people if we want a just society.

FOCUSING ON THE POINT OF SYNERGY TO INFLUENCE MORAL ACTION

When all of the forces in the hospital converge on what would be best in this situation, rather than what would be best for any one of the actors, we have a high synergy situation.[2]

The ability to work with people in a way that helps them to learn how to synergize, minimize their own needs, and focus in on the best solution in this situation calls for a high level of practice. It is not a trade-off model, nor a consensus approach, but it does require that people be able to suspend their own judgments until all the data are in and have been looked at. Our current paradigms are compromises, usually brought about by a giving in, so as not to hurt anyone's feelings, or a yielding to power because of the vulnerability of the lower status worker. To synergize is to mobilize all of the forces of the staff and the client to look for a just solution. With a supportive environment, where being willing to modify one's own decisions in the face of new knowledge is the norm, no one loses face for changing a position. In order to develop more effective practice, the staff must be willing to share their thinking with fellow professionals, to evaluate alternative views, to put their own views to hard tests, and to modify them when the evidence demands it. This is how our grounded paradigm will emerge.

Kuhn states that in the history of science, a new scientific paradigm is built when the older paradigm is unable to deal with the anomalies confronting it.[3] At this point in scientific history, a struggle ensues between the holders of the older paradigm and those of the new. The "traditionalists" continue to try to make the anomalies fit into the old paradigm, while the revolutionaries are using empirical ways to demonstrate the validity of the new model. Eventually, the traditional paradigm is dropped, and the scientists then accept the new paradigm. This is called revolutionary science.

The individual-oriented, quasi-autonomous approach can be perceived in loose terms as a paradigm for supervision of ethical decisions, and it is under broad attack.

> There has been a growing conviction that the traditional supervisory system in some hands has not been a fountain of nurture to promote the social worker's growth as much as a fountain of youth to perpetuate his childhood.[4]

This crisis of supervision creates a new level of energy for developing a more adequate model for supervision practice. The prospect of the future confronts us with anomalies for which traditional social work supervision will no longer suffice. Can a method which cannot deal with present anomalies possibly deal with those of the future?

The pieces of the puzzle do not fit together any longer. Social work articles consistently point out our problems; this implies we are faced with a new set of phenomena which our traditional paradigm cannot incorporate, to which our practice does not perform. The future is upon us, and our human services administrators and teachers need to recognize and accept that the conservative paradigm is no longer functioning and is capable of dealing with new problems. We will need to move into dialogues which lead us to a systems-transactional view of the total man, "the supervisee in the situation."

Kuhn suggests that it is the young people, or those new to the profession, that are instrumental in changing and developing the new paradigms. Perhaps some of the human services profession is viable and lively enough to engage in new social alterations. It is the younger people, tired of hierarchical decision making, who lead us in these efforts. If our resistance impedes us rather than causes us to ask hard questions, we shall no longer continue to have a proactive profession. In the following chapters we shall set forth more thoroughly our ideas for a supervision practice more relevant to our changing profession and times. These ideas are ideals to work toward. In the meantime, we can set forth some of the synergistic ideas to improve on our current models.

The synergistic process is an attempt to bring people and ideas together, to unify divergent views into a more comprehensive whole, to eliminate the isolation of the loser and the alienation of the winner from "defeated" colleagues. It is this schizophrenic separating out of people from each other which creates the anxiety and the alienation of good people who would like to work together if they could learn how.

THE NORMATIVE MODEL

1. GOALS

The historic commitment of the social work community has been for the betterment of human society and the enhancement of individual functioning. In assuming that most agencies are still functioning with that historic charter and not, as some would say, as an agent of social control, then the supervisory processes should be on behalf of these values.

The setting of such broad goals, however, is often a historic endeavor which is modified over time by emphasis on a certain population group, the elimination of a particular evil or illness, and the ravages of compromises to funding sources or available skill and knowledge. The specific goals then may change and reflect a more concentrated scope of the world, but the major broad vision—that is, the contract, the mandate of the profession—must be clear.

The professional contract. This professional contract by the institution with the community establishes that it will provide certain services to categories of clients in the most "professional" manner possible. At times these contracts are nonlegal, as in the case of a family service, counseling, or recreation center. Often they acquire strong legal restraints, as in adoption agencies or probation and juvenile courts. Because of these already existing contractual expectations, clients approach the agency with certain self-assurances that they will be treated in a certain manner and will also be expected to behave in certain ways. In a sense they say, "You have certain skills and knowledge which can help me. Since I am not in a position to judge whether you are performing correctly, particularly because some of your skills are highly technical, I will trust to the contract that your profession has made with society."

The supervisory contract. Initial contacts with staff require a reiteration of the contract, either written or in the vision of the board and staff. All parties need to be clear as to what the goals of the agency are, and the philosophy of changing which is legitimate to the achievement of those goals. As far as the goals and means can be clarified, the paths the workers must take to achieve those goals become less encumbered.

The contract then sets forth clearly the goals, means, and mutual expectations of the parties involved, as far as they can be determined at the early stages. Contract modification is anticipated and is so stated, so that no one feels committed to a process he finds alienating or a goal that might violate his sense of justice. Means of modifying the contract might also be spelled out.

Working for a just society. The historic mission of our profession has strongly been related to two major areas. The first has been service to individuals so that they could make adequate, dignified adjustments to society. The second concern has been with social reform, the restructuring of those elements of a society which in C. Wright Mills's terms become the public issues that need to be dealt with.[5] In a strong sense social work has always been a consciousness-raising profession (see Figure H) at the individual, community and societal levels.

2. STRUCTURE OF SERVICE: THE PRACTICE ENVIRONMENT

Chris Argyris began a recent monograph with a strong indictment of our institutions: "The most critical fact about present complex organizations is that they are infected with dry rot, a cancerous illness that threatens to disable and cripple seriously their effectiveness and efficiency." [6] Much of the problem is due to a lack of creativity, conservative approaches, and concretionary structures. His emphasis is that organizations need to become more human.

We would certainly agree and suggest that to be more human, agencies need to minimize status, power, and control, and emphasize instead democratic process, involvement, and respect for all ideas and people. Even where some hierarchical structuring is the mode there can be ample opportunities to minimize alienation by building in resources for decision making, appeals, and recourse grievances in an open, nonthreatening manner.

If workers come to feel alienated from that which they feel is attempting to subjugate them, then, as Etzioni points out, they may "strive to reduce the organization's control of their work by developing their own control system." [7] A possible solution to this problem is suggested by Pearlin when he states:

In order to retain its staff and maintain itself as an ongoing in-

FIGURE 4
SUPERVISION: A CONSCIOUSNESS-RAISING PROCESS

WHOM ARE WE TRYING TO INFLUENCE?	FOR WHAT PURPOSE?	GOAL
1. People (including ourselves)	To develop healthy, moral, thinking and doing people	A
A. Views of themselves, and B. Ability to act		J
2. People in relation to others. Modify roles and status, improve "the interpersonal bonds."	To improve ability of people to act in concert with others as equals	U
		S
A. Relationship between people		T,
B. Family relations		W
C. Small groups		
3. Communities Geographic (living settlements), structural, and functional	Improved setting for supportive living	O
		R
4. Temporary communities Related to (3) but less permanent: the workplace, the school	Improve the quality of life	T
		H
		W
5. Organizations A psychiatric hospital is both a temporary community for those who work there and a more permanent community for the residents	To improve their ability to be supportive and respond to the needs of people	H
		I
		L
6. Institutions A. Government, church, legal, educational, medical, etc.	To be more responsive to people and to improve quality of service	E
		S
B. Our profession	To reduce status and reward differentials	O
7. Society's thrust (THE FUTURE)	To provide the type of society which maximizes self-actualization, synergy and eliminates technological inhumanity, human destructiveness, and environmental pollution	C
		I
		E
	RECONSTRUCTION OF SOCIETY	T
		Y

stitution it must gear itself not only for the attainment of the ends for which it was established, but also for the satisfaction of the diverse aspirations and opportunities sought by its members.[8]

As he sees it, one of the important conditions which can lead to alienation is the inability of subordinates to act back upon their superordinates. Scott[9] points out the need for the establishment of many opportunities within the formal structure of the organization for just this type of "appeal."

If an agency values the contribution of all the staff in building a strong service-oriented program, there must be innovative and intelligent use made of all staff and recruitment, and training must be selective toward human-oriented people. The building of a strong institutional core "is partly a matter of selective recruiting. . . . But core building involves more than selective recruiting." Indoctrination and the sharing of experiences—especially internal conflicts and other crises—will help to create a unified group and give the organization a special identity.[10]

It is the writer's contention that the service goal and "just community" visions can be the common ground on which all workers and the administrative segments of an institution can meet in order to come to what Follet calls an integrated solution to their problems.[11] We may never entirely eliminate the need to vest accountability in one office, but we can eliminate authoritarian use of that office. There must not be a bid for power by one or the other of the groups, but rather an attempt to find solutions through mutual problem exploration, where the solution emerges from the situation to be resolved rather than from the control that each side is able to wield. The individual using the organization to fulfill his needs and simultaneously the organization using the individual to achieve its demands has been called by Bakke the "fusion process." [12] Note the similarity of this concept, coming out of industry, to synergy.

If the agency is to become the temporary society that Bennis and Slater speak of, then it must be a temporary society that reflects a community orientation. A society which reflects the evils of the rotting organization that Argyris describes will not help us in our solution. It must be a "just" community which supports the best in people and will not permit conduct which would be harmful to anyone. This can only happen when people assist each other, as partners.

3. KNOWLEDGE BASE: THE SUBSTANCE OF PRACTICE

As a new, growing profession it was necessary—in fact, it was a strength—that we could borrow ideas and techniques from the social sciences and other professions. There was a cost, however, in not having our own grounded knowledge: the cost of reacting to fashions, fads, and fallacies. Future decisions related to practice need to be researched from within our own experience. To turn to others may mean (1) buying into social science "research," which in itself is poorly conceived, nonnormative, and harmful to people, (2) locking into a formulation which, over time, loses its value for practice—such as Freud's psychoanalytic approach, or one like the medical model, which follows too narrow a view. Supervisory practice needs to grow out of documenting our own experiences, comparing results with other supervisors and practitioners, noting the "odd" case or the failures, retesting and sharing our ideas. *Then,* we can decide whether the social sciences have further insights to offer us.

The work of Virginia Robinson [13] melded her knowledge of supervision and her knowledge of what happens in the lives of students during their two years in the temporary community of a graduate school of social work, with her own theories of "functional control" into an exciting approach to supervision. It was grounded in her practice. What was missing was a comparison of her ideas with the experiences of others in other schools and subsequent reassessment of her own approaches.

It is legitimate to find some of the supports for our theory building in the fields of education, psychology, and management, but they should not be at the root of our professional practice.

4. SYNERGISTIC PROCESSES

The very best in agency practice requires that supervisors

bring out the very best in the staff. Crucial to this maximizing process is the humanistic connection integrating client worker–supervisor/administrator. The nature of the "connections" between the supervisor and the supervisee is a crucial factor in determining the amount of "growth" that can occur in the "field." If there is mutual trust, respect, and acceptance of each other's dignity, it matters not whether the supervisor is always "knowledgeable" of alternative solutions, or that the worker's actions might not always be "correct." The task of being able to work together with idiosyncratic, individualistic approaches to helping, within professional boundaries, is the vital issue. The supervisee can question the policies, the system, his own values, and contributions as well as his supervisor's expertise; and yet neither need be threatened, because the synergistic approach suggests a no-lose situation for worker, supervisor, and client. As we shall interpret it, synergy is the noncompetitive melding of two or more often conflicting ideas into an outcome which is an advance over any one of the original ideas (i.e. has better payoff for all). The term *synteraction* will suggest the process of communication which permits this advanced variation to take place. It provides a "receptive" medium or culture in which growth can take place and in which the individual feels a response from other parts of the system which are "sympatico." Synergy is the joint search with the worker for "truth," an inquiry into how two or more people, often with differing views of what the answer might be, can find a radical-effective solution to a problem.

The need for this synergising environment is particularly vital in situations where the nature of the worker-client interaction exacerbates the "environmental press" on the worker and/or the client.

Synergy suggests that when each party in the transaction maintains somewhat selfish thinking (what's best for me and the agency service), the result will be of a higher order of success than if each looks at what is only best for himself. But the task becomes one of finding a mutually satisfying solution. Maslow suggests that "self-actualizing people rise above the dichotomy between selfishness and unselfishness." [14]

Were the supervisor to look only at what is good for him, it might be to search out or support all supervisees who agree with his approaches and never question the "system." However, to look at what is best for the client and agency should mean to accept a "good" worker who also "questions," because this may lead to improved changes in the agency. What is best in *this situation* needs to be the guiding principle, and then to find a solution which approaches "what ought to be."

What is best for supervisor and supervisee is to find new effective ways to work for the client. This helps the client, improves the morale and skill of the worker, and also improves the supervisor. In addition it carries out the mandate of agency service.

In essence we are not considering what is best for *any one* segment of the subsystem, but what is best for all involved. As a supervisor, for example, my extrapersonal communication might be, "If by attempting to modify the system I can help the client and agency (worker and myself), then I have come up with a result which rewards everyone." Admittedly these solutions are difficult in a complex society *or* system, but in part they are so difficult for us because:

1. The nature of our culture implies an I-win, you-lose approach; and
2. We have not learned to practice synergistic approaches.

Changes in culture, however, are taking place, and the concept of synergy has gained increased importance in the work of psychologists such as Maslow and world "viewers" such as Buckminster Fuller.[15] On a more popular level, the O'Neills, in advocating "open marriage," suggest that the synergistic process enhances the marriage relationship:

> Synergy occurs when two organisms, or people are brought together, or combined, in such a way that the end result is enhanced—that is, when the combination of the two produces a quality or effect that is more intense than what either of the two contributing parts originally had or could independently attain.

Thus in synergy one and one makes three, not just two. It is this special effect, this enhancement, that makes it possible in open marriage for husband and wife to exist and grow as two separate individuals, yet at the same time to transcend their duality and achieve a unity on another level, beyond themselves, a unity that develops out of the love for each other and each other's growth. In a synergistic, cooperative way, each one's individual growth enhances and augments the other's growth, pleasure and fulfillment. The more of a whole person each one becomes, the more he has to offer his mate. The better he feels within himself, the more he can love; the more he can give freedom, the more he can take pleasure in seeing his mate grow; the more both partners grow, the more stimulating and dynamic each one becomes for the other.[16]

They go on to discuss the feedback potentials and actuality of this process by suggesting the following interaction process:

(1) It makes me happy to see you happy.
(2) When I see you happy because I have done something to make you happy (given you a gift, perhaps the gift of freedom), or have done something for us together, I become happier with your happiness.
(3) Through open love and open trust, I am able to take that same pleasure in your happiness even when it is someone or something else that has made you happy.
(4) Your happiness is further increased by seeing and knowing that my happiness is augmented and increased by your happiness.
(5) This mutual enhancement effect gives us synergic build-up.[17]

Industry and education have also been receptive to many of the ideas of synergy, particularly its potential for creative problem-solving methods. Two books dealing with "synectics" illustrate the use of synergistic concepts to develop new models of thinking as well as new products for industry.[18] Prince, looking at attempts at "teaching" creative thinking approaches, points out some of the difficulties caused by noncreative thinking. He suggests that we often attack new ideas because they threaten us, or we fear the people who have initiated them. We stress the bad points of an idea, attempting often to make them look worse than they might be. Naturally, when we attack someone's idea, he in turn will attack ours. That is the nature of competition and retribution. Prince suggests instead a "spectrum" approach to new ideas.

The "spectrum" approach requires that no idea that is suggested be attacked. It is assumed that if you attack my idea, I will attack yours. We must instead search for the good part of the idea in the broad spectrum of thought considered by the suggestion. It is natural in our culture to attack the bad, because that indeed is the part of the idea that would be most threatening if it were to be accepted.

The "spectrum" of an idea might be diagrammed in several ways, depending on the relative amounts of "good" and "bad" it contains:

1. |———+———————| 2. |———————+———|
  good   bad   good   bad

Only the good parts of the idea are discussed and built upon. If no one can respond by picking up a good part, the idea is ignored and fades away.

Modes of synergistic communication. The importance of communication styles and their impact on the ability to develop a synergistic mode in supervision is suggested by the work of Gregory Bateson, who pointed out that there are two major modes of communicating—symmetrical and complementary.[19]

Symmetrical relationships are based on the concept of equality. This assumes that a certain type of behavior from A brings forth more of the same type of behavior from B. This kind of process is exemplified by a series of competing communications, contests, fights, and a keeping up with the Joneses.

Complementary relationships are those in which one person occupies a "one up" position and the other a "one down," or "inferior position." These may be exemplified by the parent-child, supervisor-supervisee, or worker-client. Bateson suggests that one should not see this in value terms, but that the relationships complement each other unless something happens in the relationship to turn it into a contest or to change it into a symmetrical relationship. The mother who insists on keeping a child dependent through adolescence, or the supervisor who maintains a worker in a dependent relationship when he is prepared to move in an autonomous direction, would illustrate these "pathological" situations. They would lead to conflict and competition.

Bateson suggests that the symmetrical relationships reflect more peaceful creative types of cultures. He utilizes the concept to discuss the role of Alcoholics Anonymous as a helping tool; seeing their demands for "surrender" of the alcoholic as part of the establishment of no contest, therefore replacing a complementary relationship with something "bigger" than the alcoholic —AA, or the Group, or God.[20]

It seems clear that Bateson is dealing with an aspect of synergistic interaction or "synteraction"—those types of communication "interactions" among people in which something greater in a positive sense evolves as a result of the communication. Note the similarity between Bateson's statements and the following comments by Ruth Benedict, the "rediscoverer" of synergy.[21]

> From all comparative material the conclusion emerges that societies where nonaggression is conspicuous have social orders in which the individual by the same act and at the same time serves his own advantage and that of the group. The problem is one of social engineering and depends upon how large the areas of mutual advantage are in any society. Nonaggression occurs not because people are unselfish and put social obligations above personal desires, but when social arrangements make the two identical.[22]

Synergy is the term she uses to represent the "gamut that runs from one pole, where any act or skill that advantages the individual at the same time advantages the group, to the other pole, where every act that advantages the individual is at the expense of others."[23]

Synergistic transactions have an excellent chance of success in most supervisory situations in social work. The general norm is that the major emphasis rests on what needs to be done to be helpful to the client. The transactions between the supervisor and the supervisee need not take on the nature of a contest since neither party has anything to gain by overcoming the other, but in fact each, as well as the client and the agency, has something to gain if the transaction leads not only to better service to the client but also to increased knowledge and understanding for the worker and satisfaction for the supervisor.

Why then is there a contest situation? A partial answer may be found in some of the patterns of communication that both parties to the transaction have developed. It may be related to games they play, to a fear of being seen as dependent, or to uncertainty as to their authority.[24] A basic reason might be the person's sense of ego and loss of self-esteem. This can be minimized if people treat each other with respect.

What is important for our work, however, is not the possible motivating cause, but rather an examination of the methods through which new ways of working together toward "synteraction" might be developed and integrated into the ongoing supervisory relationship. Naturally the "culture" of the agency, as Benedict has suggested, will determine the extent to which synergistic interactions in subunits or "subcultures" can expand, survive, or influence other parts of the system.

> In all corporate societies the social order makes certain provisions for synergy. All homologous segmented societies depend upon and build up in their members an experience of social solidarity with each . . . segment of society, however small . . .
>
> If other factors in the social order make synergy low, their own group also is less dependable; but it is still there.[25]

Although it might be important for the practice of synergistic administrative transactions to be introduced and supported from the top, it is not impossible to have it start within any supervisory relationship, small society and community.

SYNERGY AS A TOOL FOR SURVIVAL

If one were to take as a metaphor for growth, innovation,

and survival the coupling bond (or the marriage bond) one would have in the nature of the reproductive process a model for synergy. Without the linkage of new genetic materials the possibilities for innovation are lost. The group becomes whole through growth and in fact enhances its own extinction by not accepting the new.

It is the synergistic approach, whether in the supervisory relationship, staff meetings, or committee work that permits innovations in the agency. It is the ability to take in new ideas and build on them which provides variation in approach and eventually in the nature of the staff.

Were all workers to remain fixed in their ideas or be required to adopt the ideas of the supervisor or the agency director, not only would there be a lack of growth in their own ability to function as autonomous workers, but the level of growth of the agency would likewise suffer. Clearly not only is it of benefit for staff growth to set the culture of the agency on a high synergy level, but it also serves agency survival. In the long run—in competition with agencies that are more flexible, creative, and able to use innovative, high synergy approaches—agency survival may require, in fact demand, a synergistic approach to administration.

What I am suggesting, therefore, is that the adoption on an agency-wide basis of a commitment to synergistic growth environment would:

1. Benefit the supervisee, by permitting and structuring autonomous, creative growth.
2. Minimize the bosslike qualities of the supervisor, which often force "good" social workers to become "bad supervisors," and permit the supervisor's own growth on the job.
3. Mobilize a "force" of workers for the agency who are creative, excited, and constantly moving to higher levels of performance.
4. Benefit the clients by providing innovative attempts to help and a sense of being worked with in a synergistic manner.

What might the procedure be for setting the proper agency culture for a synergy model? Let's explore some possibilities.

The first might be the specifying of the goals of what such a model might offer and arriving at a "contract" within the agency to use the approach, whether agency-wide or as a trial among a set of workers who feel akin to its ideas.[26] Both parties in the relationship, assuming we are starting with the traditional supervisory pair, would understand that their actions are to be mutually viewed as selfish and unselfish at the same time.

The second acknowledgment would be that the actions of both parties are reinforcing and that the direction of the thrust of their mutual actions is as a quest for the best interest of the client and the improved practice of the worker and supervisor. In fact they are partners in the quest for a synergistic solution.

The third agreement is that compromise is unacceptable. When differences in ideas as to approach arise and a dichotomy is apparent, both parties must encourage a transcendence of the dichotomy, not a profiting from the conflict.[27]

> If deadlock were the results of dichotomies between the two parties then no side would win and the result would be neither best help for the client nor the development of best practice for the worker. Deadlock could in fact result in no help for the client. If compromise were the result of dichotomies both parties would win and lose. Such a condition would result in reasonable but not optimal help for the client and a similar degree of practice for the worker. If synergy were the theme of supervision both parties would win—the best help for the client and the development of best practice for the worker would result.[28]

I believe deadlock is less apt to occur the more the parties gain the experience of working together and seeing their success. The joy of the results will become reinforcing and begin to carry the synergistic style of work. More important, perhaps, is my belief that the deadlock will decrease as the areas of dispute become subject to resolution by evidence. As we can begin to establish with increasing certainty what the "best" (statistically speaking) approach might be to the solution of the problems, we can develop a more normative practice. Synergy is at its best a mutual search for the truth. It is the art of *making people accessible* to ideas.

The areas in which deadlock is most likely to occur are those areas in which your opinion seems as good as mine because we have no evidence, but I think my way is better; or around areas in which I feel I have been threatened and must cope by defending myself. At those points I may resort to emotion and not work on finding a solution. A commitment to synergistic approaches brings me back to the cause of mutuality, a more efficient and fulfilling method of problem solving. In this respect it is hooked into the normative approach, a quest for the true solution based on the quest for additional evidence.

Synteraction as a process reflects the nature of the changes that are taking place in people's perceptions of what the nature of the working relationship should be. As Carl Rogers among others has pointed out, we are entering into the era of the "new man" (woman, too). This person deplores sham, rejects tradition, does not fit the "traditional industrial and organizational model," doesn't fit into the military, will not put up with double-talk, and reacts negatively to controls and authoritarianism.[29] Others have suggested that there is a push toward self-management; experiments with various work models in England [30] and on the kibbutzim [31] seem to bear out the success of the new person and the new models.

These new models will be evident in the social work profession as they are already in the life-styles of the people that social workers deal with. There is a new person in the nature of the client, the nature of the problems which he presents, and the nature of the contract that he is willing to make in order to obtain help. He wants in on the contract, whether it is the mechanism of "maximum feasible participation" or the demand for a nonsexist therapist. There is a growing recognition that the traditional institutions are not only in need of change, but are indeed changing.

Is it outrageous to assume that the demands for a say in decisions that affect one's life will not have repercussions in the social work profession and in the supervisory relationship? The quest for autonomy that workers have always felt as they struggled to become professionals has always had a countervailing pull for more knowledge—the need to know more, so that they can do more. Traditionally the supervisory tutorial relationship has sat-isfied in our profession. The new person of social work, however, is no longer content with the more traditional model. More inter-actional approaches have already begun to unravel the tattered model. Group supervision, peer supervision, and consultation have taken their tolls. This may not be enough, because the status differentials still remain, the supervisor is still the expert, and, even worse, the "evaluator" as well. The normative model attempts to deal with the total gestalt; it offers a new force for helping in which synergistic thinking and working play impor-tant functions.

A high synergy supervisory model would minimize the dif-ferential and would create the mutuality which could lead to autonomy for all parties in the transaction. Synteraction can become a support or substitute for the more traditional super-visory process. Rather than use the term *supervisor*, which implies the hierarchical "looking over" tasks, we might initiate and quickly substitute the role of *synergist*.

5. SELF-HELP EDUCATION

There is a growing recognition of the concept of "self-help," by which we mean people who share some concerns mobilizing as a group to do something about it. That "something" might be social action, such as getting a stop sign on the corner. It may be for personal change, such as A.A. groups, or it may be a combina-tion, like parent groups for retarded children. Many of these latter groups support the individual members' stress, give help-ful information and limits, but also attempt to change laws and build programs.

The emphasis in agency supervision should be on develop-ing groups of staff who help each other, learn how to "be," and find their own resources. If, because of advanced experience, knowledge or training, the supervisor has learned some important insights and skills related to supervision, these should be shared with *all* the staff for *all* to use.

Likewise this approach should permeate the total agency. Knowledge is not a commodity to be bought and held onto. It should be shared by all who want and can use it. Thus clients, too, should learn self-help techniques, counseling, and social action, and the agency should provide this education.

Ivan Illich, in a number of stinging articles and books, has attacked the professions for holding onto knowledge, for charging for it, or sharing it only with the worthy. In medicine, he suggests, this has created a medical nemesis, with people in worse health than ever, and an elite group of medical people holding onto knowledge that might be available to all.[32]

This is reflected in human service supervision. And we would suggest that by an open-sharing approach to our professional know-how, a nonexpert stance, if you will, in which everyone learns from everyone else, we can set the pace for an "open" approach to service.

6. PROFESSIONAL ACCOUNTABILITY

Nonnormative models of social work employ hierarchical accountability structures. These models do not make the discovery and achievement of what is good—all things considered—the concern of the profession. Instead they assign the determination of which goals are appropriately served to some extra-professional authority—the client, the agency, the legislature, the governor, or the parties in interaction. As a result, if there is to be accountability, it must be to those with authority to set values and to evaluate. The normative model of social work calls for professional, peer accountability for social practice. This requires: (1) protection of the integrity of the autonomy of social practice, and (2) *genuine* professional accountability in protection of the public.

Professional autonomy. The professional association of social workers must create policies and structures that protect against hierarchical practice accountability, for this always threatens the professional autonomy of the social worker. Hierarchical accountability for practice puts practice in the service of interests set in unprofessional ways. Needless to say, the profession as a whole will be accountable to society for the quality of its professional practice. Funding sources that do not value social work of a professional quality will not fund it; nevertheless, such sources should not determine what constitutes professional practice. If we are to achieve a truly professional status in our work we must pursue practice in a way that does not compromise with political or economic pressures. Should members of the education profession not teach unpopular political or economic theories due to threats from political powers, they act unprofessionally. Should members of the medical profession refuse to offer certain types of medical service due to political or economic pressure, they act unprofessionally. Similarly, should members of the social work profession permit their practice to be improperly distorted by political or economic pressure, they act unprofessionally. It is no more a virtue for this profession to compromise its practice in the name of political "realism" than for any other profession to do so.

Protection of the public. Protection of the public requires public documentation. Peer accountability in protection of professional autonomy must be complemented by effective supports for high quality practice. Basically what this requires is strong colleagual relationships. Practice must be effectively reviewable by peers in the profession. Effective review is review that actually succeeds in bringing about practice changes. This requires that social workers form a relationship like that of members of a scientific community. This involves the documentation of what one does in a way that seeks to achieve agreement with others on both the account of the specific act and upon its general significance and explanation. These same cognitive standards, when carefully followed, become practice standards as well. They involve us in one another's work in such a way that everything is subject to scrutiny and review. Under these conditions all practice moves upward in the direction of the best practice, for practice that is poorer than that which is known to be possible cannot survive the light of full public examination. In Blau's terms, the rewards are low, and staff will search out those supervisors who are at a high level of supervisory practice.

Consultation. A valuable element of peer accountability is the establishment of a regular practice of consultation. This fosters the documentation of cases in ways that are public and less subjectively idiosyncratic. It also provides protection against poor quality practice in an immediate, direct way at the point where it is needed, for it pushes practitioners to seek agreement in actual practice and not to split into isolated, individual practice. This would also permit a supervisee to seek assistance from more than one person, or from a selected supervisor not regularly assigned to him. Again this would serve to enlighten practitioners as to varied helping and supervising styles.

THE NORMATIVE STANCE: A SUMMARY

The normative stance sets some of the parameters related to the values within which supervision takes place.

Goals. The goals of the supervisory processes are closely related to what the functions and purposes of the social agency ought to be. In general terms these are (1) helping people arrive at sound judgments regarding what ought to be, all things considered; and (2) securing social arrangements and individual competence in conformity with such judgments.[33] We feel that agencies should be interested in evolving sound, effective, moral solutions to the problems facing society and their clients. These solutions need to be seen in the context of a restructuring of society for social justice.

Structure of service. The structure of the agency and the patterning of the interactions within the agency as well as in its relations with other agencies need to be within the framework of democratic processes and moral behavior, insuring the dignity and respect of all people involved. The structure should permit and encourage the minimizing of supervisor as expert, and should promote the concept of agency as a "just" community.

Knowledge Base. The major mode for the gathering of knowledge to be used in practice needs to be based on scientific inquiry, regardless of whether that practice is counseling, social

TABLE 1. A COMPARISON OF FOUR MODELS OF SUPERVISION

	MODELS			
	GROWTH	QUASI-AUTONOMOUS	AUTONOMOUS	NORMATIVE
Supervisor's role	Helper, administrator, teacher	Administrator, teacher	1. Administrative only 2. Professional development by outsiders	Synergist; moral scientist—practitioner
Supervisor's goals	Facilitate client services		Autonomous professional	"Just community; high level practice
Primary sources of knowledge	Education, management, casework, psychiatry	Marriage, education	Social science, small groups	Grounded practice; allied professions
Media	Individual supervision	Individual—Group	Group—Teams for professional development	Groups—self help agency as community
Supervisory structure	Executive hierarchy	Modified executive hierarchy	Team professional hierarchy	Community of colleagues
Accountable	Supervisory—hierarchy, Professional supervisor	Profession—Supervisor Administrator	Own conscience Professional ethics No other outside controls	Professional press community—clients everyone
Inherent problems	Conflict around dependency—authority		Elitist; new workers not involved	

change, teaching, or supervision. The knowledge base must be grounded in human service practice, utilizing social science research as it appears applicable and verifiable to our own grounded theory.

Synergistic processes. A synergistic process is a pattern of relationships which helps establish synergistic learning/change processes. It is a partnership between supervisor/worker, worker/client based on symmetrical relationships and permitting mutual problem solving without contest strategies.[34] The problems are not differentiated and attached to a particular individual or group, but seen as a mutual concern in which each plays a part.

Self-help education. There is a continuing responsibility to increase the ability of supervisees to practice in autonomous ways and to permit clients to develop their own self-help resources. We must promote values and practice of self-help as well as the need for a public health prevention view by the development and dissemination of materials which can be used in the community by either self-help or worker-supported groups.

Accountability and growth. In the normative approach, accountability is not necessarily to a hierarchical structure but to peers, clients, and the moral community within which one functions. There is also responsibility for a scientific evaluation of one's work and a feedback to the broader professional community for its use. This, then, would result in an ethical approach to practice in which any techniques which are not grounded in solid evidence would be identified as such to the community.

Table 1 compares the normative synergy model with other current supervisory approaches.

CHAPTER 4

ENGAGING PEOPLE IN

SUPERVISION

He who humbles himself shall be saved; He who bends shall be made straight; He who empties himself shall be filled.

A tree that it takes both arms to encircle grew from a tiny rootlet. A many-storied pagoda is built by placing one brick upon another brick. A journey of three thousand miles is begun by a single step.

LAO-TZU, TAO-TE-CHING

The passage from beginning worker to experienced professional within an agency setting requires the learning of certain skills, the acquisition of knowledge, the expression of attitudes and values in keeping with the values and the expressed goals of the agency, and the carrying out of the professional tasks effectively.[1] The acquisition and provision of this package in a manner which permits questioning, change in self, and change in the agency's perspectives is the process of socializing the new worker into the culture of the agency.

THE SOCIALIZATION PASSAGE IN AGENCY LIFE

The socialization process attempts to take into consideration vital knowledge that the worker will need as a base for sound practice. It does not limit his search. Indoctrination, on the other hand, is a limited, narrow approach to training which projects "the agency point of view" on whatever topic is being discussed. Education would hold that all knowledge is open to revision.

Figure 5

*A View of Socialization to Human Services**

ENGAGEMENT IN THE WORK OF THE AGENCY

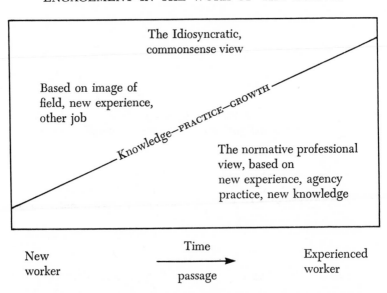

The Idiosyncratic, commonsense view

Based on image of field, new experience, other job

Knowledge—PRACTICE—GROWTH

The normative professional view, based on new experience, agency practice, new knowledge

New worker

Time

passage

Experienced worker

* George Getzels uses a similar, but more complex, model in looking at education. See "Administration as a Social Process," in *The Planning of Change*, ed. Warren G. Bennis, Robert Chin, and Kenneth Benne (New York: Holt, Rinehart & Winston, 1961), p. 376.

Figure 5 suggests that a new worker at the agency is going to work from his personal experience and ideas of what service is. His personality will strongly influence his work. Over a period of time the worker will acquire new knowledge from his practice, supervision, reading, etc., and will change his way of work in the direction of the norms (the "what should be's") of the profession. His personality will always influence his work, but it will be subject to the discipline and objectivity that he learns and that a professional needs to have. Rather than say his personality changes, we would suggest he learns which kinds of action, style, and responses are helpful to those with whom he works, and which actions get in the way of helping.

A number of authors have pointed out that any person in a new work situation is confronted with anxieties in two major areas: the task to be accomplished, and the feelings related to participation in the situation. These anxieties are situational in that they are clearly related to the newness of the situation. These are summarized in Figure 6.

Figure 6. Concerns Faced by a Worker in Individual Conferences

TASK	SOCIAL—EMOTIONAL
What do I want?	Will I like her/him?
	Will I be liked by her/him?
What can I learn?	Will it be safe?
	Will I have to change?

We can also imagine that similar concerns face the supervisor in relation to work with a new supervisee. He too might be concerned about being liked, about his ability to help, and about maintaining his self-image. This ego-oriented, but normal, human failing can get in the way of the teacher. He too must know himself.

Not only are both parties to the transaction subject to these concerns but also an additional factor enters which is of extreme importance: the phenomenon of power. To a great degree, the worker's "passage" into the agency is monitored by the supervisor. That monitoring, "overseeing" role puts one in the position of evaluation and often control of whether or not another person can proceed "upward" and complete the "rites of passage." Having such control often creates personal problems, particularly for a beginning supervisor who is uncertain how to use power. When he is aware of this intrapersonal conflict the supervisor can attempt to examine his own actions and moderate his own behavior. Unaware, however, he may not perceive how he uses power or that people are relating to him as a person occupying a powerful "role" rather than as the person he sees himself as being.

There is general acknowledgment that some people in administrative positions have difficulty using their power in relation to others. This is particularly true of new power realignments. Reynolds gives her views for the reason this may be so: "The balance which they have worked out for their personal lives between dominance and submission is upset by the new responsibility." [2] This would suggest that all people have worked out some balance related to their use of power. New situations call for a new appraisal of this balance. At times the actions of the person attempting to find his new balance may be contradictory, simply because of his constant reassessment of the proper use of authority. One might suspect that social workers will reflect some ambivalence to the use of authority with colleagues because of the nature of their understanding of what colleagual relations, or a profession, really ought to be. Conflicts between bureaucratic and professional norms will create additional problems for the supervisor as well as for the practitioner. The traditional nurturing role of the social case worker may also lead to a continued authoritative power stance even though it may appear more benign.

The supervisory transaction is a form of practice which requires knowledge, skills, and certain values and attitudes. Part of the skill of the supervisor is related first to helping the staff become aware of the vision of the agency in its efforts on behalf of people and second to working together with the staff to achieve the knowledge and skill to accomplish needed tasks. This is not to be taken lightly, for indeed the welfare of many people may be at stake. We should like the reader to view with us some of the ways in which supervisor and staff become engaged together in this process of discovery and action. For indeed it is a process, and certain segments of the process can be distinguished. We cannot separate them out, because they are parts of the whole, nor do they necessarily occur in a patterned sequence, although at times they may appear to do so. For lack of a more descriptive label, let us call this process "engagement," by which we mean the act of becoming bound to a certain idea or action process. In our model we are asking people to become engaged themselves with both ideas and action.

ENGAGEMENT IN INQUIRY AND ACTION

As in most learning situations, the key to learning in supervision is the engagement of the learners with each other and with the material to be learned. Engagement is seen as one of the key factors in the process of changing and growing.

Engagement, as we see it, consists of *awareness* of the need for change; *commitment* to a certain goal and method of action; *inquiry and knowledge* about what needs to be done and how to do it, and *movement in action* toward the accomplishment of the goal. Each of these four factors in the passage from beginner to informed practitioner contains a number of elements which need to be examined. (We do not consider these factors as time-related phases—although this is not discarded as a possibility.)

1. AWARENESS

Awareness is the increased understanding of a situation that results from the coming into consciousness and unfolding of ideas. Man exists and is free. He is free to decide whether he will change or not change. Involvement is an individual matter which starts with choice. To seek help with a problem or not, to listen or not, to reveal himself or not, to learn or not—these are choices which must remain the individual's. The choice that is made will often depend on the nature of the interaction between the individuals in the "action set," and so awareness is related to the nature of the transactions that take place between the supervisor and the worker. During this emergence to awareness process there is an attempt by the supervisor to develop a moral community and raise the level of consciousness among the staff.

There is an attempt to bridge the gap that arises between people, so that some relationship or connection can be made between them. Relationship is the "bond of feeling" communicated among the participants in the transaction. This should not be a relationship based on potential utility or power, but a relationship for the purpose of *mutual understanding* of what it is that each desires and hopes for from mutual work. Such a relationship is built through open communication and respect for each other's work and opinions. People are more readily involved when they are faced with encounters which help them think: "Change (or learn) for what?"

People are able to become more aware when faced with some conflict which creates tension or stress uncomfortable enough so that it is seen as a situation which must be modified. The initial tasks are to help the individual or group clarify what his or its tension is related to. What is it that it wishes to see changed? *Its goals.* At first, the worker may well speak of solving a specific client problem, but soon the range of goals expands. Herbert Thelen suggests:

> (1) Man is always trying to live beyond his means. Life is a sequence of reactions to stress. Man is continually meeting situations with which he cannot quite cope. (2) In stress situations energy is mobilized and a state of tension is produced. (3) The state of tension tends to be disturbing and man seeks to reduce the tension. (4) He has direct impulse to take action.[3]

It is important that the agency goals, the "just society" goals, are clarified and understood, since they provide the framework within which individual and group goals meld.

Approaches to awareness. A number of authors have discussed some of the techniques which they feel are important during the attempts to get people involved in the processes of change. Bruner has discussed the "discovery" concepts of learning, pointing out that people will become involved in the things that interest them and that in fact this might be seen as one of the strongest motivators for change.[4] Thelen, sharing this approach, has some concrete suggestions. He says that the beginning of an educative experience is an "encounter" or confrontation in which something happens to pique the interest of the person. Bion suggests the violation of expectations as one way of involving people in change.[5] Others might feel that support and reflection of some of the needs expressed by the person—clarifying some of the issues for him—may help initiate the awareness process.

Glaser and Strauss point out some of the difficulties involved in both awareness and unawareness in relation to death. In some cases people are working to keep people (i.e., the dying patients) unaware of a situation.[6]

Lewin holds for the need to unfreeze current behavior as one of the first steps in the change process.[7] More traditional approaches suggest study, action research, or the presentation of some already noted phenomenon to which people will respond. The key, however, seems to be the acceptance that something "different" must take place which can act as a catalyst for initial engagement. In addition to the "something different," there must be "human" contact and a moving out to the individual in a way that bridges the differences that many people fear and expect will be present between them. It is more than merely the development of trust—something that we in the helping professions have long felt important. It is possible to trust the professional supervisory role and the responsible actions which one anticipates from a professional person and still feel a professional detachment that comes between people. What we are seeking here is contact which reflects a mutuality of concern and an unrestricted feeling of helpfulness from the total person, not just the "professional role." There must be some joy in the relationships as well as the accomplishments. The thrust of many of the concerns of youth—encounter groups, communes, and "counterculture"—is to maintain this striving for "connections" with people on a feeling level, the development of human "bonds." We foresee the concept of "agency as community" as an important factor in cementing these bonds.

During the awareness process we ourselves become aware that the factors influencing relations among members of the transaction will play an important part in the outcomes.[8]

The Zen masters attempt to approach awareness through spontaneity of reaction. "The intuition springs forth as a wordless and thoughtless message translated into integrated and immediate action." [9]

2. COMMITMENT

The commitment process is an attempt to move from mutual understanding to a "readiness," a partialization of the problem with some plan for next steps and a commitment or contract. It is a commitment to work, and it requires the development of a work culture in the group.

The partialization of the problem around clarified needs permits one to work on the part of the problem that can be handled immediately. The planning is really a creative process that grows out of the integration of the possibilities discussed. It should lead to a mutual commitment to proceed along certain steps toward some specified goals. This mutual commitment is an initial "contract between the members and the workers related to goals and means." [10]

The contracting phase permits the development of bonds between staff members and between staff and supervisor. It permits a mutual testing and "face work." It is the "organization building" part of the process at its clearest. The mutual commitment supports the members in their "will to act." They act on each other and remind each other of the contract.

3. INQUIRY AND KNOWLEDGE

While awareness may be seen as an unfolding of new knowledge or as the understanding that a problem which needs solving exists, the knowledge we are concerned with here is the knowledge that helps us to act. This calls for an inquiry on a more scientific level, aimed at understanding the problem and what needs to be done about it.

In fact it is the newly acquired knowledge that makes the difference and permits us to alter the situation. New knowledge about ourselves as helpers, new knowledge about the environment, the worker, the agency and of what works.

The more open one is to new ideas, the more he is likely to be able to find the knowledge necessary to help the client. This knowledge can grow out of one's own practice experience, or the experiences of other human service workers. Naturally this calls for a more formal sharing of both successes and failures in supervisory practice. Creditable documentation of actual work takes experience and training. There is little produced in the literature that deals with actual "practice" examples or case records of supervisory experience.

The establishment of this knowledge base in supervision will take time, but perhaps a beginning can be found in the work done on differential supervision. A number of projects relating to the differences in supervisory and training needs between professionals and paraprofessionals have led to some evidence as to what works best (in very broad terms, such as movies rather than lectures) with each group.[11]

To act intelligently man must have sound knowledge. Action without knowledge is futile. Knowledge without action is neglect. In fact, this is generally the procedure in medicine. The investigations grow out of practice concerns. There is then a testing over time, the sharing of ideas with others (both successes and failures), and the use of other supportive fields as they are seen to have a contribution to make. In spite of the public's disenchantment with the "medical empire," there is confidence in the physician because of the *grounded*, scientific base of his data.

4. MOVEMENT IN ACTION: INFORMED PRACTICE

The commitment to goals and means—and more particularly to client services—and the inquiry after the knowledge needed to understand and act are a start on the work process and usually precede movement in action. *Action* is the public work on the problem and depends on the ability of the worker to RISK himself in change, success, and defeat.

Approaches to Action. All staff can learn to risk and to act, and this political process (decision making and social interacion) can be practiced in the group or with a supervisor through such techniques as role playing and other contrived[12] experiences which simulate the practice transactions. The supervisor and the worker become an action unit directed at change in the environmental system. The action of the supervisor, however, is constrained by the realization that he is not the major agent in the changing process: the client is not his, and the worker is not an extension of the supervisor. The supervisor in this situation is a facilitator, a back-up man to be used as needed. The worker must act from his own strengths and make his own decisions. It is gratifying for him to know, however, that he is not alone.

Generally the worker must feel comfortable in the performance of his tasks. This comfort is related to the commitments and confidence he has and to the knowledge he has been able to integrate on behalf of his action. The engagement process therefore feeds back into itself between commitment and knowledge. There will be times when information is sparse and solutions must be sought quickly without time for the type of inquiry that makes for probably successful solutions. At these times *the worker must do the best he can.*[12] He has, however, some important new inputs that can help him the next time around—one being that this is another area in which practice knowledge is scarce and in which inquiry has to be made so that future practice is based on more data.

The resulting consequences of action will often lead to new concerns and levels of awareness, and so the circle is drawn around the process in what systems engineers would call a feedback-action loop.

If things do not work, Alan Wheelis suggests, you must try harder, and try something different.[13]

THE ENGAGEMENT PROCESS

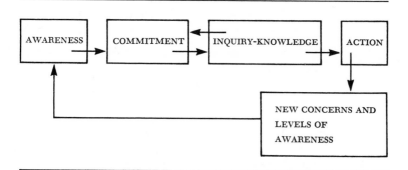

ENGAGING INDIVIDUALS

Regardless of whether the supervisor is oriented to working with groups or individuals, he must understand the dynamics of individual behavior as a response to social situations and interpersonal dynamics. The nature of individual supervision as a long-term paradigm in the social welfare field will insure its survival as a major way of learning in the agency. We feel that it is an important method of teaching and that the synergistic processes that we discuss throughout this book can be utilized in the individual conference to great advantage.

All contacts between people have the potential for enhancing one's being or detracting from it. What we used to speak of as the therapeutic stance was an attempt to give the type of response that would not detract from the individual's sense of worth, would not in fact be a put-down. We need to insure, therefore, that the individual conference respects the dignity of both parties to the transaction.

Rather than look at individual supervision as *one to one,* we would like to set the climate of *one with one,* which in fact creates the new phenomenon of two, or *we.* This can minimize the status differentials of the transaction, and, in fact, the people in this situation can be viewed as forming a group in which a third party or coalition situation is absent.

BEGINNINGS: TOWARD AWARENESS AND COMMITMENT

What does the person want? In any transaction between people, both parties are concerned with their own basic needs, with survival. We are not particularly referring to a life-and-death survival, although at times this may be at stake. We are referring to the survival of the person's image of himself as a thinking, doing, competent person. We are referring to his dream, to the things he would like to become, to the things he fears (see Figure 7).

Figure 7

WHAT DO PEOPLE WANT?   WHAT DO PEOPLE FEAR?

PEOPLE WANT TO
    achieve
    self-actualize
    become
    be respected
    have self-respect
    be accepted
    be part of something

PEOPLE FEAR NOT BEING
    a person
    an individual
    loved
    in the sense of existing
    counted for anything
    part of a group
    respected

THEY FEAR NOT HAVING A FUTURE
    death—psychological and
      physiological
    not being counted
    being alone
    being no-thing

"Man is literally split in two: he has an awareness of his own splendid uniqueness in that he sticks out of nature with a towering majesty, and yet he goes back into the ground a few feet in order blindly and dumbly to rot and disappear forever." (Ernest Becker, *The Denial of Death* [New York: The Free Press, 1973], p. 26.

Any communication, verbal or otherwise, by either party to the transaction which threatens the other person's image of what he is or wants to be will be met with apprehension, defensiveness, and withdrawal. The person may in fact attempt to return in kind the hurt that person thinks he has received, and a fight situation will ensue. Of course, for example, if I understand your approach in light of knowledge that you always act this way or that your "bark is worse than your bite," or if I react to any authority in this way, then I have knowledge that alters my perception of the situation, and I can accept your communication with less sense of threat to my image. This is one of the reasons that trust takes time to develop and why people are more likely to be open with people they know.

Realizing this, the person in the role of teacher-supervisor needs to provide the type of support which permits this trust to develop. He needs to ensure the integrity of the supervisee and avoid placing him in situations in which defensiveness replaces coping. This is of the utmost importance at the beginning of a relationship when there are many unknowns and the bonds are fragile. The processes which were discussed earlier under the section on Engagement need to be reviewed in connection with working with individuals.

The phases of group development also have similar implications for work with individuals in that there are logical projections of time and task appropriate to learning on the job. The initial phases will be related to the worker's encounter with not only the agency, but as well with his image of what social work is and perhaps his own experience with supervision. The first conferences will be related to illuminating the contract. The goals of the agency and of the supervisory experience will need to be reviewed both through written statements and open discussion. Some commitment not only to work toward the goals but also to the processes and means by which those goals will be accomplished will have to be examined in a preliminary manner. Will there be records, agendas for conferences? Where possible, these agreements should be put in writing.

One of the major objectives of the first conference should be to review the worker's job. Where a job description has been made available, this may serve as a base for discussion. If none has been formulated, one might be worked out at this initial conference. Figure 8 summarizes what such a job description should include:

Figure 8

JOB DESCRIPTION

TITLE OF JOB: Caseworker
RESPONSIBLE TO: (Title of job, specific name if known) Program Coordinator Ms. Jane Roth
PROGRAM ASSIGNMENT: (Specific department) Outreach Office
MAJOR TASKS:

Direct service
—Intake
—Counseling of unwed mothers
—Counseling with families of unwed mothers

Administrative
—Supervision of two program aides
    Administrative and educational responsibilities
—Record keeping
    practice and statistical
—Monthly program summaries

OTHER RESPONSIBILITIES
—Prepare agenda for staff meetings (with consultation) every other month
—Contacts with community to interpret agency service
—Referrals as necessary
—Participation in staff and training programs

In going over these items with the workers, the supervisor can start to assess areas of experience, strengths, and weaknesses. A worker who has not worked with unmarried mothers or done counseling with families will need help in these areas. A person who has not had experience in record writing would need to know what the supervisor expected. This would also be an opportunity for the worker to indicate aspects of the work he prefers or would rather not do. There may be some negotiation possibilities.

In addition to the job description, there can be further discussion of some of the dynamics of the supervisory relationship. How often will we meet? Why? What does the individual want to learn, how does he seem to learn best? Here is what can be expected of the supervisor. How would the person like to use the supervisor? And so on.

There will be a testing and reconnaissance phase, where both parties find out about each other and attempt to find the best way to work together. This is where trust either will start to develop or be destroyed. Are the commitments kept? How does the supervisor use the knowledge that comes out of the records or the conference? Does the style of the supervisor enhance the worker's feelings of competency or tend to minimize them? Does the supervisor create dependency or demand work?

Supervisors themselves go through phases in their attempts to make the transition from practice to supervision. Bertha Reynolds has summarized these stages succinctly.[14]

THE STAGES OF SUPERVISION AS AN EDUCATIONAL PROCESS

1. The stage of acute consciousness of self, with stage fright as the classic example.
2. The stage of sink-or-swim adaptation.
3. The stage of understanding the situation without power to control one's own activity in it.
4. The stage of relative mastery, in which one can both understand and control one's own activity in the art to be learned.
5. The stage of learning to teach what one has mastered.

Realizing that all people go through an initial stage of anxiety and stress gives the supervisor an ideal way to view the beginning of the process with a new worker. The supervisor can anticipate that the new worker will be worried about survival needs, and not be misled into assuming that the worker isn't interested in the client. In fact the worker wants to do a good job with the client, and it may be this initial anxiety which helps new people ask the "right questions." It is a situation anxiety which is appropriate to the situation. But it may also mean that the first meeting as orientation may be lost to the worker, who has his mind on other things.

> Mrs. Pond is new to the agency. She has been a homemaker for a week. She came to the job after numerous experiences as a saleslady, and as an office clerk.
> Her first assignment, a few days ago, was a call to a home of a mother who was rushed to the hospital.
> When I hired Mrs. Pond I went over with her the agency's purpose and goals. However, there doesn't seem to be much real understanding of what a homemaker really does. It has been difficult for her to understand some of the stress that a family may be under when a parent is in the hospital or not able to take care of them.
> During this time she has written a few notes of her work: "1/21—Today I worked in the home of a woman who is in the hospital for an operation. The kids cried all day."

These notes by the worker's supervisor recognize that the homemaker is not clear on what a homemaker does. But should the homemaker be expected to know what to do when she just started on the job? Even if the homemaker is engaged in her work, can she be expected to have the knowledge and skill to act? How would you proceed if you were the supervisor in this situation? Would you deal with the stress, with the tasks to be performed, with writing better records? The supervisor has a decision to make. Let us see what she does.

But first, why not jot down a few ideas about how you would start the conference you are going to have with the homemaker? What do you want to accomplish at this meeting? This is a portion of the conference dealing with this item.

> I said that I knew how difficult it must be to work in a situation in which the children were crying all day. I asked her how old the children were. She responded that they were school age. I asked her if they had gone to school that day. She said that they had, a neighbor had gotten them off to school, and she had first seen them when they came home. I asked her if she had known they would be coming home. She said she knew, but the children seemed a little surprised to see her. "I gave them some

milk and cookies and went on with some work I was doing in the house. While I was in the other room they both began crying." I asked her what she did then. She responded that "I asked them what they were crying about and sat down in the kitchen with them, but they wouldn't answer. I sat there for awhile, told them to stop, but they kept on. I told them to go out and play while it was still light." S. then asked W. if the children asked about their mother. She answered that they didn't. S. asked if the W. spoke about the mother at all. She said only when she told the children that she would be in all week until their mother got well. S. asks W. if she thought the children were worried about their mother. "Sure they were," she answered. "Who wouldn't be at their age?" W. asked why she thought the children didn't ask about the mother. W. responded that perhaps they were afraid. "Maybe I should have said something to them."

Did it go the way you expected? Why? It seems that the homemaker did a lot more than she indicated in the written record she gave to the supervisor. Why might this be? All in all the conference didn't go badly. The supervisor learned a lot, and perhaps the homemaker did, too. But does the homemaker know what to do tomorrow when she goes back to the home? Were her anxieties relieved? There also seems to be a great deal of leading of the homemaker by the use of certain questions. Yet this is a traditional approach and seems to help the workers get the answer "from themselves." But in fact these are often the answers the supervisors want them to get. It is not a mutual inquiry but a question-and-answer session.

Part of the problem may merely be supervisory style. But part of the problem might also be that the supervisor has forgotten the anxiety of being a new worker in a difficult situation. I would suggest that the old adage "start where the person is" holds, and that the main way to find out where the person is is to ask. After the greetings and recognition of the difficult situation the supervisor might ask what about the situation was of most concern to the worker.

Some further clues as to what a new person on the job needs are enumerated in a wonderful article by George Braeger. It deals with getting started and the need to engage together the meaning of a first day on the job. For example, he points out the worker's concerns following the first supervisory meeting.

> . . . He explained that he'd come out of our first conference very tense and ill at ease. He said that maybe he was wrong, but that it seemed to him that we really hadn't started much of a relationship, and I was off telling him what to do. He said that what I said sounded good, but it was so much. It was hard to take anything from me, since he really didn't know much about me. He ended by saying that he was sure that some of this feeling was due to his insecurity in the relationship.[15]

Let us review some of the items that it might be helpful to think about as an agenda for the first meeting.

THE FIRST CONFERENCE: A POSSIBLE AGENDA

1. Concerns for the basic survival and satisfaction needs of the worker. Does he have an office, desk, materials, place to live, etc. How could supervisor help?
2. Who you are. Background, interests, experience. Visions of social work, people, helping, etc.
3. The agency, its goals, means, history.
4. Job description. Start to develop the contract.
5. His first meeting coming up with clients. Has he thought about it? What can you tell him that might be helpful—e.g., cultural factors, current agency thinking, etc.
6. Other items the worker or you may want to deal with.

ORIENTATION SESSIONS

Often larger agencies, such as public welfare departments, will hire a number of new workers at about the same time. They then have general orientation sessions in which large groups of workers are introduced to various aspects of agency life, rules, and procedures, and have an opportunity to hear the agency director and a few others explain the mission of the agency (and some of its difficulties, perhaps) and are welcomed into the fold. The larger group may then be broken down into smaller units by department or interest. Eventually the new workers may get to meet their supervisor and some of the other workers in their departments.

One should not hold out too high hopes for any orientation sessions, particularly those held on a group basis. The worker new to the job has so many idiosyncratic concerns and questions that these are best handled at an initial conference with the person.

The major functions of an orientation program should be: (1) to introduce staff to the general vision of the agency; (2) to acquaint the staff with some of the administrative and other staff; (3) to handle general "important" housekeeping matters: pay, sick leave, assignments, desks, where to have lunch; and (4) to help people feel comfortable and good about the agency they are going to be working in. If possible, a fifth function would be to meet their supervisor and spend some time together. My own preference would be to stress Item Four above. Although it is important to indicate that the agency means business, it is also important to get across the feeling that this is going to be a good place to work.

THE INFORMED AND SKILLFUL WORKER: NEW KNOWLEDGE

One of the most important things that need to be said about learning is that it takes place all the time, whether or not it is planned, imposed, or sought after. It may be one of the basic survival instincts of the human being. If it is so ubiquitous, why worry about it? Why not just let nature take its course? The major reasons are: (1) we want to deal with the specific learnings which will help the worker do a more effective job at the agency; (2) we want to deal with the learnings which will help build the type of team or community which will permit all the members to work at a highly effective level, and (3) we want to minimize the forces which inhibit this goal directed learning.

One example of the natural pattern of learning is developmental theory: the infant learns the things he needs, as does the child, the adult, etc. Different stages in growth call forth different learning needs. No one expects the child to think or perform like an adult. If the PASSAGE IN THE AGENCY can likewise be seen as a developmental process, will the worker not also learn the things he needs as he grows? Unfortunately, this expectation does not take into account the physiological growth process which occurs as the individual passes from childhood to

---

Figure 9
HOW WORKERS LEARN

---

1. Workers learn in interaction with others and their environment.

2. Workers seek fulfillment of certain needs—in this case, to do an effective job, to be accepted by peers.

3. The worker will seek to learn those things which will fulfill those needs.

4. The worker's perceptions of those needs and what he needs to know will be influenced by earlier knowledge and ways of learning.

5. If these are appropriate to this situation (culture), the worker will be in a position to learn. If this culture is very different in its expectations, in order to meet the learning needs he will have to change his perception (become aware) and find new ways to learn.

6. The learning environment, peers, and supervisors can support the worker's learning attempts by setting clear and realistic norms and by helping him perceive his role in an unambiguous way.

7. Learning takes place through understanding, doing, and assessing. The worker must understand his role, have opportunities to practice, and have opportunities to evaluate what he has done.

8. Learning is most successfully accomplished in a supportive atmosphere, where threat is minimized and where creativity and discovery are the norm.

---

adulthood. In addition, and more important for our purposes, in the maturation process of normal developmental learning, many people learn things which are dysfunctional. And many are not taught some of the important things they need to know to survive and develop competence in a highly technological society. Some learning theorists hold that in fact people learn how to be sick, psychotic, evil, and nonproductive. A special assistant at NIMH would substitute a learning-theory model for the illness-medical model we now have. Ernest Becker sees psychotics as immature people who have not learned adequate roles.[16]

Our approach to learning will be simple. People learn the things they need in order to perform adequately in their culture. The first things they will need to learn are related to survival on the job, doing an effective job, and working with their colleagues. It is very important therefore that they have a clear understanding of what their job is, their role, the skills, knowledge, and attitudes needed to perform that job, and to learn how to learn (see Figure 9).

There are certain things (see Figure 10) that all workers need to know in order to function adequately in an agency setting.

Learning takes place in a situation which supports the learning needs, but in addition the material to be learned must be ego-supportive.

BLOCKS AND RESISTANCE TO LEARNING

Learning must be ego-syntonic. This means that material which violates the integrity, the values, and the personal knowledge of the learner will be resisted. Important material presented by people the learner dislikes or distrusts will be screened and resisted as well (see Figure 11). So material presented to inner-city students by middle- and upper-class faculty might be suspect.

We all filter material. In fact one of the functions of the ego is to help us filter material by (1) protecting us from material that would be too painful for us to bear, and by (2) focusing in on important survival material and screening out noise. But if

---

Figure 10
WHAT ALL WORKERS NEED TO LEARN

---

1. The tasks associated with their role: The expectations people have for someone in a particular position. For example, the worker may also learn that clients, supervisors, and colleagues may have different expectations of his role.

2. Knowledge about the people he will be working with: the culture of the community, life styles, particular problem areas of his clients (aging, alcoholism, etc.) societal problems.

3. Organizations (his particularly) and how they operate. An understanding of systems.

4. How to work with others, in particular his team or supervisor or others in the agency. How to be part of a team and community.

5. How to improve his practice and develop into a more effective worker. How to learn.

6. How to value others as well as himself. How to work toward a just society.

7. Some methods of self-evaluation and assessment of personal knowledge and feelings as they apply to the work.

8. A method of inquiry.

---

the ego has to set up such fine screens that very little material can come through—that is, if the person is so fragile that new knowledge has to be fought against—learning will be blocked. Ways will have to be found to open the screens, and this is what Karl Deutsch refers to as "openness":

> Openness—the ability to increase the sensitivity in the range of our channels of intake, the ability to interact and to receive, to learn more about the universe around us and from human beings around us—is perhaps one of the most critical and most precious qualities of any system of communication.[17]

Figure 11
PERCEPTUAL SCREENING

SOURCE OF RESISTANCE	RESISTANCE SHIELD	LEARNING
Nature of material	Can't be true	
Person presenting material	Can't be trusted	Filtered
Type of medium	Don't believe TV	
Time of presentation	Not ready yet	

People have learned to protect themselves by closing out stimuli which might be harmful. They can learn to be open by going through graduated experiences which raise their awareness, providing these are done in nonthreatening ways so that trust can develop.

Jerome Bruner makes an important point related to learning when he speaks of the differences between coping and defending.

> Coping respects the requirements of problems we encounter while still respecting our integrity. Defending is a strategy whose objective is avoiding or escaping from problems for which we believe there is no solution that does not violate our integrity of functioning.
> Integrity of functioning is some required level of self-consistency or style, a need to solve problems in a manner consistent with our most valued life enterprises.[18]

This is an important concept for the practitioner in relation to a client. If we place people in a position of having to defend themselves against what they see as our attacks, they will take flight or fight. This understanding plays an important role in the thinking of those educators related to discovery models of education, of which Bruner is a strong advocate.

The Sufi tales can also be seen as a method of teaching

which is aimed at bringing an awareness or discovery to the pupil. They are teaching stories, and the student can respond to them on many levels. For example, what is the meaning of this teaching story?

> There was once a man who did one thing right and one thing wrong, in that order.
> The first thing was to tell a fool that he was a fool.
> The second thing was not to have made sure that he was not standing beside a deep well.[19]

In addition to the various general meanings related to wisdom, tact, etc., there may also be personal meanings as well. For example, one of my supervisors would select only negatives from my recordings for discussion in conference. After I finally mustered enough courage to point out that this made me feel rather worthless, he began to bring in positives as well. His procedure, however, was to follow a negative with a positive, then a negative, etc. This was what I later labeled the yo-yo approach to supervision. First you're high, then low. Unfortunately, this becomes a game, and the student becomes confused, not sure of his real positives, and perhaps "defending" by minimizing what might be his negatives, and by recording more selectively, whether consciously or unconsciously.

THE SUPERVISOR'S PART IN THE LEARNING-TEACHING TRANSACTION

We have discussed the necessity for an early staging of the supportive grounds for learning in our section on beginnings. The supportive learning environment needs to have been already established when the new worker arrives on the job, and naturally this is not a task that the supervisor can perform on his own. There has to be agreement that all of the workers are teachers and learners, and that everyone will use an approach to inquiry which respects the visions of the agency.

The supervisor, however, must set the tone for the environment. When the supervisory process involves only himself and a worker, then the total responsibility for teaching is his. Experience with supervision will have alerted him to the fact that people learn best when the learning is related to things in which the person is interested, that will help him do a better job or are rewarding in some other way by making life more comfortable or secure. He will understand that people will learn when their anxiety levels are low, when they are not threatened, angry, or alienated. He will try to balance the thinking and the doing and will try to offer examples when theoretical matters are being discussed.

Whether he likes it or not, the supervisor must accept the fact that he becomes a role-model for the worker. Whether it be related to transfer, respect, or a need to follow lockstep because of insecurity, the worker will approach clients in the same way his supervisor approaches him, at least in the beginning. Modeling, of course, is an important way to learn, and should be recognized as such. If the supervisor, however, doesn't understand, or isn't aware of this phenomenon, it can lead to difficulties, as in the following incident.

The setting was a summer camp for handicapped children. The program director observed that one of the counselors was sitting under a tree resting. His group were straggling by themselves a few hundred feet away. The director instructed the unit head, "Will you tell that lazy so-and-so to get off his butt and get to work." The unit head then proceeded to bawl out the counselor in the same angry tone and exact words used by the program director. Other counselors overhearing the incident became angry and some of the counselor's campers were upset as well.

Should the program director have expected that the unit head who was the counselor's supervisor would be more tactful in his approach? Perhaps so, but it indicates the importance of recognizing that your style and actions are apt to be duplicated by your supervisees, and that they may not always merit that honor. It does bring into focus, however, another important factor in supervisor-supervisee interactions, and that is the matter of relationship.

RELATIONSHIP

One might assume that in the foregoing example, the bonds

of feeling between people, between the counselor and the unit head, are now strained. In addition it might not be unrealistic to assume that the unit head is also a little angry at the program director for getting him into the mess. These bonds of feeling among people, if they are friendly and warm, facilitate the work to be done. If they are cold and unfriendly, they may impair the work. We all realize how difficult it is for us to work with people we don't like, even when they are capable workers. A great deal of our energy goes into maintaining the working relationship.

Relationship can be a major variable that influences the work of the agency. When the relationship is a good one, it facilitates the ways of feeling, thinking, and doing. We must note, however, that relationships in themselves can produce anxieties. There is the matter of the authority and the emergence of ambivalence pertaining to parental figures, and the individual's own thrust for autonomy. There is the matter of trust, and the uncertainty of how far one can go in trusting a teacher who is also a boss. In balance, however, we would hold that a relationship in behalf of work in which the bonds of feeling are warm will aid the workers in identifying with the task to be done. Hilda Arndt points out:

> Identification with the instructor supports the learner in a more sustained, critical and balanced scrutiny of self, facilities and the adoption of essential ways of thinking, feeling and acting, and strengthens the integration of learning.[20]

Most writers have suggested that the nature of the relationship and actions of the teacher need to:

1. Individualize the learner. See him as an individual and assess his needs.
2. Reduce the learner's anxiety and facilitate the integrative functioning.
3. Maintain a helpful attitude toward the learner's dependence and foster the growth of independence.
4. Avoid competitiveness.
5. Have knowledge to offer the student.
6. Demand work from the student on a realistic basis.[21]

In a synergistic model of supervision, however, the assigned supervisor is not the only teacher; in fact, he may not be the major teacher. But he does carry the responsibility to attempt to coordinate the experiences so that they are integrated, logical, and appropriate for the needs of the worker.

So no matter what the problem may be that the work team may be dealing with, the learning community may have to be reminded that it is required to incorporate a new member, a person who needs to be brought on board and helped to understand what the culture of this particular work group might be. The supervisor may also have to recognize with the other workers what the new worker's contribution might be.

BUILDING THE LEARNING-DOING COMMUNITY

There have been numerous approaches to building the kind of environment that would bring out the best in people. Skinner's Walden II and numerous utopian projections and commune experiments have organized themselves around the idea that in a community that (1) demanded the best from people and (2) was set up in a way that enabled people to do their best, the members would learn no other options for behaving but the best way, and that people would indeed exhibit exemplary behavior. Their community would provide the necessary supports and rewards. This concept is at the heart of the synergy model. The more that experiences converge on doing "what ought to be" in the agency, the greater the likelihood that workers will live up to the expectations of the community, particularly if they have a say in developing and maintaining those expectations. Margaret Mead has suggested:

> As a rule an individual's behavior, beliefs and attitudes grow and change only to the minimal extent that it is called for by the demands of his immediate situation in life.[22]

Demands for a learning attitude, scientific inquiry, and effective practice will have more valence if the entire work group sees itself as a learning-doing community. This is also the basis of the therapeutic milieu approach to treatment and change.

At its best, the university offers one model for the learning-working community. We have seen, however, that competition for scarce resources can create disharmony even in such an idyllic setting, and provision must be made to permit the entire community to work out processes for the distribution of these resources.

For most of us this style of working together would become a new learning experience. Our own personal growth and educative experiences have been in the more competitive vein. Human service professionals, however, should find it somewhat easier to adapt to a community-oriented approach because of their understanding of human behavior and their commitment to service through mutual aid. The roots of this community-synergy approach can be found in some of the early settlement movement. Indeed, the settlement was a commune-type experience for those who desired to be helpful to others and at the same time expand their own life worth. The settlement was a synergistic idea. It minimized the status or pyramidal structures, even though great leaders rose to overshadow and disproportionately influence the direction of the agencies' programs.[23]

Theirs was a normative approach, both to internal living, working experience, and external programs. They had a vision of what a community ought to be, how workers ought to be treated, what health services ought to be provided, how families should survive, and how cultures might be maintained. Even if we differ with some of their "oughts," they attempted to provide the services they felt were needed. Often the services were the results of surveys which they had carried out, and often these surveys became the basis for social and political action. These surveys were their form of scientific inquiry into what ought to be.

I am not suggesting that we return to the settlement idea, but that within the best of the settlement movement and university colleagual system are the roots of a synergistic model of worker involvement and action. Let's see if we can spell these out:

> Avowed humanistic goals
> Shared experiences
> Democratic structures and decision making
> Scientific inquiry of the knowledge
> Respect for each other
> Minimal hierarchy responsible to peers
> An open community
> Action on behalf of social justice

STRUCTURING THE LEARNING AND TEACHING

In a later chapter we will deal with educational media and their use in the supervisory and staff development process. In this section I would like to look at four tools which help structure the learning situation: (1) a consistent inquiry approach; (2) the use of conference agendas and recording; (3) the educational plan; and (4) evaluation processes.

1. A SYSTEM OF INQUIRY

Scientific inquiry is based on developing commonsense ideas into testable hypotheses, actions, and proofs which can then be replicated. Usually the inquiry is built on the developing basis of previous research. Occasionally the inquiry is of a unique nature which establishes a new basis for further research. Such, for example, was the work of Freud. In the supervisory inquiry process we are involved in a type of research. It is research aimed at changing the ability of the worker to serve the client. The changes we generally seek are increased knowledge and skills and the ability to apply these.

Faced with the problem of helping a worker find what he needs to know, we can follow any number of problem-solving steps. Lippitt [24] for example suggests a seven-step problem finding and solving process:

1. Developing a need for change
2. Establishing a change relationship

3. Clarifying the problems
4. Establishing alternative ways to goals; establishing goals and intentions of action
5. Transforming the intentions into change efforts
6. Stabilizing the change
7. Achieving a terminal relationship

After examining hundreds of studies dealing with change, learning innovation, and diffusion of ideas Havelock [25] comes up with a seven stage process similar in a number of ways to the Lippitt model.

1. Building a relationship
2. Diagnosing the problem
3. Retrieving relevant information
4. Selecting the innovation
5. Developing supportive attitude and behaviors
6. Maintaining impetus for change
7. Stabilizing the innovation

As we shall see, both models are related to Lewin's action research approach. Both incorporate his basic concepts of freezing the change.

Force field analysis as an inquiry system. Following his concept of Force Field Analysis, Lewin suggested that any social situation could be perceived as being in a state of equilibrium, or balance, at any point in time, and that the nature of that equilibrium could be assessed.[26]

1. We must have a fairly accurate understanding of the worker's current level of behavior. This behavior level is part of a *field*, described in Figure 12, which is made up of a number of forces influencing whether or not the worker can move toward some common ideal we may have in mind. The goal must be individualized to the situation. The situation is held in equilibrium by a number of opposing forces which are equal in total strength.

2. Certain forces are at work which promote learning and

doing in a new way. (Change.) These are the *driving forces:* a desire to do a good job, recognition, potentials for growth, supervision, attending classes, an open mind, etc.

3. Certain forces are at work which retard change. These are the *restraining forces:* heavy job load, busy supervisor, fear of the new, stereotyping, etc.

4. In addition, there are certain blocks which are neutral but still influence the worker: building size, budget, laws.

Action. Although at any one point in time the forces may be said to be in balance, it is "quasi-stationary equilibrium"—which can be modified. For example, following our assessment, in order to reach a new level of behavior, we can (1) increase the number or intensity of the driving forces, (2) eliminate or weaken the restraining forces, and (3) modify the blocks. A change in any of these may alter the equilibrium or current level. Some of the forces may be more influential than others.

Figure 12
THE SUPERVISEE FIELD

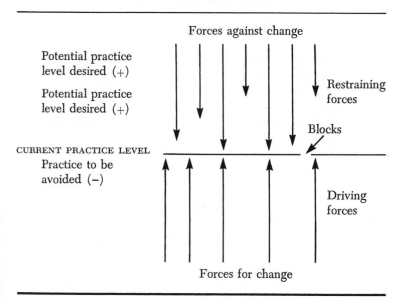

Theoretically, if the current level of functioning is in balance, an alteration in either of the driving or restraining forces should alter that balance. The addition of another driving force, or the elimination of a restraining force, should help the supervisee move closer to the goals of improved practice.

The next step in the process naturally is to strategize and work out the grand plan of how to use these forces. Which one would be a most likely force to try to alter, how might this be done, and by whom? The plan, then, which follows the search is some commitment as to (1) which ones, (2) how, and (3) who. In our example, the "which" forces selected might be classes and an open mind. The "how" forces might be more use of encounter techniques. The "who" in this case might be all the people, or a T-group expert, etc.

To be successful, the search and the strategies would have to be comprehensive, and a sound "educational diagnosis" would have to be made. Many other factors, including the agency climate, would have had to be appraised. To turn this adversary model into a synergy model we would have to meld "opposing" forces into a more mutually rewarding approach. Lewin [27] sees this change process as:

1. *Unfreezing* the current behavior. This may be done through confrontation, change of space (cultural island), presenting new facts, etc.
2. *Moving* to a new level, preferably closer to the desired level.
3. *Refreezing* the behavior at the new level. Find ways of supporting those changes that have been accomplished.
4. *Repeat the process.*

The entire process consists of five steps. It starts with (1) a *vision* of what practice might be in the agency. Then (2) a *goal* is worked out with the supervisee as to his specific needs. The force field analysis becomes (3) the *search* for the change leverage. Then (4) a *plan* is worked out and (5) is *implemented.*

Ingalls[28] incorporated a five-step decision-making model in his andragogy approach:

Problem formulation
Generation of proposals for solution
Forcasting consequences
Action planning
Evaluation of outcomes

Sonia Abels, attempting to develop an appropriate method of inquiry related to ethical practice in the human services, has come up with a four-stage process of ethical decision making.[29] She would have the learner who is confronted with a problem:

1. Specify the problem with which you are concerned.
2. Formulate an hypothesis that you think best defines the issue you are working on and shifts the problem toward a solution.
3. Indicate the conflicting aspects of the ethical problem. Describe the process you are using to make a decision, including supporting data. What is the evidence you have used to support this decision?
4. The process of inquiry includes finding the answers to the following questions. How would you check to see if your decision was right if acted upon? What would show it is a mistake? What else would have to be found to make it a better decision, or a better based decision? Who disagrees with your decision? Why do you think they disagree? What are the alternatives to the decision you HAVE MADE? Rank order of the alternatives? Who could better make this decision and why? How do you think your ethical decision contributes to the good of society?
5. The inquiry process is used both prior to making the decision and as a way of testing out the decision after it has been made.

Mrs. Abels suggests that it is not necessary to use this procedure for all decision making. Such a process would be too time-consuming, and often we know by precedent, common sense, or moral perspectives what the decision should be. The process would be used when:

1. The case or situation presented involves problematic dimensions for which there appears to be no already understood comparison cases.
2. The evidence indicating what should be done seems contradictory, given the worker's current state of knowledge.
3. The interests of different persons involved (individuals or groups) are in conflict.
4. The worker's judgment as to what should be done conflicts with those of others.
5. The expectations of the results of the actions taken are disappointing.[30]

2. THE STRUCTURED CONFERENCE

Workers should be able to seek help when they need it and from whomever they want. To that extent the learning should not necessarily be related to a fixed formal conference. But in addition to the worker's own immediate problem-solving mechanisms there needs to be a regular time when the worker meets for a more formal learning-sharing experience. These can be either individual or group conferences, but should include some basic structural supports:

1. A regularly scheduled time.
2. An agenda—mutually agreed upon and flexible.
3. Someone who takes responsibility for the direction of the meeting and sees that the needed resources are available, notices sent out, arrangements made, etc.
4. An opportunity for the workers to deal with urgent matters as well as ongoing items.
5. Consistency from meeting to meeting—a flow.
6. Shared responsibility.

This type of meeting serves a number of purposes:

1. It is an opportunity for the worker to summarize and rethink his recent experiences.
2. It permits a pulling together of the learning.
3. It exposes the worker to others' thinking.
4. It gives him experience in restructuring his ideas.
5. It gives clues to common problems and common solutions.
6. It helps the supervisor and other workers keep abreast of what is happening in the agency.
7. It promotes team building.

Agendas. For the learning worker, one of the most important aspects of the conference is the preparation of an agenda prior to the conference. This should be a part of the contract at least until some patterns of learning have been established.

The agenda forces the worker to pull his ideas together, to assign a priority ranking to his needs, and to give advance thought and preparation to the meeting. The agenda might include:

1. Items to be discussed, with some priority arrangement.
2. A summary of important actions that the supervisor might need to know about.
3. A record of inquiry around a problem that the worker is dealing with.
4. Notice of special arrangements or requests.
5. Attachments: records, if required, expense sheets, etc.

There is a mutual commitment to deal with the worker's agenda, but there is also a mutual recognition that the supervisor and other staff in the case of group supervision also have agendas. At times the group will work out priorities for work; at other times the supervisor may have to see that his agenda is also dealt with.

In individual supervision it is usually better to work through the supervisee's agenda first. There may be pressing problems which occupy the mind of the worker in a way which ties up his energy. The supervisor's agenda, though important, would be met only with half-hearted responses anyway, so why not deal with the important worker needs first?

The flow of a conference might be:

1. Worker's concerns, decisions, plans
2. Unfinished business
3. Supervisor's items
4. Summary and commitments for next meeting.

Recording as a Learning Tool. Wilensky and Lebeaux indicate that, when they made their study, about 52 percent of all agency time was spent in maintaining communication within the agency, and an additional 32 percent was accounted for by case recording.[31] Obviously, when more time is spent on these activities than on contact with clients, agency priorities are in jeopardy.

Recording serves two major purposes in an agency: (1) the ongoing records, statistics, and files that need to be kept for control, accountability, and referral purposes (maintenance records); and (2) the recording carried out to help a worker assess his work and become more effective (learning records). Often the same records serve both purposes. If the major long-term goals of supervisor are to develop autonomous, effective workers, then the recording must become a tool for this end. Both maintenance and learning records need to be kept at a minimum.

Learning Records

The function of the learning record should be to help the worker to answer the question, "How would I do it the next time?" It provides an opportunity for the worker, either alone or with a supervisor, to look at a piece of practice and see how it might have been done differently, to learn and view the possible alternative actions. The supervisor too might record on one of his supervisees to self-assess his work as a supervisor.

When the uses for the record are clear, there is less resistance to recording; in fact, the records become more focused, shorter, less time-consuming, and, one hopes, more helpful.

Focused Recording

Focused learning experiences can be provided in supervision by asking the person to focus on a specific problem area or learning need. For example, in the following exchange the task for the worker evolves as the problems emerge.

W. For the past three weeks we have been having a great deal of trouble deciding our program in the group.
S. Have the members been able to come up with ideas?
W. Yes, but nothing gets decided.
S. What happens?
W. Two of the kids continually complain and say they don't want to just as a decision is getting made.
S. How do you handle it?
W. Not well.
S. In what way?
W. Well, I usually either push or retreat.
S. How about writing down what happens the next time decisions are being made? That will help us look together at the dynamics of the situation.

From this type of exchange we see that by asking people to record on areas which represent problems to them, we help them to focus in on the problem, to think about it as they work (since it is an area of concern), and to provide material for a more effective give-and-take in the conference.

EXAMPLES OF RECORDING

These excerpts taken from a class experience are meant to give the reader some ideas about how records might be prepared.

1. SUMMARY RECORD
   NAME OF GROUP   Social Group Work Class
   DATE   Jan. 13, 1969 Session No. 1
   PRESENT X,Y,A,B,C,D,F,H,J
   ABSENT E,I.

CONTACTS AND PREPARATION PRIOR TO MEETING: Reviewed material on social group work. Prepared paper to distribute in class. Did not have any contacts with any members.

MEETING: [Usually the entire meeting would be summarized. This is a partial example] Asked for volunteers for a demonstration of "group formation." Volunteer group ignored instructions and admitted new member to the group. Discussed what happened with the class and led into a good session on "feelings" and "group process." Then talked about need to work together and trust each other if learning is to take place. Members participated in the discussion very well.

IMPRESSIONS: At first I felt a little angry that the class did not follow my instructions. Then I saw that there were things that both class and I could learn from what happened and looked at the experience with the class. I felt better after the discussion and think it was an excellent class session. Do not yet know the individuals well enough to tell much about their behavior.

THINGS TO DO: Must remember to make the point to class that what happened shows that a leader's power comes from the group. He can't make them do anything they don't want to do.

DISCUSS WITH SUPERVISOR: (1) My feelings about losing my authority when class didn't follow my instructions. (2) Was it too soon to ask for volunteers? (3) Should I have told them I was angry with them? (4) Is this part of their culture?

2. PROCESS RECORD [Highlights. Summary of most of record. Extensive recording of important incidents]
   NAME OF GROUP: Social Group Work Class
   DATE: Jan. 13, 1969 Session No. 1
   PRESENT: X,Y,A,B,C,D,F,H,J
   ABSENT: E,I.

CONTACTS AND PREPARATION PRIOR TO MEETING: [Same as Record 1]
MEETING: Introduced myself. Talked about course requirements and gave assignment. I was interested in pointing out "group formation" and member "feeling" through a demonstration of a new member coming into a group. I asked for volunteers, and to my surprise A, B, X, Y, H and J volunteered. I met briefly with the six of them and instructed them not to permit the new member to come into the group. I then told the new member she had to enter the group no matter what happened. I was surprised, then angry, when the group

turned to her and welcomed her into the group. I then decided I could use the experience to teach some other points. I asked the remainder of the class what they thought my instructions had been to the small group. Some felt that I had said let the member in, etc. I then asked the small group to tell the class what the instructions had been. I then asked the class why they thought the group did not follow the instructions. Some felt because they didn't want to hurt the member's feelings, another said because she was a friend, one said to do something to make the teacher angry, another said because the teacher was American. There was a good discussion. I then asked the group to explain why they had done what they did. One member said to show our independence. I asked if all of the group had wanted to do this. Some said no, but they did anyway. (I must remember this point when we talk about group norms and pressure to conform.) I then pointed out the following points to be learned from this experience with group, etc, etc.

[If this was a meeting later in the year, the worker would be expected to indicate the names of participants in the various actions.]

IMPRESSIONS: [Same as Record 1]
THINGS TO DO: [Same as Record 1]
DISCUSS WITH SUPERVISOR: [Same as Record 1]

3. PROCESS RECORD [Total Process]
    Same as Record 2, except that the entire record is written out extensively, with no summary. This is a very good procedure for use in teaching and learning.

4. PROBLEM FOCUS [Some process around areas of particular concern because it is a problem either the group or the worker is working on.]

    Same summary as Record 1. When I get to the part that I have been "alert" to as a problem for me, I write it in process—i.e., if I have a problem around use of authority, whenever this comes up in the meeting I write it in a process manner so I can examine (alone or with supervisor) the dynamics of the situation.

5. MINUTES
    Highlights of the decisions, motions, and proposed actions of a meeting. An ongoing record of attendance and organization action. Not necessarily for learning, except as historical review. Just enough information to transmit the flow of the meeting to a reader, very little interaction process. Used more commonly in community organization.

6. LOGS

A brief ongoing summary day to day about the experiences of the worker. Usually these are for his own use only, but at times they are shared with a supervisor for comments or evaluation.

7. REPORTS

Usually a descriptive piece of work which summarizes some action or exploratory survey, or agency analysis.

8. STATISTICAL MATERIAL

Supervisory Recording

A supervisor interested in improving his own supervisory practice should consider doing recording in relation to his supervisory conferences. One of these might be a process recording, which would help him assess his own work. He, too, would have to ask the question, "How might I do it the next time with better results?" The supervisor can focus on a specific area just as he might ask a worker to do. These might be areas he suspects are problematic for him—e.g., too authoritarian an approach, or inability to delegate responsibility.

The agendas will become an ongoing record of the conferences and the items discussed. Together with the records, these documents are valuable in the evaluation process. They become evidence for both parties as to movement, areas of difficulty, and agreed-upon problems and actions. In fact, during the evaluation conference they may be the only source of substantiation in areas of difference between the worker and the supervisor.

Group recording is a little more difficult than individual conferences, particularly if process is to be recorded. It requires some experience or practice to follow the trends and interactive patterns. At group sessions it might be important to ask all of the group members to record. Comparing their action with different perceptions is a valuable way of learning and understanding not only the group process, but why certain things register with certain people and not with others. The supervisor can record as well or follow the patterns of one of the members whom he wishes to work with around certain educational needs.

3. THE EDUCATIONAL PLAN

Although it is important to individualize the learner, it is also important to make some generalizations around educational planning. It is best to start with the job description, and during the first few contacts with the worker to review the knowledge attitudes and skills that might be necessary to perform each task. For example, if one of the tasks relates to counseling unmarried mothers, we might either visually or on paper try to chart, as in Figure 13, the information we have about a particular worker.

Figure 13

TASK:	ATTITUDES		KNOWLEDGE		SKILLS	
Counseling	Accepting	x	Adolescent	____	Referrals	____
unmarried	Warmth	____	Women	____	Relationship	____
mothers	Nonjudge	____	Adoptions	x	Interviewing	x

The X's indicate areas in which there seem to be satisfactory knowledge and approach. The other areas would need some working on. This would be repeated for the major tasks. Some of the factors might be assumed by previous experience. Shortcomings indicated by references, of course, need to be confirmed. But the major way to assess would be through the supervisor's own experiences with the worker and his own knowledge of what a person in that particular level of experience might need. These have to be determined with some of the same inquiry methods discussed earlier, but some authors have attempted to develop procedures for such assessment. A great deal of assessment research has been done in the area of education.

Hester [32] suggests a five-step approach:
1. Determine the learning problem.
2. Identify the cause of the problem (Is it a lack of under-

standing, a difficult client, or the nature of the problem? Or does the worker lack skill?).

3. Identify the worker's strengths.
4. Set some priorities for action.
5. Determine the method and approach (focused recording, reading, talking through, etc.).

Group work and community organization practice is more open and available to supervisor appraisal. Community people are more likely to mention to the agency executive their feelings about the competence of the new worker. They have more access to the agency and are usually more involved. Clients in most casework agencies, however, are not involved in the ongoing work of the agency, and most of their sessions are behind closed doors. This is an important factor in requiring the writing of adequate records, so that practice can be reviewed and can be accountable to peers.

In group supervision the application of an individual educational plan is limited by the needs and actions of the entire group. Where special problems need to be confronted, it may be necessary to arrange individual conferences or group sessions which focus on a particular problem that needs work.

Differing Styles in Supervisory Transactions. Just as the supervisor will approach supervision in the way most natural to his personality, experience, and culture, so too will supervisees reflect some of the special impacts of their culture. Even within professional groups, schools of thought will be reflected in the views of the teacher held by the student. The worker trained in behavior modification will look for this type of training approach. The psychodynamic approach will lead a worker to expect to be analyzed. The supervisor needs to be aware of some special group concerns, and the educational plan needs to take these differences into consideration.

Paraprofessionals. There has been a great deal of material during the past decade relating to the training of paraprofessionals in the human services, as well as to their mobility and career ladder.[33] Although at one time there was a great deal of concern about their use, paraprofessionals or agency-trained workers have now come to be accepted and their contributions recognized. Clearly they should be integrated into the life of the agency and not be seen as a special group. This type of stereotyping can create problems for them, the agency, and the supervisor, who may find himself dealing with a hierarchical system among his staff.

The reason for paying special attention to paraprofessionals here is to alert the supervisor to some of the training differences which may be required. There is some indication that level of education, although not reflecting effectiveness, may reflect the amount of helping experience.

Concrete training media such as films are more generally successful at the early training sessions than abstract discussions about psychological and moral concepts. Case records and their own life experiences are also very useful in training paraprofessionals.

There seems to be some agreement that beginning with concrete life experience is important. Some paraprofessionals have not had enough experience in concept thinking. Of course it might be best to start all training programs with concrete material. Pearl and Riessman suggest that the training methodology of nonprofessionals should stress the following seven points:

1. Continuous on-the-job training and almost immediate initiation to work.
2. An activity rather than lecture approach ("do rather than write") with a heavy emphasis on role playing and role training.
3. An intensive team approach aimed at building strong group solidarity among the nonprofessional workers in any given project.
4. Informal individual supervision at any time on request, supplemented by group discussion and group supervision.
5. A down-to-earth teaching style, emphasizing concrete tasks presented in clarity and detail, which recognizes that concepts and theory, if properly presented, are definitely within the reach of indigenous personnel . . .

6. Utilization of the "helper principle." Whenever possible more experienced nonprofessionals should assist and teach their less advanced colleagues in dealing with various tasks.
7. Freedom for the nonprofessional to develop his personal style.

The chief hazard in supervising, training, and administering an indigenous staff and program was that of molding workers in the professional image and thereby dissipating their ability to help the client group.[34]

The caution is a sound one, but if the trainer uses the basic concept of "educational assessment" and a natural approach to training, which permits discovery and creativity, "molding" will not be a concern.

The Volunteer. The range of service volunteers perform, from board members to big brothers, leaves an analysis of their training needs problematic. One thing is certain, however. They should be prepared for the tasks they are to perform with the same intensity, quality, and demands as the paid worker. Expectations of performance need to be high in order to insure quality service and to show the volunteers that their best will be expected.

During the orientation period for the volunteers, the importance of regular attendance at the training program should be stressed, but they should be treated just like any staff person as regards to their right to suggest content program ideas and to offer their talents. Although there are a number of clichés about the volunteer as partner, these are only clichés. The more the volunteer is expected to meet the norms maintained for all staff, the more satisfied the agency is likely to be, the less resistance from other staff, and the more the self-image of the volunteer will be enhanced.

Just like all staff, volunteers can be expected to maintain a regular work schedule, record their work, have regular conferences, and go through periodic evaluations. They should know that they will be held accountable for their work. The only difference between them and other staff is the matter of salary. Since they are not paid, however, other forms of recognition for their work should be found. Most volunteers are serving because they want to help people. Certainly there's something in it for them—a feeling of accomplishment, growth, self-actualization. It's an opportunity to do something useful for others and for themselves. Many women have become volunteers because volunteering provides an opportunity to move out of the dull routine of housewife in a society which offers all too little opportunity for women to assert themselves. Many men, also feeling a need to do more than a dull job, will volunteer. We all want to be treated with dignity and to feel valuable. It is important therefore that volunteers not just be given the dull, repetitive, mechanistic, baby-sitting jobs. For example: Freudian and neo-Freudian therapeutic approaches are losing their importance for a large portion of our profession. New treatment approaches—T.A., Gestalt, reality therapy, behavior modification, Kohlberg's moral development—are replacing them. These are helping methods which are easier to learn and easier to apply. They can be taught quickly to volunteers and professionals. Social work education is compacting. The bachelor's degree with a one-year master's is on the horizon. The gap between the professional and the nonprofessional as far as education is concerned is closing. Most social workers are still focusing on counseling—they are neglecting advocacy roles—and volunteers can fill that gap. Where we had administrative and service volunteers, we will now have advocacy volunteers.[35] Agencies can assess how volunteers can be most helpful and truly partners by being open to new ideas and seeking synergistic solutions.

4. EVALUATION AS A LEARNING TOOL

THE ASSESSMENT PROCESS OF
WORKER PERFORMANCE *

I. DEFINITION. Appraisal of worker's performance in various aspects of the job. Use of the job description statement of standards of performance provided by the agency.

* This outline was developed out of a course in supervision and staff development at Case Western Reserve University and is based on the work of Professor Ester Test, who taught the course for a number of years.

    II. PURPOSE. To provide worker and agency an opportunity to review the degree to which the worker has met expectations and to detect areas in which he needs further help and follow-up by supervisor and/or other appropriate persons.

    III. BASIC ASSUMPTIONS

      A. That all areas included in the summation will stem from the ongoing assessment done jointly by worker and supervisor within the regular supervisory conferences.

      B. That it is a shared process in which the client's welfare takes precedence and the worker's professional skills will be enhanced.

      C. That it is based on contract goals.

      D. That administratively it forms a solid basis on which recommendations are to be made for promotions, merit increases, or separation from the job.

      E. That it will be used as a basis for reference letters to employing agencies, etc.

      F. That some emotional impact is always present for both the supervisor and the worker and should be expected.

      G. That there are always subjective as well as objective aspects present.

    IV. BASIC PRINCIPLES AS GUIDES IN THE PROCESS

      A. Supervisor should be expected and ready to carry major responsibility for:
        1. Setting the process in motion.
        2. Moving the process along to completion.
        3. Recording final statements of judgment in written form and sharing same with worker.

      B. The worker should be expected to participate actively in the process through careful preparation, ego involvement, and reading of the final evaluative statement in presence of supervisor.

      C. Evaluative statements by either party must be supported through concrete evidence, and supervisor must feel a professional commitment to this.

      D. The process should indicate some future direction.

It is crucial to remember that evaluations of any kind call forth anxiety and emotion for both parties. It is difficult to have to make people face their limitations, but often people are aware of them. It is difficult as well for a supervisor to have to face limitations within himself. There is uncertainty and fear, even when one is fairly certain that he has been performing adequately. In addition there is a mutual concern as to how the material written up in evaluations will be used at a future date.

Naturally the thoughtful supervisor will realize that any evaluation of another person is in part an evaluation of himself.

Some of the above concerns can be discussed at a pre-evaluation conference. Let us examine the possible procedure of an agency evaluation of a worker.

Pre-evaluation conference: (1) The concerns related to evaluations are discussed. (2) The manner in which the evaluation will take place is spelled out. (3) Items to be covered are discussed—e.g., use of resources, counseling ability, use of supervision. The job assignment should be reviewed.

Evaluation conference: Each party might prepare some items on each point; the supervisor's certainly might be written out. The points are discussed, differences noted and at times resolved.

Written evaluation conference: The worker should now have an opportunity to see the entire evaluation in its semi-final form. Differences might still be negotiated, but where the difference is too wide to be reconciled, the worker should have the opportunity to note on the form his views. The evaluation should be signed and the worker should be given a copy. If indeed the evaluation is to be used by the worker for his own further development, what he needs to work on should be made clear, and this should be a major part of the evaluation.[36]

There should be no other items taken up at the evaluation session, and there should be no items discussed that have not been previously dealt with in supervisory conferences. There should be no nasty surprises. It would be mandatory for the supervisor to support his statements, particularly those considered to be unfavorable, with evidence such as written records, dated supervisory notes, and/or conference agendas.

The evaluations can be extremely helpful in aiding the worker to understand the directions he must take in order to become more effective, but this needs to be handled in an extremely sensitive manner. This is particularly true in larger, more mechanically oriented agencies, in which evaluations are used for automatic raises, promotions, or firings.

Even agencies which use official checklists rather than process evaluations can follow the above procedures. There is no reason that the supervisor cannot fill out the mandated checklist in conjunction with the worker and still go through a more educationally oriented and professional evaluation process. Considering that a worker's career can rest on the nature of the evaluation material, every effort needs to be made to make it as comprehensive, clear, and honest as possible.

ETHICAL SUPERVISORY PRACTICE

Discussion of evaluation seems an appropriate point to look at some of the ethical concerns involved in the supervisory transaction.

Ethics is related to the selection of appropriate actions based on some common understanding and expectations of what is "good" or what "ought to be." These behaviors reflect principles established by a society or community. Our profession's code of ethics reflects the priorities social work adheres to.[37]

Beck and Orr [38] suggest that four things are involved in ethical decision making:

1. CHOICE: There are alternatives; you are called upon to choose; you could have acted otherwise.
2. VALUES: Things valued are at stake.
3. OBLIGATION: What ought to be, or some feeling that some things are right or wrong.
4. THE RULE: Some moral principle to which debaters refer.

What makes the supervisor vulnerable to ethical contradictions is the fact that he is in a power position. Not only can he make decisions that affect the future of the worker within the agency, but a reference, for example, can have impact beyond the current position far into the future. Levy states:

> Because the supervisor has power over the supervisee, it is his ethical responsibility to make sure that written evaluations and references based on them are accurate, relevant to the supervisee's job and expectations of him in it, considerate of the circumstances under which the job was done, and sensitive to the possibility that such information may be misused, misinterpreted, or outdated.[39]

The supervisor is also in a position to receive information, some of which might be incriminating to the worker if confidentiality is not maintained. The use of this information must be clearly defined and decisions adhered to.

In general, the supervisor should respect all agreements, and in case there are difficulties in doing so, the circumstances need to be examined with the worker. Supervisors should not discuss workers with other staff except when absolutely required to because of the nature of the job, nor should they use their worker's case material in staffings without the worker's permission. One might expect that any ethical procedures important in work with clients would hold for staff as well.

Concerns with ethical behavior in the agency will lead to sound policies in relation to service to clients. Concerns with ethical supervisory values should also lead to sound personnel policies.

Personnel practices play an important part in ethical conduct within an agency. The NASW suggests that agencies should have personnel standards which are written and available to all. Most NASW professional adjudication procedures are related to violations of the agency personnel practices.

In their policy statement related to personnel standards, NASW states:

> These standards are based on the principles that (1) effective social service depends on qualified staff and (2) staff mem-

bers can give their best service when they work under conditions of employment that are conducive to the maintenance of high quality and quantity of production. Since the provision of responsible services to individuals and groups is the paramount concern of the social work profession, these standards are issued with the understanding that they will always be applied within the framework of this fundamental concern of the profession . . .

In order that social workers may function at their best, every organization employing them should have policies pertaining to personnel administration developed by an appropriate process. These policies should be in writing and should be available to all members of the staff and governing boards. Staff should participate in the development of these policies and in regular, periodic review of them. The policies should include provision for hearing staff members' grievances and other provisions substantially similar to those that follow. These policies are endorsed by the National Association of Social Workers and recommended by the association to practicing social workers, to employing agencies, and to the supporting public as being basic to good personnel administration and good social work practice . . .

These standards represent principles of desirable personnel policies and practices.[40]

It is also seen as important for agencies to maintain standards in staff development:

An orientation period shall be provided for any employee newly appointed to a position, whether coming from within or outside the agency, for the purpose of informing him of the specific job duties and their relationship to agency functions . . .

Opportunity for continued staff development shall be afforded through provision for the following:
1. Qualified supervision and consultation
2. Professional literature
3. Regular planned staff meetings for discussion of agency program and social work problems and methods
4. Absence during working hours to attend conferences, institutes, workshops, or classes to advance employee skills related to the functions and goals of the employing agency. Such attendance shall result in no loss of pay or vacation time.[41]

In regards to evaluation, their recommendations are:

> As a basis for objective evaluation of performance, the agency should set forth written standards of performance for all positions in its classification plan. Such standards should describe the quality and quantity of performance expected for each job duty. The evaluation shall be made by the person or persons who directly supervise(s) the employee . . .
>
> The time of the evaluation shall be known in advance. Evaluation shall engage the joint participation of the employee and supervisor. However, the authority of the evaluator must be recognized on both sides and final authority belongs to him . . .
>
> The evaluation shall be in writing and shall cover the points discussed in the evaluation conference. The employee shall be given the opportunity to read the evaluation, to sign it (signifying that he has read it), and to file a statement covering any points with which he disagrees. A copy of the evaluation shall be furnished to the employee.[42]

Currently, by law, all evaluations and staff files should be available to the worker. It is important to note that ethical codes and personnel policies usually set minimum standards and cannot anticipate all contingencies. Our profession needs to raise ethical standards by supporting "good" decisions with sound evidence.

> An ethical code serves as a guide to practice based on the values and the knowledge of a particular profession. Although there is always some balance between the decisions we make based on our professional values and knowledge and our feelings, the stronger the knowledge base, the more that knowledge is likely to influence our decision and our ethical code.
>
> Some fear that scientific ethical decision making would replace our value of humanity. The contrary is true. Scientific decision making is truly humanistic. It permits us to make decisions that are genuinely ethical, and permits the client to make real choices. It truly licenses us to serve humanity in the best professional manner. (There is no relationship between a more scientific approach to ethical decisions and a hasty introduction of semi-scientific results from the social sciences into social practice.)

The future professional will not only have to develop an effective ethical code, but he will have the additional task of advocating his code in the face of growing technological advances and pressures to adopt these advances in his practice with people. Only the achievement of clear ethical agreements in the social work profession can hold welfare decision-makers and supervisors accountable when they are under the pressures of political expediency and technological change.[43]

CHAPTER 5

ENGAGING

GROUPS

We are all in the same boat in a stormy sea and we owe each other a terrible loyalty.

G. K. CHESTERTON

Without the conscious acknowledgment and acceptance of our kinship with those around us there can be no synthesis of personality.

CARL G. JUNG

Although it is beyond the scope of this book to deal adequately with the field of group dynamics, it is important for the supervisor and staff development specialist to have some perspectives on the small group.

1. WHAT IS A GROUP?

The groups we will be talking about generally fall under the label of "small group." We will not be dealing with mass movements or mobs. We are thinking of groups small enough

to work together. The following attributes are generally identified as representative of the small working group:

1. A size of 2 to 20 members (certainly the larger groups are
   more appropriate in staff development programs)
2. Small enough to permit face-to-face interaction (communication)
3. Meetings with some continuity over a period of time
4. Some boundaries or regulations which establish who is in
   or out. This may just mean that certain members recognize
   each other as belonging, or that people with certain job
   assignments are included
5. Some distribution of roles, leaders, trainers, etc.
6. Some common interest, a goal, a clear reason for existing

One author has pointed out that in all groups certain uni-
versal aspects of behavior can be observed. The members have
certain *sentiments* about each other. They perform certain *actions* like working, and they communicate or *interact* with
each other. And these three aspects of behavior are influenced
by the *norms* or patterns of expected behavior that evolve in
the group.[1] We might thus define a group as a number of individuals who interact with each other over a period of time,
with feelings toward each other holding them together as they
work toward some common goal, and who identify themselves as
connected or bound to each other in some way.

2. THE GROUP AS A SYSTEM

To the extent that any group is a bounded "set" of people
in interaction who are out to accomplish some common task,
Figure 14 shows how we might consider a group as a system.
"Systems are made up of sets of components that work together
for the overall objective of the whole."[2] We may categorize
groups in a broad range from:

1. Task-oriented groups, in which the group becomes a way of
   solving some environmental problem; to

2. Internal-oriented change; to
3. Socioemotional groups, in which the rewards come from within the group itself.

	Figure 14	
SOCIOEMOTIONAL TASK ORIENTATION	INTERNAL TASK ORIENTATION	EXTERNAL TASK ORIENTATION

	Encounter	Drug abuse group	Community
Athletic club	group	Patient group	action
Social club		Patient government	
Bridge club			

CLASS   T-GROUPS   POLITICAL ACTION

←————————————— SUPERVISORY ——————————————→

Naturally there are no sharp lines dividing one type of group from another, and some groups perform a number of functions. Thus a person in a dance class learns to dance (one of his stated or avowed goals) and may also feel less lonely because he meets other people (a goal which may be unavowed). Patient government groups are seen as therapeutic for the members but also often bring about some changes in the institutional structure and procedures; they may be seen as task oriented. A supervisory group in some ways resembles a class in that the rewards come out of the learning experience, but they also move in to more effective problem solving on behalf of the client through both new knowledge and additional change. In that respect they can cross all three categories.

3. WHY THIS GROUP?

When they have a choice, people join into groups with people who *they think can furnish the rewards* they want. All of us operate from a base of selecting those activities which we feel are pleasurable or rewarding, and avoiding those which are costly to us. *Conscious decisions are generally made by weighing the costs against the rewards.* Such decisions may require a process of careful consideration, or may take place almost instantaneously. What kinds of things influence people to join with others in a group? A may join with B because he sees in B certain qualities he would like for himself (role models, heroes). He may join with B because they are both in the same boat and need reinforcement from each other (self-help groups —A.A., for example). He may join with B because A feels B can help solve certain problems (classes, yoga, meditation, supervision). Or because he needs large numbers of people to present a powerful force (social action, and social movements).

When people join together in groups, they explore their similarities and discover common concerns and causes. They can support and help each other. They feel stronger and less alone. The more they interact with one another as equals, the more likely they are to like each other, and to become like each other in their behavior. Because people joining groups have varied goals, one of the first tasks for the worker is to help the group find a common goal. A common goal is something the members will achieve as a group at some future time. In a supervisory group, the common goal is more visible, and there is better service to the client.

However, it is important for the worker to remember that in addition to achieving the tasks for which the group was organized, the group must also meet the needs of its individual members. Where he has a choice, the member will remain in the group as long as the rewards of being a member are greater than the costs. As the rewards become fewer, the member will tend to feel ambivalent toward the group. If the rewards should disappear, so, in all likelihood, will the member.

Rewards seem to be related to two major areas (see Figure 16):

1. SATISFACTION: The feeling that the group is accomplishing its tasks. It is getting the job done that it started out to do.
2. SECURITY: The feeling of acceptance as a member of part of the group. Comfortable group climate.

Where members treat each other with respect, value each

Figure 15

MEMBERS' PERCEPTION OF TASK ACCOM- PLISHMENT	NO SATISFACTION	NO SATISFACTION	SATISFACTION	SATISFACTION
Group climate	Threatening	Comfortable	Threatening	Comfortable
Probable chance of group success	None	50%	50%	100%

These probabilities are for illustrative purposes only

other's needs and contributions, and where the goals are clear and agreed upon by the membership, the chances of having a successful and productive group are enhanced.

The amount of rebuff that a member in a group will take is often related to ease of access to other groups. "How much a particular group means to a member" may depend on other groups he has access to. A retarded child with only one group open to him may stay in that group even if he is treated badly.

Leadership roles are important in all groups, and these roles are generally related to carrying out the two functions of a group: the accomplishment of the *task* and the *maintenance* of the group so that the task can be accomplished.

All groups carry on both functions simultaneously in order to accomplish their goals. The fact is often overlooked that, in truth, groups often cannot accomplish their goals if members' personal concerns—i.e., process—are neglected. Barber, discussing committee decision-making procedures, points out:

> Numerous studies of initially leaderless small groups show a marked differentiation between a "task leader" who contributes ideas and guidance but is not well liked, and a social-emotional leader who has the opposite characteristic. But in seventy-two

real communities in business and government the chairman ordinarily performed both roles, and members were dissatisfied when he failed to do so.[3]

His comments are supported by Heslin and Dunphy, who reported on the Kahn and Katz studies.

These authors attempted to identify the characteristics of supervisors in industry who led productive, in contrast to less productive crews . . . Supervisors of high-producing groups . . . possessed both the technological skills needed to support group tasks and the ability to help members to satisfy their important needs.[4]

Thelen suggests four problems which all groups continually face: the publicly stated problem the group was brought together to solve, the hidden problems of dealing with *shared* anxieties which usually are not explicitly formulated; individual efforts to achieve publicly stated ends; and individuals' efforts to deal with their own hidden problems of membership anxiety, self-integration, and adaptation.[5]

The worker who recognizes the systematic relationships among these factors cannot *consider process and task in any way as a real dichotomy, and must accept their functional relationship.*

4. STRUCTURE FOLLOWS FUNCTION

Structure is the manner in which the group organizes itself to get its work done. Structure starts to develop in small groups as roles evolve over time (patterns of association: like-dislike; status-interests). Some people will volunteer to carry out tasks, and they start to be seen as leaders.

What is the function of structure? Efficient job performance seems to be the major benefit. But it also:
—serves to control both tasks and behavior at meetings,
—provides a division of labor (who-does-what begins to become institutionalized),
—helps internalize obligations: to lead, to communicate,

—supports psychological processes, such as tension reduction and a common need to predict group behavior.

—supports individual needs to count on stability of attendance times and of meetings.

The structure of a group affects its work (ability to solve the task of the group) and the mental health of the members. It helps to solve the social problems of the group. Some research has shown that a person's position in the group is related to his feeling that the group is worthwhile and his feeling of his own self-worth.

Research on behavior settings indicates that what a group looks like can often be influenced and even deduced by other factors, such as meeting time, the space it acts within, and the mode of dress. Thus, we expect groups meeting in a gym to do physical things, a group meeting in a small room to talk, a well-dressed group not to fight, a group meeting at 12 noon to eat, a group meeting at 5:00 P.M. to drink.

Roles are seen as basic units for understanding some of the behavior of members of groups of all types. A great many personal and societal problems are interpreted in terms of role analysis. In addition to the roles which appear on tables of organizations, roles evolve in groups over time as members begin to develop patterns of actions. Some volunteer to do certain tasks, some become "jokers," etc. Roles tend to fall into three major areas: task-oriented roles, group maintenance roles, and individual-oriented roles.

Tables of organization usually indicate what the *formal* structure of a group looks like. Often, however, there is an informal structure made up of subgroups, or cliques, which may differ from the formal power structure but which may be equally or even more influential in decision making.

When the roles taken by members of the informal subgroups subvert the goals of the formal structure, the group can become disoriented and disintegrate, or it can alter its actions to be more in keeping with the needs of all its members.

Often in supervisory groups the supervisor assumes or is delegated the roles of leader, expert, judge, parent, boss, evaluator, friend, etc. Can one person carry all of these roles equally well? Should he? A major asset of a supervisory group is that there are many people who can assume supervisory roles if urged to, permitted, and rewarded. There is a need to understand the roles of various actors in the environmental arena.

> In practice, for example in negotiating a mental health program with a superintendent of schools it is at least as important to be familiar with the role of the superintendent in modern American communities as to be aware of the particular superintendent's personality and characteristic ways of coping. For it is the role of the superintendent and the norms of his functional community of educators, and the goals of the education program that will determine, far more than will his personality, the ways in which he can respond to the mental health field.[6]

5. COMMUNICATION AND THE GROUP

The structure of the group not only helps define tasks but permits certain channels of *communication* to operate. Communication is the art of getting information from the mind of one person to another. The purpose of communication is to get the needed information processed through the group so that the job can be done (see Figure 16).

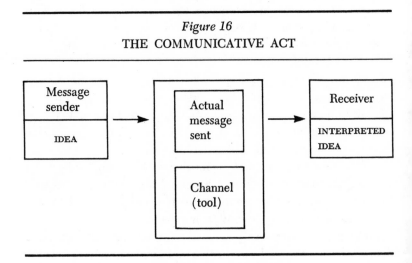

Figure 16
THE COMMUNICATIVE ACT

This information may be facts: "The group will meet at 8:00." "Supervision is an educative process." "I want help." This information may be feeling: "You make me so mad." "I didn't feel I helped the client." It may be spoken, written, musical, or gesture (making a face, a fist, a smile, or a frown).

Communication also influences the structure of the group. Members tend to direct their messages toward the higher status member or to the leader rather than to the lower status members.

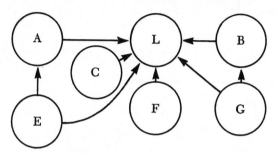

In some organizations communication always comes down the line from the leader to the lieutenants to the members.

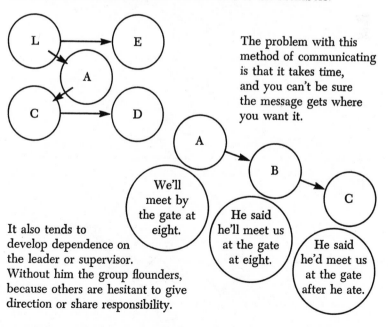

The problem with this method of communicating is that it takes time, and you can't be sure the message gets where you want it.

It also tends to develop dependence on the leader or supervisor. Without him the group flounders, because others are hesitant to give direction or share responsibility.

In most small groups communication is more informal. The members also send messages back to the leaders. This is known as feedback.

Another way of communicating is *the circle:* sooner or later

FEEDBACK LOOP

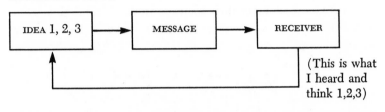

THE CIRCLE

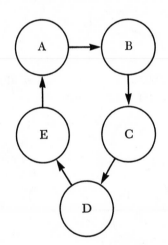

THE WHEEL

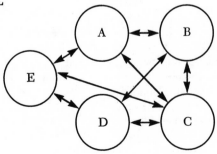

everyone gets a chance to talk to someone. But *the wheel* might be better. Communication is free and everyone gets the message. The members know what the leader thinks, and the feedback can be quick—provided that the culture of the group permits free discussion.

Some people find it very difficult to talk to other people in one-to-one conversation. Often it is safer to talk about things in groups than when you are alone: You find out other people have the same problem, or you see nothing happens to them when they talk—it's safe.

Some people have decided it's better not to talk. They have found out that they never "read" messages right, no matter how hard they try. Some therapists refer to them as victims of the "double bind," illustrated in Figure 17. It is a common phenomenon in family problems. Some say it is a cause of schizophrenia.

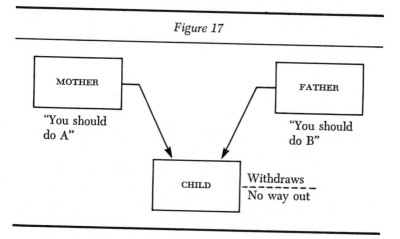

Figure 17

(Or mother says, "Go out and enjoy yourself, but don't get dirty.") Thinking of mental illness in communication terms has led some therapists to consider therapy as basically a communications concern. In a work group it may work like this:

CHAIRMAN: I don't think we'll have a meeting tonight. What do you think, Bill?

BILL: I don't think we should have a meeting tonight.

CHAIRMAN: You never want to have meetings. No wonder the committee is breaking up.

BILL: But . . . you asked me.

CHAIRMAN: I wanted your honest opinion. Not just what you thought I wanted to hear.

BILL: I . . . didn't think we should have a meeting.

CHAIRMAN: That's what I mean. You never want to have meetings. I'll have to tell the staff you suggested we shouldn't have a meeting.

BILL: Well . . . maybe we should have a meeting.

CHAIRMAN: You never stick to anything. No wonder the committee is breaking up . . .

Bill can't win. He decides the only way to survive is to be quiet. Imagine a child in a family that communicates like that! or workers in an agency in which the director responds in such a manner.

Unless the group is able to communicate information about *what it wants* to do and *how it wants* to do it, as well as *how it feels* about what is happening in the group, it will not be able to become a productive, *cohesive* group.

6. GROUP COHESION

Group cohesion suggests the degree of attractiveness that a group has for its members. In a cohesive group the members feel they want to belong and they have a part to play. Cohesive groups satisfy the needs of their members. This satisfaction might be due to the high status of the group, its accomplishments, opportunities to participate and be accepted, having a leadership role in the group, or safety from outside attack. On the other hand, a too domineering leadership, disrespect for a member's ideas, or constant fighting weakens the group bonds. There is generally a "zone of indifference" within which unhappy members will still maintain a working interest in the group. When things get beyond this zone, however, the members will drop out psychologically and/or physically. (See Figure 18.)

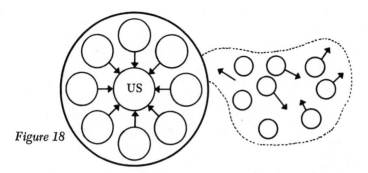

Figure 18

Cohesive groups tend to be able to make stronger demands on their members to conform to the group's norms. Therefore, in a work-oriented situation, cohesive groups will be highly productive. In order to make themselves more attractive to prospective members, groups will offer a wide variety of programs, hoping to meet needs. For example, church groups not only attempt to meet religious needs but educational and social needs as well.

In a work group such as in a group supervision situation, cohesiveness often develops around the agreement on social goals, synergistic techniques for decision making, and minimizing status differentials.

7. GROUP NORMS

Just as role defines the expected behavior for individuals filling certain positions, norms set the expected behavior for all the members of the group. Norms are the "rules of the game" that the members of the group evolve for themselves. All groups have some norms, which members must adhere to. Clarity of group norms often helps new members learn what is acceptable behavior in the group. The group often helps you determine which line is longer, A or B (see Figure 19).

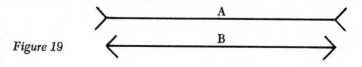

Figure 19

Groups tend to create "conformity" to the norms of the group, not only in actions, but in dress, speech, food habits, etc. Conformity, however, may not necessarily be seen negatively. For example, if the norms of a ward group are such that patients are expected to participate in activities rather than hang around in bed, this can be used for therapeutic purposes. In large institutions, the norms of various subgroups often differ. Goffman has pointed out that the differences of doctor norms and aide norms can immobilize the treatment process.[7]

Deviance from the norms of the group presents special problems. The deviant can often force the group to examine its own behavior. As Figure 20 makes clear, the group can (1) mobilize against the deviant; (2) change some of its own limits of behavior in relation to the deviant; or (3) accept the deviant's ideas.

Figure 20

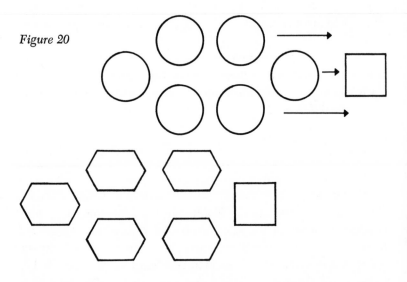

People belong to many groups, and the influences of these groups affect the member's actions in other situations. They often become his reference groups. Reference groups are those groups to which a person aspires, and from which he tends to take clues for behaving. Members and prospective members tend to conform to the expected behavior of their reference groups. These groups tend to be socializing influences on the individual. Where the expected behavior is fairly clear, as in a professional group, it is easier to learn correct actions.

The expectations that the members have of each other mold many of the norms of the group. As it meets over a period of time, there are recurrent interactions among members. These tend to build up a pool of common symbols—ways of perceiving and thinking—which leads to:

> Common ways of looking at things
> Consistent ways of communication
> Shared attitudes
> Mutually accepted obligations
> Mutual expectations regarding the behavior of others

8. DEMANDING WORK: CREATING A CULTURE FOR EFFECTIVE SUPERVISION

Picture, if you will, a group supervisory meeting attempting to decide what type of procedures might be developed to make referrals from the Intake Department more helpful.

SUPERVISOR: There have been a number of complaints that the intake process does not operate in a way that is helpful to clients and staff. A number of staff people feel they don't get enough information, while clients feel they have to go over the same ground twice. At our last meeting we said we would look at the process.

WORKER A: Part of the problem is that we don't have consistency in the Intake Department.

WORKER B: They don't want to cooperate.

WORKER C: They should be given clear directions as to what to look for.

WORKER B: That's been tried; it doesn't work.

WORKER C: Try again.

WORKER B: It's a waste of time.

SUPERVISOR: Are there other ideas?

WORKER A: Why not find out how they do it at Family Service?

WORKER C: Who cares?

WORKER B: (*whispering to Worker A*) Did you hear about what happened to Joe on the way to work?

WORKER D: I think a subcommittee should take this up; I want to talk about the new regulations.
SUPERVISOR: I don't feel we're getting anywhere . . .

And so it goes . . . Many of us have been at meetings that go round and round and never seem to get anywhere.

An analysis of the "forces" at work may be impossible, as there seems to be a maze of individual paths to follow. Transactional analysis doesn't quite do it, either. Everyone appears to be acting adult. Wilfred R. Bion's approach gives us an alternative tool for looking at the group's dynamics.

Bion suggests that a group in a broad sense can be seen as doing either of two things: work or non-work.[8] If they are working on the task for which they have gathered, there is no problem. If they are not working, we need to assess what is happening and why. He provides a framework (see Figure 21) for looking at non-work:

Figure 21
BION'S MODEL

WORK	NON-WORK
	Fight-flight (FT-FLT)
	Dependency (D)
	Pairing (P)

Nonwork: This consists of three ways of behaving: The first is *fight-flight*. The response to any idea is that it is "not good, won't work, absurd, not worth the effort, dumb," etc. Or the other side of the coin is, "Too hard—we can't do it, we don't have the power-skill-time." Either represents an attempt to run away from the problem.

Another way of not working is to be *dependent*. "You tell us what to do." "Let's get an expert from Chicago." Anything as long as we don't have to work. "Let's get a beer."

The third technique of not working is what Bion calls *pair-*

ing. People talk among themselves, tell jokes, love, romance, form cliques. It shows that the group is a warm, friendly group, but little work gets done.

It should be noted that some of these forces of nonwork are natural and take place in most groups. In some groups, however, it becomes a "way of life" and a learned way of not working. It becomes their style—a culture—or what Bion refers to as the *basic assumption* of the group. Once this is learned, it is difficult to alter the group's basic assumption. For this reason, from the start of their relationship, there must be a *demand for work* from those in the worker role.

In any reciprocal relationship, such as supervision, the mood of the group will influence the supervisor and vice versa. The group not wanting to work will try to get him not to demand work of them. If the supervisor doesn't want to work or wants them to be dependent, he will "set them up" for that experience. "Know yourself" is a worthy piece of advice in analyzing any experience with people.

If the group is fighting, am I joining in or am I demanding work? If they seem dependent, is it because I have been lecturing for twenty minutes? If a client is flirting, have I been showing some "preening" behavior? In the course of a supervisory conference, I can assess what the basic assumption seems to be. If nonwork happens at two or three meetings, I have to change the nature of the transaction. Some confrontation to demand work would be necessary. For example, the worker might sit and say nothing at a first meeting. The group would say, "When are you going to do something?" He would respond, "What do you want me to do?" After a few rounds of this, they become angry and tell him what to do. He has violated their expectations, and they may work.

The concept of reciprocity (my setting the stage by what I do) is reminiscent of an underlying (nonverbal) contract. It was never agreed upon but seems to be an effect. The supervisor needs to get back to the verbal contract and demand that the work of the group be accomplished.

9. THE GROUP CONTRACT

> GROUPS WHICH ARE CLEAR ON THEIR GOALS HAVE A BETTER
> CHANCE OF ACHIEVING THEIR GOALS THAN GROUPS WHICH ARE
> UNCLEAR.

> GROUPS WHICH HAVE AN IDEA OF THE MEANS TO THEIR GOALS
> HAVE A BETTER CHANCE OF ACHIEVING THEIR GOALS THAN
> THOSE WITH NO IDEA.

When a group works out its goals and means and decides
how its members will use each other to achieve these goals, it
has dealt with some of the dynamics related to the establishment
of the "bonds" of organization or contract.

GROUP SUPERVISION

Groups have been used successfully as a medium for learning in staffings, staff meetings, orientation, and training; but the
use of the learning group as a major tool for supervision and
teaching has had a slower acceptance as an educational resource
by agencies and field teachers.

Group supervision is an educative process in which the
major supervisory tasks (teaching, administration, and enabling)
are carried on in and with the group. Mutual (though not equal)
responsibilities for the content and teaching are shared by the
teacher and student.

The usual supportive teaching opportunities—such as individual evaluations, staff meetings, and individual conferences—
are needed and made available to the student.

If supervision can be seen as behavior which affects the
educational group toward the learning objectives, then the responsibilities for teaching become the joint responsibilities of all
the instructional group members, and not only the formal
teacher. The latter's authority comes from the institution and his

competence. The student's authority to teach comes primarily from the instructional group but also from the formal teacher.

THE SMALL GROUP AS EDUCATIVE SYSTEM

The nature of the small group as both an educative, socialization, and supportive force has been documented and discussed by a number of writers in the fields of social work, education and social psychology.[9] The quest is for the solution of some problem, although often the motivation might be unknown—e.g., "autonomy" and "self-actualization." [10]

The small group offers a natural setting in which this quest can be carried out. For the practitioner, the quest is for a professional competence in common search with others and the help of a supervisor-teacher. Together they share responsibility for this common quest, each according to what he has to offer and his function in being there.

One of the major tasks of the supervisor is enabling the group to develop the kind of working relationships among the members which expedite the learning situation. Sensitivity and concern for the individual, or what Towle calls "individualization," must be practiced by the supervisor in group supervision just as in individual supervision. Although the increased interaction and opportunities may at times seem to make this more difficult, it must be noted that other group members also practice this same concern and under synergistic conditions help sustain the learning community.

THE GROUP AS A MUTUAL AID SYSTEM

The function of the group is to serve as a mediator between the members and society. In so doing, each group is faced with three major problems: (1) achieving the task which it set for itself; (2) maintaining itself as a group long enough to achieve its goals; and (3) coming to terms with the environment or systems of which it is a part.

The goals of the supervisor and the goals of the members are brought into focus for the group members as far as these can be explicated. The needs of both are taken into account, and the resulting transaction becomes the working agreement. Out of the common concerns of the individuals emerges an acceptable "group goal," which becomes an "interdependent need system which arouses, maintains and directs group behavior." [11]

The purpose for the group's existence is its reality-oriented task, and one of the first assignments for the group is to confront itself with what its task is to be. Although the group members may come with their own goals in mind and their own views of what the group can offer, there needs to be some soliciting by the group of a "common goal" which the group has set for itself. When this common goal is linked to discussion of agreed-upon ways of achieving these goals, we have the "group contract." [12]

The motivation to achieve both the individual and group goals is tied in with:

1. The involvement of the individual in the interaction process or "life of the group."
2. His own individual need system and his understanding of the link between his need fulfillment and the group's achievement.
3. The ability of the individual to find both security and satisfaction in the group.
4. The enabling ability of the supervisor.
5. The commitment of the individual to the goals of the agency.

In order to achieve their goals the members assume various roles based on their own need systems and what this particular group requires in order to work on its goal-directed tasks. The group serves as a tool by which the group members are able to achieve the goals which brought them together.

We know, however, that for a number of reasons which may be related to the abstract nature of the goal, the imposition of goals from the outside, the inability of the members to function with each other, or the hostility of the environment, groups do not always achieve their goals. Often in their search for solutions to these problems, groups have sought the consultation or leadership of nonmembers who in some planned way attempt to affect the group process so that the members' goals can be achieved. The supervisor or teacher is one such nonmember, who because of his position, experience, and task focus can help the members achieve their goals.

THE SYSTEM WITH SUPERVISOR

In addition to the provision of educational resources, the major tasks for the supervisor are: (1) to help create the conditions under which learning can take place; (2) to help the worker to focus and integrate some of the learning experiences that are vital to the learning of the professional role; and (3) to help the workers make the best use of the group learning situation.

As with all groups and learning processes, certain obstacles to learning are apt to appear, and it becomes the function of the supervisor to help the students discern the nature of these obstacles and find ways of dealing with them. These obstacles may include: (1) the inability to look at one's own or fellow workers' practice in an objective manner; (2) the manner in which one presents or interprets material; or (3) a lack of ability to work on a problem that has "loaded" meaning to the supervisee.[13] The supervisor, in addition to presenting material and helping the group utilize this material, must be able to help the group deal with some of the blocks to its learning.

The responsibility for keeping the group focused on the material to be learned lies in the hands of the supervisor, who must continually hold the group to the purpose for its existence. The responsibility for working on the learning problems, however, lies primarily in the hands of the group members, just as in a one-to-one supervisory conference, the responsibility to assume the learning role and to work at learning is the student's.

PHASES IN THE TEACHER-LEARNER TRANSACTION

We have already commented on some of the initial tasks of emerging groups, such as group formation and goal setting. These, however, are preliminary to some of the developmental tasks still facing the group as it seeks its goal.

Many practitioners and researchers concerned with small groups have noted that there appears to be a natural progression in the development of a group's life: (1) initial group formation; (2) a period of testing of the group and its limits; (3) a period of rather productive accomplishments on the part of the group; and (4) a phase which is generally seen as the termination of or change in the purpose or activity of the group.

The stages in the supervisor transaction can also be perceived in this manner. The various stages call for different action patterns on the part of the group members and discreet action responses from the supervisor.

1. THE ENCOUNTER

At this stage in the life or prelife of the group, the nature of the supervisory relationship is brought to the attention of the supervisee. This exposure may be through (1) a brochure which describes the agency or the nature of field work instruction; (2) contact with staff in other agencies; and (3) contact in some way with the agency. In essence, this exposure acts as an advance signal that something unusual may transpire in this learning situation. All contacts with new staff must be seen as part of an ongoing interpretation part of the learning process.

All groups must be concerned with two major factors as they work together for the accomplishment of their goals. Both are closely interrelated: they can be distinguished but not separated. (See Figure 22.) The first such factor is the ongoing relationships among the members, the social-emotional factors related to keeping the group together so that the work can be accomplished. The second factor is the accomplishment of the

Figure 22

CONCERNS FACED AT GROUP FORMATION
BY INDIVIDUALS AND GROUPS *

	TASK	SOCIAL-EMOTIONAL
GROUP	"What do we want to do together?" Purpose Expectations Rewards "How?" Activities Structure (control) Members	"How to deal with stress?" "Can we function?" "Will we be permitted?" "Will the leader let us?"
INDIVIDUAL	"What do I want to do?" "What can I give the agency, group?" "What can I learn?"	"My role?" "Will I be liked?" "Will I like them?" "Will the supervisor like me?" "Will he help me?" "Do I like him/her?" "How much does this group mean to me?"

* Adapted from material presented in lecture by Herbert Thelen, University of Chicago, 1965.

tasks, the work to be done to reach the goals. Both of these enter into the minds of the members, perhaps even prior to the first meeting.

2. CONTRACTING

The initial contact between supervisee and supervisor is a start in a relationship in which the initial goals of the transaction are worked out and the means of achieving these goals are discussed. Some of the reasons for selecting the group as a method of teaching in the field should be pointed out, and the value of the participation of the members as a prerequisite for success should be emphasized. The building of trust to enhance learning must start immediately, because the nature of the beginning relationship has an important bearing on the subsequent frame of reference of both the learner and the teacher.

The supervisor has the responsibility for interpreting and clarifying the nature of the group and the values inherent in the group situation for learning. He helps define the goal of the group, clarifies the expectations both of the members and the supervisor, and discusses the individual learning assignments as well as some of the responsibilities inherent in a supervisor-teacher and supervisee-learner situation for both parties to the transaction. The supervisor may also discuss with the group some of the teaching techniques that will be used in the field and the part each will be expected to play if the learning experiences are to be most beneficial to all. Some of the guidelines for the types of concerns that may be brought to or excluded from the group—at least initially—are discussed.

The supervisor points out some of the common learning needs of the group and broadly sketches the direction and type of cases that the learners are likely to have as well as some of the anticipated problem areas. Some discussion should follow as to how the supervisor can be used both in the group and for individual conferences. The matter of confidentiality should be discussed, both for case and conference material. The supervisor should point out his responsibility to use the material brought up in the group with the agency.

The expectations and responsibilities of each of the actors need to be discussed. The initial contract is the first in a series. It attempts to establish some of the rules of the game with the group and also to gain "credit" from the group while they learn to trust both the group and the supervisor so that some initial learning experiences can be mutually worked at as the group develops.

3. THE RECONNAISSANCE

This refers to the "scouting" period as group members get to know each other and the supervisor, while the supervisor in turn gets to know them. There is a mutual testing of members, limits, and the supervisor.

The new worker is uncertain of what is expected of him in the agency and the group, and he is often dependent on the supervisor and other members for direction. This is a "normal" development and should be so noted, but efforts to utilize the supervisor as expert and to negate the value of the group should be discouraged. At first, there may be few attempts at risking of self, but as the group starts to be helpful and supportive of the member, the risk of self increases.

The supervisor must assume some of the initial responsibility for bringing material to the group which he knows will be of immediate and common concern, such as intake, recording of material, discussion of agency policies and clientele, etc. He immediately begins to make demands on the group that they work on some of these problem areas by calling on the group to work and by using the contributions of the group members in the problem-solving or exploration process. The nature of the material needed to make an adequate assessment of client need is an item which lends itself to this type of discussion.

The supervisor helps the group bring out some of the factors which they as beginners feel they most urgently need in order to start working with the client, and their concerns become significant parts of the group's agenda. He permits differences of opinion, even with his, and helps the group see that it can handle differences within the group and still function productively.

Toward the end of this phase the group is able to take risks, and members freely bring in their practice for discussion in front of the group.

4. AUTONOMOUS LEARNING

As the trust both in the group and the supervisor grows, the ability of the group members to risk themselves increases. The group members are able to deal with "more significant" material and can bring in items about their practice which at first might have been too threatening. The supervisor encourages this and can act as a mediator when this material may be too threatening to any one individual or when scapegoating seems to be occurring and the group is not able to work. The supervisor starts to demand increased work from the supervisees and often brings in material which another learner has brought up in a record. This should be generally discussed with him beforehand if it is material that the learner might not want to share in public.

As the material is fed into the group, the supervisor and the members share in the solving of the problems, with the supervisor pointing out implications of action that might have been overlooked, helping the group move in the direction that is related to the current piece of practice being discussed by the group, and holding the group to this focus. This does not mean that the group cannot look at other things that may in their opinion be important, but they should be helped to deal with this at a point where it may be most useful to the group. At times the group might help a colleague with a problem which is not necessarily one common to the group, but is related to the field experience.

INDIVIDUAL CONFERENCES

Although the group is the medium by which the supervisor has selected to help, there are times when individual conferences are in order and in fact may be the recommended course of action.

1. EVALUATIONS

The periodic evaluations of the learners that are aimed at assessing their growth and problems during the past period of time should be done individually with each learner. This becomes a private matter in which some of his strengths and weaknesses, his performance with the client, and his total learning experiences are discussed.

Needless to say, the group as a group must also have periodic assessments of its own developments and ability to work on some of the problems with which it has been confronted.

2. REQUESTS FOR INDIVIDUAL CONFERENCES

When the member makes a specific request of the supervisor for a discussion of material which the supervisee feels cannot be discussed in the group, an individual conference should be arranged. It may be that the supervisor will attempt to have the learner bring this up in the group after hearing and discussing the matter with the individual. If this type of request from the supervisee is repeated too often, the reasons for this have to be examined with the supervisee.

3. INITIAL ENCOUNTERS WITH THE AGENCY AND SUPERVISOR

In addition to the group orientation sessions, there should be individual sessions in which the worker can discuss at his own pace some of his concerns with the experience that he is about to enter, his past experiences, his goals, etc.

4. AT SUPERVISOR'S DISCRETION

At times the supervisor may feel that individual conferences are needed because the supervisee is not making progress in the group or is not able to use the group as the medium. The supervisor can then help him work on this problem on an individual conference basis for as long as this is needed. The member should still be expected to work and learn in the group.

THE CONTRACT WITH THE GROUP

The contract which the supervisor makes with the group is basically that this is a work group and that both the supervisor and the supervisees are there to work. The goal of the group is to learn how to be competent social workers even though their initial attempts may be naïve and fumbling.

In this agreement there are expectations that the supervisor will bring his advanced knowledge, educational skills, and understanding of behavior. The worker has to bring his time, interest, knowledge, and the desire to participate in the work of the group, learning how to be more effective. This work is accomplished not only through work with the clients in the field, but through work in the supervisory group, by contributing examples, questions, concerns, insights, and differing views to be worked by himself, by other group members, and the supervisor.

Just as in individual supervision, the ability to give of oneself in supervision develops as one feels that he can trust the experience and the people he is involved with. Konopka, in discussing the role of the worker, points out, "Nothing significant can happen until the members have learned to trust him." [14] Just as the supervisor in the individual supervisory sessions cannot expect this trust to develop on initial contact, it cannot happen immediately in the group sessions.

There is a possibility, however, that the involvement of members in a situation with their peers—all with common goals and concerns, all "in the same boat"—helps speed up the climate for trust. From the group they gain strength to share their concerns and the knowledge that this is a group expectation. There is less concern with authority and control as the group shares with the supervisor authority for teaching and control. The control rests in the problem to be worked on and in the combined efforts of the members to deal with their concerns of control and authority. The members become dependent on each other and not only on the supervisor. The group will demand of its members that they participate and carry their fair share in the work group. They, as well as the supervisor, will confront the learner who is not able to share his experiences or contribute to the analysis of the material under discussion. They will point out the seeming overdependence of a worker on the group or supervisor and wrestle with similar concerns within themselves.

CHAPTER 6

APPROACHES TO STAFF

DEVELOPMENT

Nothing astonishes men so much as common sense and plain dealing.

EMERSON

Larger social welfare and human service agencies have established a specific job responsibility for the staff development specialist. The functional responsibilities of this position often include:

1. the recruitment and selection of staff;
2. the orienting of new employees to their positions;
3. the development in employees of the knowledge, attitudes, and skills necessary to do the job;
4. the maximizing of all the employees in the agency's job performances; and
5. consultation with other agencies, departments, and organizations around the training needs of staff.

In addition to identifying the training needs, the staff development specialist is often in the position of having to develop, monitor, and—on occasion—train the staff. In addition to understanding how people learn, the specialist has to be a teacher, workshop leader, and training program organizer. For this purpose, it would be essential for the staff development person to examine a number of approaches to training. There are important considerations here for the supervisor as well; he can then translate some of the group learning orientations into work with individuals or smaller learning groups.

MODELS OF STAFF DEVELOPMENT

We will begin this section by examining four different training models. We will briefly look at how each might train staff around the concept of poverty and its impact on the family. The reader will note that comparisons are made more extensively between the Thelen and the Tyler models. The reasons for this is that those two models are fairly opposite in their approach.

THE THELEN (NATURAL) MODEL [1]

1. Confrontation:	Thelen believes that the initial experience must permit the worker to relate to the material in his own way. Something needs to take place which invites speculation and thinking in new ways.
Examples:	The workers may be taken on a bus trip through the poverty area, see a film, or be confronted by welfare clients who "tell it like it is."
2. Emergence to Awareness:	People who have been stimulated by new ideas or experiences need the opportunity to think and talk about them. This helps them to legitimize the ideas, bring them into sharper focus, and think about what the ideas mean to them.

Examples:	Open discussion or question-and-answer period, then writing a short summary of the experience. Breaking into smaller groups to discuss the meaning, or talking to a neighbor.

3. Eliciting of Testimony: The trainer then calls the groups together, or solicits the individual thoughts, so that everyone begins to see the different meanings the experience called forth. He helps them examine the similarities and differences, the implications, the varied philosophical or social science base that may be involved. They examine the truth, source, or means of proof for some of the statements. Many of these ideas are listed on the board with an attempt to frame large or significant concerns and questions, some of which are to be investigated by individuals or groups of staff according to their interests.

Examples: Family Breakup: How do you keep families together? The image of the father. Why do children feel hopeless? Can poor families rise out of poverty? What can a worker do that helps? The male worker's role in fatherless families.

4. The Task: In an attempt to discover the answers to some of the questions that the trainer and the students have raised, the students set out on tasks. This may be individual work or in groups. The teacher is available to help, and other students are used as resources. The work is bound by agreements made with the staff. Of course, time is an important factor in this model, but even in one-day training programs, parts of the model can be followed.

Examples: Staff might interview a family, read

some material, search out other's views. Groups can split up assignments.

5. Organization of Material: The students must decide how they are going to put their findings together. In what way will they approach their search and their reporting? Ongoing progress reports in the staff provide constant feedback; they utilize other staff and teacher to help.

Examples: In a two-day session, the morning of the second day could be used to ask the other trainees if they have information which might be useful in the groups. These are incorporated in the afternoon presentations.

6. Reporting to Staff: The report might be oral or written— a play, song, newspapers, panel, etc. This reporting may be the beginning of another confrontation.

Examples: Following a presentation in the form of a scenario of "the poor family of the future," staff asked for a future session on black family life styles. Dialogues around the material presented are again solicited by the trainer.

As staff goes through the process of selecting the material they are interested in, it becomes the trainer's responsibility to present the material of importance that is not covered. So if no one selects "hopelessness," and this is an important concept to be taught, the trainer presents that area.

THE TYLER TRAINING FRAMEWORK

Tyler has no doubt been one of the most influential educators in recent years in helping staff development specialists in social welfare formulate their programs. There are two reasons for this. First, his model was widely used in the training programs for social welfare trainers sponsored over a number of years by the Welfare Administration of the Department of

Health, Education, and Welfare.[2] Second, it was also the formulation used in the curriculum studies used by the Council on Social Work Education.[3] The particular example analyzed here was developed to explore the impact of poverty.

1. Formulate training objectives

What is it you hope to accomplish? Start with as high a level of abstraction as possible with the group you are going to train. What behavior patterns do we want? What are the most important things to be learned? What roles do we want the workers to play?

Examples:

Not just understanding the Joneses as a family, but poor families, and what poverty does to families in our society.

2. Devising the training means

People learn best by doing and thinking about doing. Skill learning means doing something which helps you utilize that skill. There must be motivation for learning. What present motivations exist or can evolve? The trainee must see the new as better.

Examples:

We might learn about poor families by reading, movies, interviews, or role play. If we were dealing with working rather than understanding, we would want to do more role play, video-taping, practice under supervision, or use of records.

3. Organizing the learning experiences

In what way can the training methods be put together so that they make the most sense to the learner? Should there be a presentation, then discussion, then a role play? Materials need to be gathered. How much time for the program, for each topic? Who should do the training? Ways of guiding the learner through experiencing need to be developed. There must be opportunities for practice.

Examples:

Introduce the family by looking at it as a historic institution, then by looking at

	the status of the members, then at what happens to the father's status when he loses his job. A father may talk about his experiences.
4. Evaluating	Some way to measure whether the learning experiences have indeed been met. This can be a written test, observing a meeting or a role play, etc. It is important that the evaluation be closely linked to the objectives.
	Evaluation may be done during the programs as checks to whether or not the goals of the training are being met. The evaluation may also take place at a time subsequent to the program to see whether the training is being used.
Examples:	A questionnaire two weeks after a program to see if workers were able to use anything they learned. It may also ask for ideas for future training.

Tyler generally sees four basic purposes for staff training programs:[4]

1. to help staff members develop the understanding, skills, and attitudes required to perform their work effectively;

2. to help them keep up to date where new research and new practices are developing rapidly;

3. to provide opportunities for each individual to develop increased competence and to assume increasing responsibility in improving services; and

4. to provide a warm, dynamic environment for growth and improvement by both clients and staff.

In a sense we can view Tyler's model as a building backward approach. We start with where we want to be at the end and plan our experiences from there.

THE THELEN AND TYLER MODES COMPARED

Similarities
1. Both would involve staff in determining what they need to be trained for.
2. Both would be specific about the groups to be trained.
3. Both would try to clarify their objectives.
4. Both would involve participants in learning and doing.
5. Both would evaluate and look for feedback.

Differences
1. Thelen would present a confrontation related to objectives from which content would evolve.
   Tyler would present content.
2. Thelen would pressure class to develop ways of working. His approach is more student-directed.
   Tyler's approach is more teacher-directed.
3. Thelen's content is more open.
   Tyler's content is fairly fixed in advance.
4. Thelen uses the class as a group and promotes small group work.
   Tyler has a more traditional view of the class.
5. Thelen's approach calls for more interaction with other students.
6. Thelen's approach calls for more self-learning and teaching by class members.
7. Tyler offers the class more structure.

ANDRAGOGY

Malcolm Knowles has developed an educational model which he calls *andragogy,* (see Figure 23) the art and science of teaching adults. Knowles has been involved in exploring the differences in youth and adult education and has reported his work in a fine book on andragogy.[5] He suggests that in adult learning the goals are clearer for the learner. Generally the adult learner knows what he needs as well as his learning style. He is also learning for immediate use on the job. The trainer has to make use of this knowledge in his teaching.

"The primary function of the teacher (or facilitator) in an andragogical activity is that of managing or guiding the andra-

---

Figure 23
THE ANDRAGOGY MODEL

---

1. Setting a climate for learning.
2. Establishing a structure for mutual planning.
3. Assessing interests, needs, and values.
4. Formulating objectives.
5. Designing learning activities.
6. Implementing learning activities.
7. Evaluating results.

---

gogical process itself, rather than managing the 'content' of the learning as in traditional pedagogy." [6]

The important contribution is that it respects the individual as an adult who can take responsibility for his own learning yet can use the knowledge of the expert. A summary of Knowles's thoughts on pedagogy and andragogy appears in Chart I, which will be found on pages 176 and 177.

This model might start by discussing the trainees' experience with poverty, or discuss how they intend to find out about the poor. It would facilitate the "class" to develop a structure of work and define its needs and direction.

A SYNERGY MODEL FOR STAFF DEVELOPMENT

The synergy model utilizes procedures from other models, but in addition focuses on developing the whole person in concert with others.

1. Engaging the trainees (transitionary orientation): Any beginning situation creates a mixture of excited expectation and situational anxiety. An initial period should be provided to move from the security of the known to the anticipated new.

(Prior to the start of the meeting, have coffee, etc., available, with materials lying around the room; use roving introductions.)

Set the contract for what the training program has been set up to do and some of the prospective things that will happen. Point out some of the fixed items and the open periods. Solicit from the trainees what they think the program "ought to be."

Set up the mechanisms by which they make their wishes known: committee, notes, questions, meetings, etc.

Example:

"The outline you received last week covers the major topics. As I see it we can modify the program as we go along so long as we touch on some of the important points. That would leave us about one-third of the sessions still open. After the opening session you will have some time to think about some other things you might want to do."

2. Initial bridging content:

The content, material, and methods in the training program should be related to:

    a. the nature of the idea to be taught,

    b. the capabilities, experience, comfort, and receptivity of the learners,

    c. the availability of resources (including people),

    d. some assessment of the impact.

Much of this is not known until the program has gotten under way, and an assessment of these factors needs to be made as the trainer attempts to involve the learners as doers and mutual-trainers. It is necessary therefore to help them warm up to involvement. They have to be taught to use the synergistic approach. In essence

CHART I
A COMPARISON OF ASSUMPTIONS AND PROCESSES OF PEDAGOGY AND ANDRAGOGY

| | ASSUMPTIONS | | | PROCESS ELEMENTS | |
	PEDAGOGY	ANDRAGOGY		PEDAGOGY	ANDRAGOGY
Self-concept	Dependency	Increasing self-directiveness	Climate	Authority-oriented Formal Competitive	Mutual Respectful Collaborative, informal
Experience	Of little worth	Learners are a rich resource for learning	Planning	By teacher	Mechanism for mutual planning
Readiness	Biological development, social pressure	Developmental tasks of social roles	Diagnosis of needs	By teacher	Mutual self-diagnosis
Time perspective	Postponed application	Immediacy of application	Formulation of objectives	By teacher	Mutual negotiation

CHART 1 (continued)

| | ASSUMPTIONS | | | PROCESS ELEMENTS | |
	PEDAGOGY	ANDRAGOGY		PEDAGOGY	ANDRAGOGY
Orientation to learning	Subject-centered	Problem-centered			
			Design	Logic of the subject matter	Sequenced in terms of readiness
				Content units	Problem units
			Activities	Transmittal techniques	Experiential techniques (inquiry)
			Evaluation	By teacher	Mutual rediagnosis of needs
					Mutual measurement of program

SOURCE: Malcolm Knowles, "Issues in Adult Learning," *Adult Leadership* 22, no. 9 (March 1974), p. 315.

they have to learn to learn, and the initial material should be the kind that will call forth easy responses, raise their interest, and yet not be too risky for them.

Example:

In a training program with the goal of learning how to supervise, the following excerpt was passed out at the first session, and the learners were asked to think about who might have said it— what kind of a person? "What was he like?" The responses were listed on the board. No one had to be an expert to respond, nor were there wrong answers:

"Society stands in the same relation to them [welfare recipients] as that of parent to child . . . Just as the child is expected to attend classes, so also the 'child adult' must be expected to meet his responsibilities to the community. In short, 'social uplifting'—even if begun on the adult level—cannot be expected to meet with success unless it is combined with a certain amount of social disciplining—just as it is on the pre-adult level" *

The excerpt is used to discuss what kind of supervisor they feel this person would make, and whether they would like to have him for a supervisor. Why? How might he act? It is planned to fit into subsequent relevant material.

3. Synergistic learning experiences:

The training program should be set up in a way that balances the need for structure—which many of the people

* Statement by a former welfare director of major city program. Quoted from a journal article.

involved in training desire—with the desires of the trainers to involve the trainees in discovery, creative thinking, and assuming responsibility for their own learning and training. By not forcing or permitting one over the other, the resulting program melds both into a unity in which people grow into the ability to create "live" programs with meaning for them.

There is an emphasis on work groups following the presentation of material to the total group. This opens new knowledge so that the work groups are purposeful and related to content and the goals and tasks are clear to the participants. This emphasis is used to expand the learning situation and increase the consciousness related to the material under review by having significant others share their views, learn from, and teach each other. The trainer here is a facilitator rather than a teacher.

Part of the underpinning of this model is that in addition to the training content goals, some training is in synergistic approaches: synectics, spectrum thinking, brainstorming, etc.

Example:

The training group had been discussing the McGregor X and Y management styles. They were asked if they thought the person in the excerpt above would be an X type supervisor or a Y type. Following this discussion they were asked to meld the X and Y. Were there things they would like to see in a supervisor that could be drawn from both? (The attempt here was to get away from dichotomies— to think more synergistically.) They were then asked to work in small groups, considering how they would help two people (an X- and a Y-oriented) to work together if they were on a team.

Example:

The task here was to deal with the concept of creativity. How would they get their staff to think differently about things? The synectics idea was tried. First they were asked to think of themselves as a can of fruit, vegetables, etc. Their visions were listed—with some prompting. They were then asked, "If you were a can of fruit, how would you want to be opened?" This led to a great deal of interest, ideas, the concept of power, denial, death.

We went on to "If you were a client how would you want your check to come?" We discussed empathy and analogy. We decided a good way to teach the concept of acceptance would be to ask, "What is the similarity between the idea of acceptance and an electric toaster?"

4. Organized Sharing

The ideas that come out of the small group discussions need to be organized by them and presented to the total group. This permits another type of work to take place in the groups, increases the knowledge bank of the total group, and also helps them feel they haven't lost out on anything.

The trainer lists these ideas, and organizes them as other groups report, commenting, expanding the ideas, and linking with things that have been on the previous sessions.

He reviews the lists, pointing out how the ideas tie in with items yet to be covered and with the group's. He sets some priorities on how to spend future sessions.

5. Evaluation:

Although evaluation does usually take place at the close of the session, it is important to evaluate at an earlier stage so that the program can be modified. In addition there may be an evaluation after each day's program with the total group or with the staff. The learners may want to meet on their own and feed in comments. The trainers might share their views as well.

Example:

"We have three more sessions left and I have two items I feel we have to deal with. Are there other things that you want to touch on, review, or get another viewpoint on?"

(Some programs evaluate at a later date and ask for comment sheets.)

If the evaluations are to be more formal, an attempt at a before-and-after questionnaire can be made to see what has been learned, or there can be a follow-up to see if practice has changed at all because of the training. Both of these require skilled planning and scheduling.

"The other trainers and I would like to give you our views of how the training program went."

In a later section of this chapter, we will discuss some of the approaches to evaluating the training program, both during the training process and at the program's conclusion.

THE TOOLS OF THE TRAINER:
EDUCATIONAL MEDIA

Obviously the most important tool that the trainer has is himself. His ability to relate himself to the task at hand, to the material, and most important to the people, can make the difference between a lackluster, boring session, and an exciting process of growth for all involved. Regardless of the approach he uses, the trainer can make use of various media to help make important data known, to increase the sensitivity of trainees to a problem, or to elicit feedback and thought. We will now explore some of these teaching tools. It is important to note that although we will deal primarily with verbal approaches, the awareness of nonverbal communication is important. Staff will be sensitive to all types of cues from the trainer. His verbal and nonverbal messages should complement each other.

This modeling role is an extremely important one in the learning-teaching process. The way the trainees are supervised may very well be the model they use to supervise. Beyond that, however, the trainer cannot talk about human ways of working with people while he himself neglects basic considerations due to staff, or talks about clients in a manner which degrades them. The trainer cannot count on teaching techniques to pull him through. The media are tools, extensions of himself.

The training specialist, whether he trains directly or consults, or hires trainers, should have familiarity with a range of learning media and their prospective uses in training. In this section we try briefly to review media and their differential use.*

In any learning situation, media are extensions of the teacher. They are tools which can be used as educative devices for transmitting information among people and for exposing students and supervisees to planned learning experiences.

---

* Portions of this section were presented at the Council on Social Work Education Annual Program, Cleveland, January 1969, and published in *Teaching and Learning in Social Work Education,* Marguerite Pohek, ed. (New York: CSWE, 1969).

This section will touch briefly on the use of certain media in staff development. It emphasizes the learning-teaching aspects of supervision and staff development. It will touch on teaching patterns, learning patterns, practice patterns, and the search for meaning. We will spar together with "motivation" and wrestle with "inquiry-discovery" models of learning. We will then explore examples of "experiential" media.

MEDIA

McLuhan has categorized media as "hot" or "cold," the cold being the media which furnish sparse information and thus demand of the receiver that he involve himself more completely in the communication exchange. "Cool media are high in participation or completion by the audience." [7] We are searching for media that call for high participation on the part of the trainee in the teaching-learning transaction.

An impressive long list of devices may be defined as educational media: television, books, flannel boards, chalk boards, projection machines of all types, case records, video tapes, lectures, teaching machines, etc. It is obvious that many of these devices have important uses aside from education. With such a wide range of possibilities, what criteria can we use in order to decide which media would be most appropriate to our teaching objectives in social work education?

TACTICS

First we should examine the concept that selections of specific media for staff training are in essence "tactical" decisions. This is part of a decision-making process related to the goals of the teacher,[8] his educational strategy, and the means or tactics he selects to carry out his strategy. Approaching the selection of media in this manner alerts us to consider the probabilities that specific media will achieve specific goals. Certain objectives are defined, and the media become tools to meet those objectives.

The teaching-learning process includes numerous actions on

the part of the teacher designed to influence the learner. Smith has defined teaching as "a system of actions intended to induce learning." [9] This pattern of actions, or teacher behavior, suggests the second important area of concern. What pattern of teacher actions maximizes achievement by the student?

Our patterns of supervising are closely related to the patterns of supervision to which we have been exposed; to our philosophical outlook, to our own needs; to conditions generated by the need to individualize the supervisee; to the agency and the community; to the client; and finally to research on learning which is available to us.[10] Thus, the selection of media is related first to tactical decisions related to the accomplishment of specific learning objectives and the individualization of the learner, and secondly to the pattern of teacher behavior which has become second nature to the teacher.

Learning is a personal experience, a unique relationship among learner, content, and teacher. The content will have different meaning to each supervisee because of his own life experiences and his experience with the material, the agency, and the teacher. Teaching is student-centered; the content must have meaning to the student, and so is individualized. As Charlotte Towle has noted, "The central principle in social work at all operating levels and in all its helping processes is that of individualizing persons, groups, and communities." [11]

THE QUEST FOR MEANING

Meaning evolves from encounters between the learner and his environment. These encounters, relative to the content we teach, result in selection, sorting, and internalizing through the patterns of learning unique to the student. These patterns are his organizers.[12] The key to meaning is in the breadth, depth, and flexibility of the learner's organizers as they sift through his storehouse of data. His organizers control what he perceives and what meaning his perceptions can have for him.

The meaning of an encounter with a poor client may be illustrated as follows: A worker's encounter with a poor person on the street or in his own office is fed into his data bank, or storehouse of experiences. He has seen poor people before and has certain stored data related to the poor, including abstract information about them. His organizers provide his pattern of how he will perceive this person; what meaning this will have for him.

$$E \longrightarrow D \longrightarrow O \longrightarrow M$$

| Encounter | Data | Organizer | Meaning |

In any encounter, the data derived is dependent not only on the information generated by the encounter, but also by the "organizer patterns" of how one looks at the poor. "The main point of the preceding analysis is that the key to the generation of meaning is the interaction between organizer and encounters." [13] If we wish to foster meaningful learning, we must increase the number and types of encounters that the learner will have. This allows his organizers to derive meaning from one of the encounters if another is meaningless to him. This is the reason for giving illustrations after a point has been made in a discussion. It presents a different type of encounter around the same information and presents the data in a different way. Two or three examples around the same idea may have more spread and make the content more meaningful. It is also important, however, to enlarge the learner's repertoire of available organizers. We say to him, "Look at it in a different way; analyze it from *this* point of view." We are attempting here to create conditions which will bring more of the available organizers into use for the generation of meaning. We are attempting in the short run to make the supervisee "open" in examining the content. As Deutsch puts it:

> Openness—the ability to increase the sensitivity in the range of channels of intake; the ability to interact and to receive; to learn more about the universe around us from the human beings around us—is perhaps one of the most critical and most precious qualities of any system of communication. [14]

When we are able to present the content in a manner which calls upon the worker to experience the meaning of some material, and we permit this meaning to become manifest, we increase his range of sensitivity. We do not tell him *how* to relate to the material; we attempt to look *with* him at the meaning it may have. We are permitting his organizers to scan the material for clues and to evolve new organizers, or ways of perceiving and reacting.

Basically we are confronted with the differences between *delivered* meaning and *derived* meaning. In the former, the material is presented without the students having much opportunity to derive their own meaning. In a classroom, feedback usually is minimal, and when there is any it is used in relation to specific questions thought by the teacher to be of importance. This feedback usually is in the form of a paper or exam, often at the end of the course. Derived meaning is an attempt to have the student struggle with the content and discover the meaning it has for him. Feedback for the supervisor is ongoing as he mediates between the supervisee's ability and the needs of the job.

The content itself is chosen in order to move the class along the directions professional education must take: (1) the development of autonomous professionals who can perceive problems from a wide view and have a range of tactics to call on in problem solving; and (2) the ability to relate to people in "helpful" ways.

Derived knowledge may be compared to "personal knowledge" or phenomenological knowledge, that which I know to be so because I have personally experienced it and believe it, regardless of any "book" knowledge you may have at hand to contradict it. There are times when "that which *I* know to be so" differs from what the supervisee "knows to be so." This can lead to mutual quests for the discovery of points of agreement, common ground, different ways of looking at the material and/or more knowledge. This is the beginning of an educative experience.

The opportunity to make discoveries is part of a method which holds that there is a natural bent toward discovery and learning and that we should make use of these natural tendencies by putting the learning experience to a greater extent in the hands of the student. This natural thrust toward learning takes us into the "wilds" of motivation—an immense topic beyond the scope of this discussion. Perhaps it would suffice to mention some of the ideas of theorists who have seen this "will to learn" as an intrinsic motive. Bruner speaks to this point and lists four intrinsic motives for learning: curiosity, competence (accomplishment), identification, and reciprocity.[15]

> The early helplessness of man, for example, seems to be accompanied by a propelling curiosity about the environment and by much self-reinforcing activity seemingly designed to achieve competence in that environment.[16]

White discusses competence motivation quite fully in his brilliant work on motivation; he points out:

> The thesis is then proposed that all of these behaviors (visual exploration, grasping, crawling and walking attention . . . language and thinking . . . and producing effective changes in the environment) have a common biological significance: they all form part of the process whereby the animal or child learns to interact with his environment. The word *competence* is chosen as suitable to indicate this common property.[17]

Efforts to make use of these natural tendencies have led to the development of the discovery or inquiry "models" of learning. "Inquiry has been defined as the controlled use of interaction in the pursuit of meaning." [18] Building on the work of Dewey, the proponents of inquiry and discovery suggest that it is the "natural" way of learning. Thelen calls his model the "natural inquiry" model. These educators suggest that it is natural to want to learn, particularly around things that catch your fancy or which are needed to gain competence. Suchman states: "It can be argued that free inquiry is the most naturalistic form of learning behavior." [19]

Starting from the belief that that motivation for learning is most potent which comes directly from the internalized needs of the students, and that students have a natural desire for competence, these authors have evolved the "discovery" approach. As Bruner points out:

> Whether one speaks to mathematicians or physicists or historians, one encounters repeatedly an expression of faith in the powerful effects that come from permitting the student to put things together for himself, to be his own discoverer.[20]

The discovery method is a "cool" method. It permits the student to fill in with the material he needs and to seek out this material with as much self-directed independent work as possible. Its benefits are perhaps summarized by the following statement:

> In short, what White, Bruner, and Dewey are saying is that concepts are the most meaningful, are retained the longest and are most available for future thinking, when the learner actively gathers and processes data from which concepts emerge.[21]

Thelen's "Natural Model of Inquiry" is an attempt to put the theoretical concepts of learning into practice in the classroom. His approach consists of the six phases in a learning process discussed earlier in this chapter. It is important to note that Thelen's model insists that the student have time to think. Throughout all of this, suggests Thelen, there must be ample opportunity for meditation.

The beginning phases are of greatest importance for us at this point. The method used here consists of a number of tactics utilizing whatever media we think to be instrumental in achieving our goals. The teacher must know the particular content involved and which medium might be the *most* suitable. In the confrontation stage there are limitless media available. Should it be a tape of a politician pointing out the dishonesty of "ADC" mothers? The trainer reading a statement referring to the poor as "children" and then soliciting from the trainees their ideas on who might have made the statement? Should it be a movie, ghetto field trip, or a case? The medium, like the confrontation, should permit the student to react on a personal level. A violation of expectations, such as occurs when a ghetto leader at an opening staff development session says, "Social workers don't help," faces the worker with a gap between the data available from the confrontation and the conceptual organizers available in storage.

If he is to find meaning in the situation, the learner must take some action. This may mean asking questions of others as he tries to make sense out of the situation. In the "emergence to awareness" phase, the trainer makes use of these tendencies through such media as the small group discussion or work group, open dialogue in the classroom, or student examples from their own experiences in helping the poor, etc. The process can continue with the students following through by studying historical attempts by social workers to help the poor, successful helping techniques, manpower issues, utilization of indigenous workers, etc., depending on the focus of the course and the students' interests and time.

COOL MEDIA

Carl Rogers has written:

> You can trust the student. You can trust him to desire to learn in every way which will maintain or enhance self; you can trust him to make use of resources which will serve his end; you can trust him to evaluate himself in ways which will make for self-progress; you can trust him to grow, provided the atmosphere for growing is available to him.[22]

We should start with the worker. He is an unusual and primary resource. Any selection of a medium must involve a feedback mechanism which can alert us to just how "cool" the medium really is. The lecture, for example, can be "hot" or "cool." If properly handled it leaves a great deal of room for the student to fill in material. But it can be used oppressively, too, as when a speaker covers too much or is so involved with what he is saying that he runs five minutes beyond the class period. We are then faced with the "nonlecture"—the point at which the trainees tune him out. Thelen suggests that twenty-minute lecturettes are more likely to produce change than eight hours of lecturing. He feels that "people come together to be taught voluntarily when there is something important for them to learn, when there is real use for the information, when some valuable activity over and beyond the activity of listening is contemplated." [23]

In other words, they will listen and become involved in the lecture if there is some immediate payoff involved. Will they be asked to react to it? Will there be an opportunity to add their experiences, etc.?

The lecture can help organize the material and stimulate the action to come. As Bruner points out:

> Teaching specific topics or skills without making clear their content in the broader fundamental structure of the field of knowledge is uneconomical in several deep senses . . . An unconnected set of facts has a pitiably short half-life in memory. Organizing facts in terms of principles and ideas from which they may be inferred is the only known way of reducing the quick rate of loss of human memory.[24]

Lectures are also valuable when guests are invited in to speak. But even then, only if they are great people or great speakers should the major portion of the session be given over to lecture.

THE CASE FOR THE CASE

Many workers labor over, but rarely work on, case records—particularly "dead" cases of past client-worker interactions. On the other hand, they involve themselves with relish in "live" cases, such as the ones they are currently carrying. Some cases are exciting, some parts of cases are exciting, and some things that look like cases are exciting: these we should use.

Analogs, critical incidents, or minicases which carry the impact of a point you are trying to teach can be very effective. Reading portions of records out loud in the session also permits the instructor to involve the class in assessing what it thinks will happen in such a context without having access to the actual material in the record. It permits the class to do its own filling out of the process. Certain materials simulate cases—plays, for example. In one class, portions of "One Third of a Nation"—a living play written in the late thirties—was used to demonstrate the roles of workers and tenants in community groups dealing with housing problems. Not only were the students made aware of the history of public housing, tenant union roots, and approaches to work with ghetto residents, but in reading out the parts in class they were brought closer to the actual feelings of people in those situations.

Legal cases are also valuable for the teaching of certain information. They are written differently from social work case records, but many of them deal with social welfare problems. The legal proceedings and decisions around the Newburgh incident and Parrish case, for example, can be augmented with social work articles related to the case.

Some recent attempts to join theory and practice which present some extremely useful material are available as a series put out by the United Neighborhood Houses in New York.[25] This material enables the student to see current practice and the theory behind it. If the class discussion focuses on experiences from the students' own practice, it provides further opportunity to provide meaning.

EXPERIENTIAL "GAMING"

The development of competence is related to the opportunities the individual has to interact effectively with his environment. Where the student does not have these opportunities, they must be provided; at times this may mean offering simulated experiences as a substitute for the "real thing." As Bruner points out, "the provision of vicarious experience is a necessary adjunct to other modes of learning." These experiences can be accomplished by various "model" and "dramatizing" devices such as role play.[26]

Episodes. Although some of the more successful role-playing situations call for careful planning and warming up on the part of the class, there are a number of occasions when role play arises spontaneously out of the classroom give-and-take among students and between teacher and student.

As this spontaneous use becomes a familiar and nonthreatening part of the classroom experience, it becomes simple to shift from teacher into the role of worker or supervisor, saying "O.K., I am the supervisor—how would you feel and respond to this. . . ?" At times it has been possible to achieve the transition without any introductory statement. As you are discussing with a worker her group's concern about paying the agency thirty dollars they owe it, the trainer says, "It must be hard to know that all the money you make at the cookie sale is going to have to be paid to the agency." "We ought to be able to keep some of it," responds the student, falling into the role without any hesitation. And so it goes. We might look at these learning experiences more as "episodes" rather than role-playing. These are fairly spontaneous verbal exchanges between two or more people in which each assumes a role.

Role-playing. Attempts are made in this technique to act out experiences. Students are asked to assume certain roles: client, supervisor, worker, parent, etc., and they proceed to interact according to their roles. There may be a script for part of the action, or the plot may be described and the action improvised. This approach has been used quite frequently, and there is a great deal of literature available on the technique.[27]

Certain variations might be mentioned. In one, certain actors are sent into the role-playing after the action starts. They are instructed to move in a certain direction, to support, to push a point of view, etc. The effect on the group by added actors can be very significant.

Coaching from the side is another interesting approach. The coach, teacher, or student talks to the actors as they are role-playing.[28] He tells the worker he is "coming on too strong," or "losing the focus." The role-player hears but does not stop the action—he keeps the movement going but can accept or reject the instructions and observations. In this way the teacher can help the student learn the role as he is carrying it out, not just by discussion afterwards.

Empathetic moving. This method might be considered a mini–role-playing situation. Two students are assigned a role. They might be client and worker, supervisor and supervisee, or trainer and trainee. They are given two words on a continuum. "Hopeless—encouraged." "Fearful—confident." The client has to move from one position—e.g., "hopeless"—to the other—"encouraged." The worker has to move from "fearful" to "confident." They are to help each other move.

The major values of role-playing and simulation experiences are the opportunities they offer the student to know what it feels like to be in that position and to "practice."

FANCY "GAMING": SIMULATION

A simulation is a model. It is an attempt to represent some aspect of reality with varying degrees of exactness. For our purpose the simulations are "human interaction" models. They represent some aspect of an organization or event which duplicates as nearly as possible the factors appropriate to the experiences and environment of people who may come into contact with social workers. When "played out," the simulation permits the trainee to enter into the environment, take a role in the organization or experience, adopt attitudes, make decisions, and take action appropriate to the experimental requirements. (The terms *games* and *gaming* have often been used interchangeably with *simulation.*)[29]

Simulation is currently being used primarily for teaching and research. The range of simulation studies runs from those closely resembling role-playing situations familiar to most of us to complex computer simulations of international problems. Its major values seem to be: (1) its ability to increase the students' interest, motivation, and participation; (2) the testing out in controlled situations of certain actions and their possible repercussions; (3) the insights furnished to decision-making processes; (4) the insights it furnishes the teacher as to the learners' needs, and (5) its research potential.

Simulations have been used in staff development programs aimed at helping staff to learn how to work with "new" people moving into a changing area, and to simulate the "team" approach to dealing with social work problems. The agency situation is duplicated as closely as possible. Simulated staff minutes are read, memos are sent, and replies required. Various teams can work the exercise and their approaches can be compared. When there is a gap that cannot be filled in by records, readings, or classroom discussion, the simulation exercise can be extremely valuable.

The "moot court" competitions in which law students "practice" before distinguished panels of judges are simulations. Teams representing various schools are selected for national competition after competing with fellow students on a local level.

OPEN AND CLOSED CIRCUITS: THE AUDIO-VISUALS

These media can be "cool" if they provide the stimulus for active participation with the student. If not, there may be a repetition of the giving-taking process, or, as Bruner says, films, audio-visual aids and other such devices may have the short run effect of catching attention. In the long run, they may produce a passive person waiting for some sort of curtain to go up and arouse him.[30] We then wonder why, since we are using the latest media available to the electronic age, we are faced with a blank wall of apathy.

Generally the videotapes have been used to tape meetings with client systems which then can be played back and evaluated by the worker or a supervisor.[31] This may be a conference with an actual client or role-played. Following the evaluation, the worker can try again in a similar interview or group situation. This adds something to the dimension of role-play, since the student can actually see what he has done. He can even see if he does it better the second time. Lectures have also been video-taped. But this adds very little to our teaching repertoire unless we utilize tapes by "great men." Some videotapes have been used with client groups in which the viewers are taped as they react to seeing themselves on the tape. This adds still another dimension to self-understanding. The potential is vast, but limitations set by cost, mobility, and imagination have so far minimized the uses of this medium in social work education except in the few schools able to set up laboratories for it.

In one experiment the videotape was used to demonstrate the Thelen model by simulating a training program on the use of this medium. The television equipment became the stimulus for the confrontation. Its major value seems to be to increase self-awareness—allowing one to see oneself at work. It is also valuable for showing the student how this can be used as a helping device with the client. In addition, it can bring into the classroom current work with clients for observation by the students.

Audiotapes have also been developed for classroom use.[32] Listening to lengthy taped sessions is laborious and is probably more helpful to a researcher than to a task-oriented social work student. Playing short excerpts, particularly of student or faculty practice and discussing that practice, does have impact on the class. But there are tapes that need to be "played out," and there should be areas where individuals or groups can listen to those tapes that support learning.

FEEDBACK MEDIA

The assessment of student learning calls for some method of "tuning in" on whether or not the group is receiving and decoding the message. Where there are opportunities to involve trainees directly either through chosen representatives or open assessment, feedback is ongoing. Most often, however, the feedback takes place through an assigned paper. When these latter devices are used during the course rather than at the end, they offer clues for necessary adjustments. They also help the learner pull together the knowledge he has acquired. In one institute the participants were given ten questions which they were asked to respond to and return whenever they wanted to on a voluntary basis. This also served to reinforce the learning by bringing it back into their minds. A similar attempt also included taped responses to each question by the teacher which the student could refer to after he reacted to the questions.

THE LEARNING GROUP AS A MEDIUM

The concept of the group as the mediator between the individual and society and concept of the classroom as a group have been documented many times by many writers in small group and educational research.[33] The view that the class is a group opens new potentials for teaching-learning transactions. A recent report, "The Student in Higher Education," states:

> The most effective teachers usually are other students. While classroom instructors obviously have more knowledge and greater skills than a student's classmates, his classmates interact with him more frequently and at a deeper and more intimate level. They therefore contribute greatly to the level of reception he turns on in the classroom . . . While our knowledge of how the friendship group can contribute positively to the educational process is still meager, the importance of peer group influence is so obvious that we must rapidly acquire more knowledge of how it works and integrate it into the educational experience.[34]

Thelen points out that there are certain tendencies in the classroom that the teacher has going for him. One of these is the tendency for students to associate with one another. They do this, he says, "in order to cope with [their] own feelings, doubts and anxieties . . . When members of a large group, such as a class, are forced to associate with one another day after day, smaller psyche groups form; students, we say, begin to 'relate' to one another . . ."[35] In his model Thelen uses these natural tendencies of association as aids to the "emergence of awareness" phase, but he allows for individual work for those who would prefer it. The group does, however, offer many opportunities for mutual aid and mutual learning.

In addition to the pooled knowledge available among the workers, there is their ability to perceive content, problems, and teachings in different ways. When they are free to interact with each other, point out facts, blocks, and evaluate their own contributions in the sessions, a new dimension of learning is added. But there are also some new role demands on the trainer. In addition to skills in discussion method and the ability to be a catalyst, the trainer may also have to call on his role as a mediator. In this role he helps the worker not only to deal with the content but with the trainer and the other workers as well. Through this process the worker is helped to negotiate the "politics of interaction." He learns to relate helpfully to people. His fellow students in the program become the medium which helps the worker learn this skill. When the culture of a training program becomes one of an honest give-and-take—with the goal of learning clearly in focus—then experiences are shared freely and praise and criticism welcomed. When the *common* purpose is foremost, the class becomes a work group. The growing use of group supervision, originally projected as a time-saving device, has had secondary benefits in terms of group and individual productivity, and its utilization in agency and field teaching is expanding.[36]

Although I am suggesting that all staff development programs should take advantage of the small group power available to it, sessions dealing with interaction among people need especially to use this resource. One teacher concerned with the stereotyped answers he would get continually in his organizational behavior courses at Harvard and UCLA sought solutions in T-groups. He states:

> I personally conclude from this that what is needed, in part at least, is an educational experience which is usually involving to the individual and which occurs in a group that develops the members' capacity to give explicit assistance and support to one another's enlarging experiences.[37]

Kenneth Keniston says that youth "seeks not only new knowledge, but new ways of learning and knowing:

> [They are] committed to a search for new forms of groups, of organization, and of action, where decision-making is collective, arguments are resolved by "talking them out"—self-examination, interpersonal criticism and group decision making are fused. The objective is to create new styles of life and new types of organization that humanize rather than dehumanize, that activate and strengthen the participants rather than undermining or weakening them, and the primary vehicle for participation is the small face-to-face primary group of peers.[38]

Previously we have discussed how students, when involved in an interaction process with other trainees and trainers toward a common purpose, will come up with ideas that will help one another learn. We have known about this phenomenon in social work education for a long time. Bertha Reynolds pointed it out in 1942:

> In relation to the teacher's learning, it has been a comforting thought to many . . . that "you can always trust a group to teach you what you may teach them." The statement is met with incredulity at first. The skills necessary to evoke from a group this revelation of their needs are not inconsiderable . . . At first these skills seem unattainable. Soon, however—very soon if a leader is capable of some trust in people even when the outcome is in doubt—a group begins to respond and make itself known. The joy of seeing that a relationship of trust actually works is second to no other joy in a teacher's life.[39]

Miss Reynolds, a great teacher, would have found her task easier today, for the workers are more ready, it seems to me, to tell their supervisors what it is they want and need to learn. They have worked on their part of the problem. We must work on ours, developing a trust in the group as a teaching medium, and the willingness to risk ourselves in some new experiences.

EVALUATING STAFF DEVELOPMENT PROGRAMS

Regardless of what form the evaluation of a program takes, it should be related to the original objectives. Some programs are evaluated at the conclusion of the program, others only after its conclusion, generally to see if the workers have retained the material used or have been able to use what they learned. Perhaps the most comprehensive type of evaluation would be to try to assess the workers' knowledge at the start of the program, measure what they seem to be learning in the course of the training program, and assess their knowledge and skills at the close of the program. These were the evaluation procedures attempted in the program which we will describe below. There was no opportunity to do a follow-up later than two months after training.

THE NURSE GROUP-WORKER (A CASE IN POINT)

This was a program set up in a children's psychiatric hospital to train nurses to work with groups toward therapeutic aims.[40] Within the concept of milieu therapy there is considerable support for a significant therapeutic role for the nurse. Whether one takes the position that the psychiatric nurse should be ready to lead treatment groups based on the resolution of personality conflict, or the position that her role should be to help patients learn to operate more effectively in the social groupings which exist spontaneously in any institution, it seems clear that knowledge and skills in working with groups of people are relevant and important.

The knowledge upon which the training program was based can be partialized into two major areas: (1) determinants of behavior, and (2) interventive techniques which modify patients' behavior. An underlying theme permeates the whole training program—namely, the content presented has implications for the establishment and operation of a *therapeutic milieu*.

The basic sequence of actual content areas presented to the psychiatric nurses in the training program is as follows:

1. An introduction to group behavior
2. Human growth and development
3. An introduction to social group work
4. Communication
5. Milieu therapy

Obviously there is additional material that would be pertinent and helpful to nurses in a psychiatric hospital, but there are practical limits as to what can be covered in an in-service training program, even when the content is not provided in depth. Choices have to be made as to the most crucial areas impinging on the day-to-day operations of the nursing personnel if the training program is to be immediately relevant to the nurses and help them to perform their therapeutic roles adequately.

Major emphasis was thus placed upon small group theory and group work. Using the nurses' existing training and understanding of individual needs, we moved to the individual in the group, the worker's role, and to the nurse in the group and her role in helping the individuals in it.

Training Techniques. For in-service training purposes the most productive learning of skills is probably inductive, rather than deductive. This implies that drawing principles out of everyday personal and work experiences would be the most meaningful and effective way to promote such learning. The very concept of in-service training connotes and supports this notion.

The training design calls for restructuring classes into small groups whenever possible so that the trainees might get the "feel" of the group concepts and contexts that they are dealing with. Demands made on the class by the teacher are compared to the demands for work that the group worker makes on the group. When class members demonstrate the *fight-flight, dependency* or *pairing* behavior described by Bion,[41] this is identified and compared to similar situations in patient groups. Communications in the class which demonstrate the principles of "games people play" [42] are related to Berne's concepts and compared with expected similar communications in treatment groups. Other treatment group experiences are stimulated through the use of confrontation, role-playing, "games," and simulation techniques that help the trainees "feel" and become involved in the experience.

The organizational and administrative content presented in the classes is also related to real life experiences. For example, discussions of the dynamics of apathy on the part of patients have led to consideration of apathy by staff. This, in turn, has resulted in actions aimed at eliminating some of the causes of apathy— e.g., the belief that "administration" might resist projected group work programs. Simulation of organizational problems in the classroom has led to discussion of actual administrative problems in the hospital. This, in turn, has led to the consideration of operational changes in the institution.

The actual experiences of the trainees in the class have also been used to demonstrate other milieu concepts—e.g., "our class" is part of a total system in which a *part* influences the *whole* system, and in turn is influenced by it. One operational example of the systems approach (which is emphasized) was pointed out to trainees: other members of the hospital system—the child care workers, recreational therapists, and teachers—want to participate in the training program and share in the learning. This is an organizational outcome which can influence a total institutional system.

Evaluation and Research. The program built in plans for both research and evaluation from the start. The forms below, in addition to showing current practice, were used to assess worker change and the training program's effectiveness.

This questionnaire was administered at the start of the training program and at six-month intervals over the two years that the training program was carried out. The final evaluation was administered two months prior to the end of the program, and additional questions about their actual use of the content were covered. We have selected a sample of the questions for illustrative purposes here.

CONFIDENTIAL

We want to determine whether the material being presented to you in the Training Program is at the most useful level (i.e., not too elementary; not too advanced). We are, therefore, asking you to help us by indicating your current understanding of the content covered in the Program.

In addition, some information on the hospital program is required as part of the Training Project. Part of this questionnaire asks for your personal judgments as to various aspects of the nurse's professional role in an institution such as this. There are no "right" answers to the questions, only valid answers in the sense that you mean what you say.

❁   ❁   ❁

NOTE: Your answers to this and to other questionnaires that you might complete during the Training Program will, of course, remain confidential in that no person's individual answers will be revealed by the Research Coordinator. We are only interested in the responses of the whole nursing staff.

Sample No. ――――――
(do not fill in)

FOR EACH OF THE ITEMS WHICH FOLLOW CHECK THE BOX WHICH MOST CLOSELY REPRESENTS YOUR CURRENT UNDERSTANDING OF THE SUBJECT INVOLVED

1. Understanding of the principles of how people interact in groups and the dynamics of the group itself—i.e., "group dynamics."

Little or no understanding				Advanced understanding or expertise	
☐	☐	☐	☐	☐	☐
0	1	2	3	4	5

2. Skill in working with groups.

Little or   Advanced skill
  no skill   or expertise

☐   ☐   ☐   ☐   ☐   ☐
0   1   2   3   4   5

3. Understanding of the principles of "milieu therapy."

   Little or   Advanced understanding
no understanding   or expertise

☐   ☐   ☐   ☐   ☐   ☐
0   1   2   3   4   5

4. Knowledge of the processes and principles of human growth and development.

   Little or   Advanced knowledge
no knowledge   or expertise

☐   ☐   ☐   ☐   ☐   ☐
0   1   2   3   4   5

5. Understanding of the dynamics of the nurse-patient relationship.

☐   ☐   ☐   ☐   ☐   ☐
0   1   2   3   4   5

6. Understanding of nurse-staff relationships (i.e., child care workers, doctors, etc.)

   Little or   Advanced understanding
no understanding   or expertise

☐   ☐   ☐   ☐   ☐   ☐
0   1   2   3   4   5

7. How comfortable would you feel at this point in working with an ongoing group?

Very uncomfortable   Very comfortable

☐   ☐   ☐   ☐   ☐   ☐
0   1   2   3   4   5

THESE ITEMS ARE CONCERNED WITH THE NURSES' SATISFACTION WITH THEIR CURRENT PROFESSIONAL PERFORMANCE. CHECK THE BOX WHICH MOST CLOSELY REPRESENTS YOUR CURRENT LEVEL OF SATISFACTION.

8. How satisfied are you with your ability to understand the meaning of patient behavior?

Totally
dissatisfied

Completely
satisfied

☐ ☐ ☐ ☐ ☐ ☐
0 1 2 3 4 5

9. How satisfied are you with your ability to help patients?

Totally
dissatisfied

Completely
satisfied

☐ ☐ ☐ ☐ ☐ ☐
0 1 2 3 4 5

10. How satisfied are you with the hospital's ability to help?

☐ ☐ ☐ ☐ ☐ ☐
0 1 2 3 4 5

11. How satisfied are you with the responsibilities and duties (i.e., the professional "role") of the nurse in this hospital?

Totally
dissatisfied

Completely
satisfied

☐ ☐ ☐ ☐ ☐ ☐
0 1 2 3 4 5

12. What gives you the greatest professional satisfaction in your current work?

1. _____

2. _____

3. _____

13. What gives you the least professional satisfaction in your current work?

1. ————————————————————————————————————

2. ————————————————————————————————————

3. ————————————————————————————————————

14. What groups have you worked with?

Number of groups ———————————————————————

About when did they start meeting? ————————————

Are they still meeting? ——————————————————

How often did they meet? —————————————————

Briefly describe program or activities of the group: ————

——

How successful do you feel the group was in meeting some of its goals? ————————————————————————

For the following questions please circle the answer that more nearly represents your idea.

15. Do you believe the program to have nurses work with patients in groups is:

		somewhat		very		
a. not helpful		helpful		helpful		to your understanding of
1	2	3	4	5	6	7	groups.

		somewhat		very		
b. not helpful		helpful		helpful		to your ability to work
1	2	3	4	5	6	7	with groups.

		somewhat		very		
c. not helpful		helpful		helpful		to the children in the hos-
1	2	3	4	5	6	7	pital.

17. Do you believe children can be helped by working with them in groups?

not at all		somewhat			very much	
1	2	3	4	5	6	7

18. Please give us some of your ideas about the Federal Program to use nurses to work with groups. What do you think of the program?

_____

19. What do you see as the program's major strengths? _____

_____

20. What do you see as the program's major problems? _____

_____

21. What should the program have done differently? _____

_____

22. Other comments. _____

_____

23. Please rank the following subject areas covered in the Program according to their value and relevance for you. Indicate the most valuable with 1, the next most valuable with 2, etc., until you have ranked all six subject areas.

RANK
_____ Group behavior and dynamics (theory)
_____ Growth and development of the individual
_____ Group work techniques (how to work with groups)
_____ Communications
_____ Milieu therapy (family treatment, crisis treatment, use of the organization, community, etc.)
_____ Organizational behavior

24. Considering the Training Program as a whole, please rate each of the following items on a seven-point scale from "very low," 1, to "very high," 7.

_____ a. Extent to which the training was useful in your actual work.
_____ b. Relevance to future practice in psychiatric nursing.

———— c. Amount of duplication with previous education (*1* is very
    low duplication).
———— d. Extent to which content was intellectually demanding.

ASSESSING CHANGE

One area of concern in training programs is to establish a
baseline from which to judge whether or not staff has increased
its ability to be helpful. Not only Did they learn anything? but
also Where were they when we started? One such attempt was
made by presenting child care workers with vignettes at the
start of the program and following up by repeating the experience six months into the program to see if there was any change
in the workers' handling of the problem. Some examples appear
below.*

I

During dinner Mary accidentally spilled gravy on Kathy's new
sweater. Kathy was furious. She called Mary "a big fat slob" and
slapped her in the face. By the time the child care worker got to the
table, Mary and Kathy were wrestling on the floor, scratching, slap-
ping, kicking, and pulling each other's hair.

The other girls were egging Mary and Kathy on, calling, "Don't
let her get away with that." "Hit the bitch." etc.

What would you do?

(Check your *first* choice among the following)

———— (a) Separate Kathy and Mary immediately and later have
        a group discussion about what happened.
———— (b) Send Kathy to her room and punish her by taking her
        privileges away.
———— (c) Punish both Kathy and Mary.
———— (d) Take both of the girls aside and talk to them together.
———— (e) Insist that the whole group discuss the incident right
        then and there. (P)
———— (f) Send Kathy and Mary to separate rooms and talk to each
        of them later.

* These vignettes and the earlier evaluation focus on nursing were developed by Paul Abels and Serapio Zalba. The preferred response (P) is
added for current purpose only.

II

Jimmy is a poorly coordinated, overtalkative boy who is a wise guy both with the other kids and with adults. He just doesn't know when to shut up. He tends also to be a crybaby. The other kids pick on him and blame him for whatever goes wrong.

During a kickball game this afternoon he dropped the ball at a crucial time and his team lost. The members of his team were very angry at him and told him he could never play with them again. He started to cry and ran to the child care worker.

What should the child care worker do?

(Check your *first* choice among the following)

———— (a) Tell the other boys that they cannot play unless Jimmy is allowed to play with them.
———— (b) Take him aside and practice kickball with him.
———— (c) Talk to the boys about their disappointment in losing the game, and discuss their anger toward Jimmy. (P)
———— (d) Make Jimmy the scorekeeper.
———— (e) Comfort Jimmy and talk with him about why the boys are angry.

III

Yesterday there was a pillow fight on Ward E which got out of hand. Some pillows were destroyed, and the boys would not obey when you tried to stop them. You told them at that time that they would have to miss today's baseball game as a punishment for their misbehavior.

Today at 3 P.M. they started to go to the baseball game and you stopped them. They said that Nurse X had given them special permission to play, since Ward G could not play unless Ward E also played. Nurse X was off from work today, so you could not discuss it with her.

What would you do?

(Check your *first* choice among the following)

———— (a) Tell the boys you don't care what anybody else says, no baseball today.
———— (b) Call the child care worker of Ward G and ask to postpone the game to some time when the boys are not being punished.

———— (c) Call the head of nursing and find out if it is okay to keep the boys from playing today.

———— (d) Let the boys go to play baseball.

———— (e) Discuss with the boys the fact that they manipulated Nurse X and ask how they feel about getting away with having destroyed the pillows. (P)

Another way to use these brief experiences is to have open discussions about how to work with the particular problem, what might cause the problem, and what a synergistic solution would involve.

The following questionnaire was developed for trainers in a police training program aimed at expanding the policemen's sensitivity to human needs. Such a questionnaire helps the group trainer assess his ongoing approach to work with the group, and in fact it acts as a "self-supervisory" process. It is also used by the training director to help the leader with his concerns.

QUESTIONNAIRE FOR GROUP LEADERS

1. What are your present objectives for your group? More specifically:

   A. What do you want them to accomplish?

   B. What do you expect they will actually be able to accomplish by the end of this training program (which will probably last 27 weeks)?

   C. What are the factors most likely to help you accomplish your objectives?

   D. What are the factors most likely to hinder you in accomplishing your objectives?

2. Have your objectives changed since the beginning of the program?

   A. If so, why and how?

   B. What were your objectives originally?

3. What tends to "turn on" the participants in your group?

   A. In terms of "themes," subjects, or problem areas?

B. In terms of format—e.g., discussion, small group tasks, role-playing, lectures, outside speakers, etc?

C. Other factors?

4. What do you think are the most salient needs of the participants in your group?

5. What are the personally most rewarding things about leading this group?

6. What are the most difficult things about leading this group?

7. What are your plans for your group for the next month?

At times the training director may want the group to assess some of its own processes. One brief form for such an activity appears below.* (See Figure 24.)

Figure 24
GROUP DYNAMICS EFFECTIVENESS

The items below may be used to rate group dynamics effectiveness. Circle the number on the scale below that most accurately reflects your evaluation of your experience in your group.

1. COMMUNICATIONS: Are people really listening, hearing what's said, and understanding meanings?

LOW   1   2   3   4   5   6   7   8   9   HIGH

2. MEMBERSHIP (RESPONSIBILITY): Are all people helping to get group's work done: Do all have feeling of belonging? Is there initial respect for all?

LOW   1   2   3   4   5   6   7   8   9   HIGH

3. LEADERSHIP (AUTHORITY): Is the group democratic or like a dictatorship? Do members feel they have authority and can play a leadership role?

LOW   1   2   3   4   5   6   7   8   9   HIGH

---

* The use of any "form" is enhanced by some discussion of the tabulated material so that the group members have an opportunity to hear the thinking of others and test it against their own ideas. This too becomes a tool for change.

4. DECISION MAKING: Do all members participate fully in decision making? Do they feel they can influence group decisions?

LOW   1   2   3   4   5   6   7   8   9   HIGH

5. GROUP NORMS AND GROWTH: Are members able to question group norms and facilitate change leading toward group growth?

LOW   1   2   3   4   5   6   7   8   9   HIGH

6. INTER-GROUP COMMUNICATION: Are groups collaborating and sharing resources and information?

LOW   1   2   3   4   5   6   7   8   9   HIGH

SOURCE: Developed by the Continuing Education Program, School of Applied Social Sciences, Case Western Reserve University.

OTHER STAFF DEVELOPMENT RESOURCES

At times agencies use outside consultants or trainers. These programs, too, should also be carefully evaluated. A professionally oriented trainer will usually build such an evaluation into the program. An agency which is situated close to universities may have access to a good continuing education program—in fact, may have the services of an excellent staff development program without having to place its consultants or trainers on the payroll. The continuing education specialist is "everybody's staff development specialist." Such persons usually have special training in teaching and workshop development and are continually trying to evaluate their programs so as to meet the needs of agencies. The evaluation scheduled below is a regular, integrated requirement of one program.* (See Figure 25.)

* This material was developed by Lois Swack, Director of Continuing Education, School of Applied Social Sciences, Case Western Reserve University. For some of her thoughts on how such programs serve the agencies and the human services profession, see Lois Swack, "Continuing Education and changing needs," Social Work 20 (Nov. 1975): p. 474.

Figure 25
COURSE EVALUATION

1. What did you expect of the course when you enrolled?

2. To what extent were your expectations met?

———————— To a great extent
———————— Somewhat
———————— Very little
———————— Not at all

3. Was the content useful in relation to any specific problems or areas of practice? Specify. ————————————————————————

4. What do you consider the three most important content areas? ——
——

5. What do you think should be included in the course which was not included? ————————————————————————

6. To what extent was:	To great extent	Somewhat	Very little
Classroom presentation interesting	————	————	————
Material well organized	————	————	————

7. What teaching methods did you like best? (lecture, class discussion, small group discussion, films, role-play, etc.) ————————————
——

8. What teaching methods did you like least? ————————————

9. Do you have any SUGGESTIONS FOR OTHER COURSES which would be helpful to you? ————————————————————————

Blake and Mouton's Management Grid is another tool that can be used for evaluative purposes. It is based on a series of questions, and the individual can use it to evaluate or assess his own levels of concern. He can use the results for self-improvement or share them with the group. He can also be asked to assess his group as a group or even the agency by use of the same grid (See Figure 26.)

Figure 26
MANAGERIAL GRID

LOCATING YOURSELF ON THE GRID:

DIRECTIONS: In order to locate yourself on the Managerial Grid below, find your score for *Concern for Production* on the horizontal axis of the Grid. Next, move up the column corresponding to your *Production* score to the point of intersection with your *Concern for People* score. Place an "X" at the intersection that represents your two scores. Numbers in parentheses correspond to the major styles on the Managerial Grid.

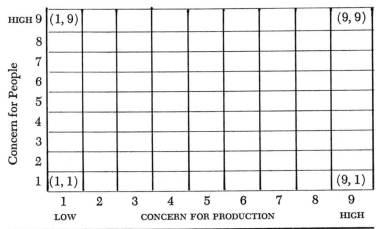

SOURCE: Robert R. Blake and Jane Srygley Mouton, *The Managerial Grid* (Houston: Gulf Publishing Company, 1964), p. 10.

A similar self-appraisal can be used related to X and Y styles of supervision by asking trainees to put themselves, and their supervisors' agencies, on an X-Y scale.

This exemplifies how we see the use of evaluation in staff

development. It is not meant as a *judgment* but as a guide to where we are, with particular reference to where we want to be or feel we ought to be.

> The very act of judgment implies a comparison and condemnation . . .
> In place of judgment there must be an awareness . . .[43]

It may be that the staff development person does not collect all of the evaluations. Some may remain the property of the trainee or be discussed when the trainer is not present. The goal is awareness. In order to modify his own training, he needs feedback, but that is only one use for the evaluative material.

CHAPTER 7

BEYOND

SUPERVISION

Heaven and earth unite: The image of PEACE.
THE BOOK OF CHANGES

Can a social agency become a "just" community? Can it develop normative stance?

Does life in social agencies reflect our society? Is it the real world? To what extent is it a reasonably accurate reflection of modern-day life-styles? Status relationships and ritualistic practice are not unlike the relationships and work performed in thousands of factories and offices by people of all ages, who "pass the time." [1] Reich has found us impoverished by a "loss of self or death in life—stripped of imagination, creativity . . . personal uniqueness . . ." Marcus Raskin sees us all as victims of the colonized, pyramidal society and suggests a number of projects to start to move our society to a community of equals. [2]

Thinking of ourselves as either captives or powerless, human service professionals take on the patterns of institutionalized-ritualistic behavior reminiscent of their clients, who in reality do have fewer *decision making* opportunities.

Jules Henry helps us see the similarities between workers and clients as he concludes his description of patient life:

> As for patients, they live out their last days in long stretches of anxiety and silent reminiscing, punctuated by outbursts of petulance at one another, by TV viewing and by visits from their relatives. There is no inner peace, and social life is minimal . . . There is a yearning after communion but no real ability to achieve it. In this we are all very much like them.[3]

Many institutions portray the kind of life which is prevalent in the society, its residents carrying on as before and its staff doing as has been done to them. Some are isolated, and have always been so. Others are able to forge close and meaningful ties. But similar problems face the staff in their relationships with each other.

Each supervisor then, because of his critical position and the leverage he has in controlling the thrust of the relationships among staff and between staff and client, needs to use this power for the betterment of the human condition. Thus, to view our society as alienating, or the institution as depersonalizing, is to recognize a truth, but only a partial truth. As much as one is acted upon, one also acts. "With the noose around our neck, there still are options—to curse God or to pray, to weep or to slap the executioner in the face." [4]

We have held in this book the view that supervisory practice needs to reconstruct itself around a new approach to working with people which minimizes status differentials and attempts to establish a moral community in which teacher and learner, helper and helped, are indeed one. We have suggested that although there are many who share this vision, it is only now beginning to find its way into practice in western organizations. What we have come to realize is that the visions of the administrator are useless unless the visions can be shared by all. As Walt Whitman said, "To have great poets there must be great audiences too."

Normative supervision can exist without a normative practice, but only as a shadow maintaining an island of humanism and social justice in a sea of disillusionment. Although it is outside the scope of this book to establish a reconstructed practice in the human services, we clearly see this as an important step. Indeed, in their beginnings, the social reform and settlement movements were attempts to establish a normative approach in the human service professions.

Earlier it was suggested that normative supervisory practice is new to our Western organizations. It is not totally new, however, if one takes a worldwide perspective and a historical view. There have been proscriptive-normative orientations growing out of Eastern approaches to administration and governance.

One such approach was evident in the work of Confucius, who taught a way of life in which morality occupied a supreme position. One of his views on the totality of the human experience is reflected by the following:

> The ancients, who wished to preserve the clear and good character of the world, first set about to regulate their national life. In order to regulate their national life, they cultivated their family life. In order to cultivate their family life, they rectified their personal life. In order to rectify their personal life, they elevated their heart. In order to elevate their heart they made their will sincere. In order to make their will sincere, they enlightened their mind. In order to enlighten their mind, they conducted research. Their research being conducted, their mind was enlightened. Their mind being enlightened, their will was made sincere. Their will being sincere, their heart was elevated. Their heart being elevated, their personal life was rectified. Their personal life being rectified, their family life was cultivated. Their family life being cultivated, their national life was regulated. Their national life being regulated, the good and clear character of the world was preserved and peace and tranquility reigned thereafter.[5]

His thoughts on administrators might be summarized by the following anecdote. When asked "Wouldn't it be good if everyone in the village loved the mayor?" he responded, "It would be better if the good people loved him and the evil ones hated him."

A later development in Chinese thinking was reflected by the work of Lao-tzu in his Tao-te-ching or tao (the Way). There was a recognition here that leadership was important, the state and people fragile, and that the ruler should model himself on the tao. "One who has the tao will be inwardly a sage and outwardly a true being." 6

The basic stance of this eastern philosophy was the idea that through a minimum intervention of the administrator, and through his delegation of authority to others, the "best" administration would result. "Desiring to rule over the people, one must, in one's works humble oneself before them; and, desiring to lead the people, one must in one's person, follow behind them." 7

Interesting offshoots of this approach were references which could be consulted as guides to proper decision making in regard to one's own life and the process of political life.

The I Ching, or Book of Changes, was one such guide. Recently, with our revived interest in other approaches to the good life and in self-actualization, the I Ching once more has become a popular source. It has entered the human service literature in relation to supervision by way of an interesting article by Stambler and Pearlman, who used it as a supervisory-analytic guide in order to assess a case previously reported in a journal.8

As a result of this report, I have used the I Ching experimentally with a group of supervisors working for a state welfare department. At a session at a state conference, over forty workers dealing with the concept of synergy worked on an I Ching forecast, coming up with number 11, Peace. To quote just a few lines from the I Ching statement:

HEAVEN AND EARTH UNITE: THE IMAGE OF PEACE

The Receptive, which moves downward, stands above; the creative, which moves upward, is below. Hence their influences meet and are in harmony, so that all living things bloom and prosper . . .

In the world of man it is a time of social harmony; those in high places show favor to the lowly, and the lowly and inferior in their turn are well disposed toward the highly placed. There is an end to all feuds.9

For many, the statements reflected what we had been

dealing with so closely that they were amazed. I must admit I was too. Subsequent use has confirmed verisimilitude, but never with such closeness to the material under consideration.

One reason for presenting the experiment was to influence the group toward creative ways of thinking about their own supervision. It served as a point of discussion around the constant search for effective ways of working with people, and the difficulties encountered when status differences and power relationships are present. The I Ching was a guide to help those in "ruling" positions make "just decisions" thoughtfully and in harmony with what then was the most moral focus of thinking. Not only does it link us to the past by indicating the historic search for help in decision making, but it also shows us that administrator-staff relationships have always called for thoughtful handling.

We are faced with similar problems today. In fact, we seem not to have moved too far from some of these earlier concerns of the interrelatedness of people in hierarchies and the use of power. Nor have we found many more scientific guidelines in our own decision-making approaches. We are still in need of framing what one does in a way that achieves agreement with others on both specific supervisory experience and upon its general significance and explanation. Stambler and Pearlman conclude that "in our opinion, use of I Ching as a consultant/supervisor deserves further exploration." [10] We might add that consultation can take place in many ways. The I Ching can serve as a consciousness-raising device. The important factor, however, lies in the willingness to assess one's work and remain open to new ideas. The I Ching, in ancient Chinese culture, and even more recently, could be used as a resource for contemplating future actions related to important personal and work situations. What one finds in the analysis of course will depend on what one brings.[11]

In one sense it was a tool which was universally used, and could be used by *all* people. It was what Illich would call a convivial tool.[12] We might compare it with a modern compendium or handbook on administrative techniques. The difference would be that because of the element of chance, the answers might more likely be seen as "fateful," therefore carrying a weight to be reckoned with. Convivial tools would permit workers to supervise themselves or to make use of their peers for consultation. Of course not all situations would call for peer supervision. An important factor, of course, would be the degree of direct control the supervisor is able and willing to relinquish, and this too reflects his view of population.

As would be expected, individual decisions as to basic supervisory strategies are closely related to the supervisor's philosophical approach toward work with people, and *his style develops from his philosophical base.* Pappell and Rothman, in an excellent article, have attempted to demonstrate three ways of working with groups—the social goals, remedial, and reciprocal models.[13] Similarly, Joseph Eaton lists three models in community development: social Darwinism, expertism, and mutualism.[14] One's philosophical base molds one's practice.

I would suggest there are two underlying polarities of worker philosophies: (1) the expert, who makes decisions which the client or supervisee then carries out; and (2) the supervisor as partner, a human being with certain skills which are at the disposal of another, to be used as they mutually agree upon. I have labeled these two philosophical emphases the "status-manager" and the "contract-synergist." [15]

The status-manager approach stresses the expertness and authority of the person who has the skills necessary both to diagnose and to treat or educate the worker, who is not enlightened. He uses the authority of his credentials, the force of his personality, his skill and ability, to decide what the worker actually needs and how the supervision should be delivered. He "directs" the action toward his goals. The process is supervisor- or agency-centered rather than worker- or group-centered. He is a manager who maintains a "line" relationship and uses "relationship" as a means of furthering *his* goals. The medical model fits perfectly. In social work the managerial philosophy can be identified by such statements as:

> The group work practitioner can . . . encourage the development of those patterns that will best suit the particular characteristics

of each group and that will facilitate *his* treatment goals for the clients [emphasis added].[16]

If we substitute "educational goals" for "treatment goals," we can see how the expert approach fits into the traditional supervisory paradigm.

The perceptions by staff or community members of being pushed, pulled, or manipulated into positions or self-images which do not reflect their own desires, are legend.[17]

The contract-synergist model is the approach most likely to maximize worker participation in the decision-making process within the community. This approach does not see the worker as underdeveloped or subject to manipulations by experts who know the answers. It accepts the premises that people are seeking solutions to problems for which they do not have the answers and that they can be helped to learn either the technical skills, political interaction techniques, or interpersonal competence necessary to deal with these problems. The function of the contract-synergist is to help these things happen. His actions are not *on* the individuals. Always they are *with* individuals. Decisions are jointly arrived at, and for the most part the relationship is a reciprocal one. There is a quest between worker and supervisor for an authenticity of relationship, a reaching out for each other in a way that permits the development of that sense of "community" among the staff and the administrators which permits authentic and satisfactory use of one another.

The position of the supervisor is close to what Siu describes as the "philosopher-executive":

> To discharge his various obligations in style, the philosopher-executive covers the integrated whole of experience with a triple insight—the dreaming, the understanding, the acting.
>
> To begin with, the philosopher-executive is able to join his researchers in their dreams. It is mostly in dreams that one finds the delightful overtones that make life decorative, the ideals that spur man's efforts, the genial sensitivity to the nobler aspects of life, the soothing charm and heroic wit that cheer men's lives, the grace notes that beautify the theme of the laboratory, the glimpses of the ever-receding and reappearing patterns that fuse

THE SUPERVISOR AS MANAGER AND SYNERGIST:
TWO MODELS OF SUPERVISION

Supervising as: *Status-manager* Ends-oriented	*Contract-synergist* People-oriented
GOALS:	
Help people learn specific skills necessary to do the job as defined.	Helping people learn how to work together in the interest of the best solution in the situation.
Goals defined by agency power structure	Goals defined by all involved.
Supervisory Styles: Instructor Manager-boss Giving to/Telling Communication: unidirection persuading—advising	Teacher-enabler-synergist Member of community Learning and doing with Communication: reciprocal inquiry listening
Judging	Mutual discovery
Values Focus on what's good for agency and client.	Focus on "just society" as reflected in this agency.
Outcome-centered—i.e., M.B.O. as a feeling—objective	"What ought to be." Process/outcome centered related to "Are these objectives good?"
Ends justify means	Means as important as ends.
Cost-benefit analysis	
Implicit definitions of agency Good as established	Good as it functions justly
Collection of hierarchical roles in interaction.	Collection of people in growing-learning situations.
Agency as an organization	Agency as a temporary community

into the unity of the universe. Without dreams one is bound to the ordinary conventions of the waking hours. There is no inspiration. After all, are not scientific concepts but dreams petrified? Inability to dream strangles the source of the raw stuff of science . . .

. . . In his no-knowledge, the philosopher-executive does not seek perfection among his associates. He recognizes the slimy trap of harping on deficiences. He understands the simple truth that mortals are full of defects. Criticizing the obvious lends neither prestige to the critic nor aid to the recipient. . . .

The philosopher-executive recognizes that great works emanate from dedicated sincerity. If the creator is actuated by the will to goodness, he will untiringly pursue the hidden vagueness of unfinished experiments until he penetrates to the very heart of the problem. He will ferret answers from the far reaches of his mind. Ideas dredged from the very bowels of his soul are bound to bear the stamp of originality, for no two investigators are prototypes to such depths. He will also be impelled to communicate the fullness of his findings in the clearest expression so that others may be infected with the same enthusiasm and share in their use. When the lust for discovery is enkindled by quick adulation and quick gold, there will be trolling only in shallow waters.[18]

REAWAKENING THE VISION

How is it that something can remain invisible for centuries? Material, concrete objects that can be seen and touched, walked on, through, and past—yet remain invisible? Only a few can see the gestalt, the totality. Perhaps only a few can visualize the old with a new vision. If the vision blurs with tangible objects, how much more difficult must it be to deal with the nontangible, with concepts and ideas, and to view them in a different way.

Just after Christmas in 1648, John Aubrey, out hunting with some friends, rode through the Wiltshire Village of Avebury and there saw a vast prehistoric temple, the greatest of its age in Europe, which up to then had remained undiscovered. It was not hidden in some remote and desolate spot, for a thriving village stood within its ramparts, nor at that date was it particularly ruinous. Yet Aubrey was the first of his age to notice it . . .

Before Aubrey's visit untold thousands had passed their lives within the walls of the Avebury temple without noticing in its fabric anything more than a random assembly of mounds and boulders. But the moment Aubrey saw it, it became visible to all. Now every year crowds of visitors marvel at the huge scale of the work, the size and precision of the great stones, which three hundred years ago were considered merely an impediment to agriculture, and were broken up to clear the ground.[19]

Avebury is a stone circle, similar to Stonehenge, and possibly the largest of its kind in the world.

Let us imagine there is a group of people whose responsibility, desire, wish, and need is to further humanity by helping other people resolve their problems, by eliminating poverty, by building moral communities, by seeking for peace, by demanding of other professions that they carry out their mandates. By restructuring society for good, let us imagine also, this group of people is advanced on the evolutionary scale, either genetically or by self-selection. Assuming, of course, that evolution is working toward higher humanistic development.[20] Imagine also that this group evolves into the social work profession. These human service professionals still would need exceptional administrative, management, and supervisory processes which reflected this higher level of development. These practices would reflect democracy at its highest.

This idea may not be as farfetched as it might first appear. The Sufis, who number about 50 million, have for generations assumed the task of illustrating the "Sufi idea that man has the possibility of conscious self-development, becoming able—with his own efforts and under a certain kind of expert guidance . . . to serve mankind on its path of planned evolution." [21]

John Friedman, in his book *Retracking America*, outlined an approach to working with people in the planning sphere which he calls "transactive planning." [22] He believes this approach is apppropriate to the conditions of a postindustrial society. It is a process of mutual learning between the "expert" and the client group. The style requires a dialogue through which "knowledge becomes morally engaged and embedded in a matrix of ongoing actions." What he is attempting to do is narrow the gulf between planners and their clients. The two perceive things differently because they have different ways of knowing. The planners know from processed knowledge, and the client knows from personal knowledge. Learning to see things on a parallel level requires a new *inquiry into what is good,* and a process of learning together.

In a similar vein, Ivan Illich has been developing a position based on important data which suggest that society is in danger from the growing process of professionalization.[23] His major targets so far have been education and medicine, but he also directs his aim at social work, and, in fact, at all service professions. He, too, feels that the people in need can learn how to provide their own services, whether it be medicine or social work. Knowledge should not be treated as a commodity and should be openly available to all equally for all services. This might serve as a base for a just society.

The uniqueness of social work as a profession has been its concept of unity. It has avoided the dichotomy of thinking versus doing: it is a thinking-doing profession. Social work deals with questions of action, requiring an action vocabulary. If we are to be successful, we need to know what to do, and to know what we are doing, in complex and difficult circumstances. The vocabulary of action is the vocabulary of values. Knowing what to do is knowing what *should* be done, what *ought* to be brought about, what it would be *good* to achieve, what would be *right*. This vocabulary is the vocabulary of ethical or normative theory. The social sciences that have provided the cognitive base of social work in the past have, however, been especially careful to skirt this vocabulary. As a result we have no clear record, from even well-documented social work, of success in achieving what is good. What we have achieved is at best ego-supportive structures, higher levels of consciousness, and psychological acceptance. In view of this, colleagues and I have proposed the development of human service supervision as an explicitly normative or value-oriented practice.[24]

The problem, however, is that our current knowledge of values and how they change is still at the primitive level. Baier defines a value as an "attitude for or against an event or phenomenon, based on a belief that it benefits or penalizes some individual, group or institution." [25]

There have been a number of attempts to help people make their values explicit so that they can be assessed and modified. The value-clarification approach tries to help people answer value-oriented questions and reconstruct their own value systems.

Values clarification "enhances the ability of people to communicate their ideas, beliefs, values and feelings." [26] It is felt that through better communication, they are more able to consider alternative opinions. It "enhances the ability of people to engage in decision making." [27] One of its shortcomings is its lack of explicating "higher" value thinking and systematic methods of raising the level of thinking on moral issues.

Lawrence Kohlberg's approach, "moral development theory," attempts to formulate exact levels of moral thinking as well as explicating processes of raising the moral level of participants. There are three major levels of thinking, broken into six stages.[28]

PRECONVENTIONAL LEVEL

Stage 1:   Right is obedience to power and avoidance of punishment.
Stage 2:   Right is to take responsibility for oneself in meeting one's own needs and leave to others the responsibility for themselves. Fairness is: "You do something for me; I'll do something for you."

CONVENTIONAL LEVEL

Stage 3:   Right is being good in the sense of having good motives, having concern for others, and "putting yourself in the other person's shoes."
Stage 4:   Right is to maintain the rules of a society and to serve the welfare of the group or society.

POSTCONVENTIONAL LEVEL

Stage 5:   Right is based on recognizing individual rights within a society with agreed-upon rules, a social contract.
Stage 6:   Right is obligation to principles applying to all humankind,

principles of respect for human personality and justice and equality.

The indications of his research suggest that peers, such as agency colleagues, can help raise the individual's moral reasoning levels. His work in correctional institutions has important repercussions for supervisory practice.

In the following example taken from the manual, we can see how a discussion of this type involving inmates, guards, probation officers, and supervisory staff might open important new insights and lead to conditional, rather than rigid, decision-making patterns.

> Like most correctional officers, Carol Owens is actively concerned with the women assigned to her. During a several-month period she had developed a particularly close relationship with Inmate Ina Martin. On the basis of Officer Owens' strong recommendation, Inmate Martin was approved for a Christmas furlough. However, after the furlough, Martin confided in Officer Owens that she had violated the rules of the furlough by going to another state.[29]

On the basis of such an example, it would be possible to discuss such things as, "Under what conditions would you let things go and not tell you supervisor?" "Should a worker develop such a close relationship?" Because of Kohlberg's systematization of countless responses to such an example we can assess the level of functioning of the people in the vignette, and also the discussants.

> For instance, Martin sees Owens as having an obligation to keep a trust, she does not see that Owens has an obligation to maintain the institution's rules impartially. Martin is Stage 3, she thinks that morality means being nice to other people and keeping good relationships with them. She does not understand obligations to the society and the maintenance of its rules.

> Owens is Stage 4, she understands the importance of good personal relations but also considers her obligations to society and puts them ahead of personal feelings. Owens' decision is at a higher or more mature level of moral reasoning. Martin, because she is not at that level, does not understand Owens' decision and

thinks it is wrong and unfair. On the other hand, Owens does not understand why Martin does not think she is right and does not know how to communicate her thinking to someone at a different level. Even Owens' thinking has its limits in failing to recognize that inmates have rights even when they violate the rules of the institution (an awareness worked out at Stage 5).

It would be useful to resolve this conflict by moral discussion within a small group of other inmates and staff members. Group members could then help Martin and Owens understand each other's thinking by presenting that thinking in their own terms. The matter thus could become an issue for discussion and clarification of what is the fairest solution to the problem, rather than remaining a source of hostility. By coming to see each other's points of view, the misunderstanding could be at least partly resolved.[30]

In a paper evaluating Kohlberg's approach, Butler, Sonia Abels, and Richmond have discussed how such an approach could lead to improved educational processes, ethical practice, agency autonomy, and professional support. They suggest that empirical moral reasoning would be a higher level than Stage 6.[31] We would concur with Richmond to the extent that moral decisions based on grounded theory and evidence would be a valuable higher level of decision making.

Supervision as a helping process has always been concerned with (1) problem identification and problem solving; and (2) consciousness raising of both practitioners and society. There is a continual interplay between these two forces in the human service professions. The supervisor not only must provide the help needed in acquiring practice skills, but must constantly work at raising the sensitivity and consciousness level of the staff. In fact there may not be any difference between the two. The supervisor, in addition, must also be concerned with helping the agency arrange itself for effective practice towards the ends of social justice.

It is time for the human service professions to reestablish a learning society, to once again develop the sense of community among staff, administration, and clients. To do this, we will have to reestablish our normative stance. Only then can we have a profession which knows what needs to be done either because of facts scientifically explored and arrived at with the client, or because it is in keeping with higher moral principles yet to be scientifically established.

Whatever secrets we have need to be opened to the public. Staff and clients can share thinking processes. A normative model of social work containing a dialogue and scientific inquiry with the parties who seek help would focus more clearly on the future and the direction that needs to be taken in order for change to take place. It would be a model that would minimize status, diagnosis, and the clinical stance. The approach would focus on the environmental factors to be changed and the skills to be learned. It would, following Kohlberg's model, attempt to evolve "proper" levels of moral development for all parties involved.[32] It would focus on mutual data gathering and decisions based more on fact than on whimsy.

Currently, the humanistic approach is again being challenged in the name of "science" and particularly by developments in less-advanced, evolving professions. The managers are pushing for management, cost benefits, and efficiency models. From the psychologists has come the behavior-modification approach, which partializes the person as an object to be manipulated.

The roots of transactive-learning society have always been present in our profession. But growth has been neglected as we fancied the more beautiful blossoms of psychiatry, great men, and—now—the large corporation style. The flowers are fading, the great men are gone, and the corporations go bankrupt. The people are left, searching for meaning in their lives and faced with a postindustrial society quickly growing out of control. A learning community can start to cope with these problems. The human approach to human problems requires dedicated professionals who are themselves autonomous and willing to join with others in search of the just community.

We can start the processes toward a normative practice of supervision right now if we are willing to make a commitment to attempt to try this approach. Let's review the process.

THE NORMATIVE STANCE

1. GOALS

The goals of supervisory practice are closely related to what the functions and purposes of the social agency ought to be. In general terms these are: (1) helping people arrive at sound judgments regarding what ought to be, all things considered; and (2) securing social arrangements and individual competence in conformity with such judgments. Agencies should be interested in evolving sound, effective, moral, solutions to the problems facing society and their clients. These solutions need to be seen in the context of a restructuring of society for social justice.

You might want to start by asking, If I were to return to this agency five years from now and be able to look in, what would I want to see going on? What type of service? What would supervision look like? Would it look like this?

2. STRUCTURE OF SERVICE

The structure of the agency and the patterning of the interactions within the agency, as well as its relations with other agencies, need to be within the framework of democratic processes and moral behavior; this insures the dignity and respect of all people involved. The structure should permit and encourage the minimizing of the supervisor as expert and should promote the concept of agency as a "just" community.

What would be the base for some of our decision making?

3. KNOWLEDGE BASE

The major mode for the gathering of knowledge to be used in practice needs to be based on scientific inquiry, regardless of whether that practice is counseling, social change, teaching, or supervision. Is our knowledge base grounded in human service practice?

And how are we helping people learn to use this knowledge to make "good" decisions?

4. SYNERGISTIC PROCESSES

Is there a partnership between supervisor-worker, worker-client based on symmetrical relationships, one that permits mutual problem solving without encouraging the development of contest strategies? The problems should not be differentiated or attached to a particular individual or group, but seen as a mutual concern in which each plays a part. Is the agency following the concept of synergy? Are mutually satisfying solutions found when there are two or more conflicting ideas? Are the solutions an advance over the original ideas? What does client and worker autonomy look like?

5. SELF-HELP EDUCATION

Is there an increase in the ability of supervisees to practice in autonomous ways and to permit clients to develop their own self-help resources? Are the values and uses of self-help as well as the dissemination of materials which can be used by the community by either self-help or worker-supported groups being promoted? And, finally, where is the locus of accountability?

6. ACCOUNTABILITY AND GROWTH

Within the normative stance, accountability is not necessarily to a hierarchical structure but to self, peers, clients, and the moral community within which one functions. There is also responsibility for a scientific evaluation of one's work and for a feedback to the broader professional community for its use.

Some of the things you see in your vision can become alternatives to current practice if you are willing to work for your vision, and of course it need not follow all the details of my normative vision. What is important is a commitment to what ought to be.

If we are to have vision, we must learn to participate in the object of the vision. The apprenticeship is hard.

ANTOINE DE SAINT-EXUPÉRY

We must act as well as think, and now that we have some vision of the future we want, it is necessary to take the second step. We must select one thing, no matter how small it may seem, that we as students, workers, or administrators might do to start us toward that vision.

CONCLUSION

We have come full circle. The profession cannot change unless the professionals, particularly those with experience and administrative responsibility—the teachers and supervisors—are willing to operate differently. And they will not operate differently without the commitments and the supports and pressures to do so. Yet the future demands new approaches.

We have tried to establish that supervision is a vital, integrated part of the profession, requiring skill, experience, sensitivity, and commitment. It has been both a creative force for the growth of the profession and a force slowing down and regulating its growth. Perhaps that has been because we have accepted the traditional teaching, enabling, administrative, functions of the supervisor. It may be time for a fourth function, the reconstructional role. This function would highlight the higher moral function, the quest for the "just community." With this as a guide there is little question that the synergistic techniques would play a vital part in the supervisory processes. We are not suggesting that this function replace the others. They are vital to the continued growth of the profession. But we must synergize the new reconstruction function with the old, to achieve something greater. As Jane Addams noted:

> Life has taught me at least one hard-earned lesson, that existing arrangements and the hoped-for improvements must be mediated and reconciled to each other, that the new must be dove-tailed into the old as it were if it were to endure.[33]

The supervisor has a vital role to play in making this profession a leading force in the struggle for a just community. In this he will have the support of the countless numbers of social workers, young and old, who have recognized that regardless of the shortcomings of our profession, there is no other which is prepared to battle the whole society if necessary on behalf of just treatment for all people.

The definition of the word "finished" is: "this word means finished."

(PROVERB)

NOTES

CHAPTER 1

1. *Closing the Gap in Social Work Manpower* (Washington, D.C.: Department of Health, Education and Welfare, 1965), p. 73.
2. Carol H. Meyer, *Staff Development in Public Welfare Agencies* (New York: Columbia University Press, 1966), p. 98.
3. West C. Churchman, *The Systems Approach* (New York: Dell Publishing Co., 1968), p. 25.
4. Daniel Katz and Robert L. Kahn, *The Social Psychology of Organization* (New York: John Wiley & Sons, 1966), pp. 14–29.
5. Ludwig Bertalanffy, "General Systems Theory: A Critical Review," in *Modern Systems Research for the Behavioral Scientist*, ed. Walter Buckley (Chicago: Aldine, 1968), p. 15.
6. See Paul Abels, "The Managers Are Coming! The Managers Are Coming!" *Public Welfare* 31, no. 4 (Fall 1973), p. 13. In addition, the value of systems theory as a way of perceiving things as a whole or in interaction is still unproven. See "General Systems Theory," in *A Current Appraisal of the Behavioral Sciences*, ed. Rollo Handy and E. C. Harwood (Great Barrington, Mass.: Behavioral Research Council, 1973), pp. 118–19.

7. Churchman, *Systems Approach,* p. 11.
8. Garrett Hardin, *Exploring New Ethics for Survival: The Voyage of the Spaceship Beagle* (Baltimore: Penguin Books, 1973), p. 38.
9. For another view of service systems, see Marvin Rosenberg and Ralph Brody, *Systems Serving People* (Cleveland: Case Western Reserve University, School of Applied Social Sciences, 1974).
10. Lillian Rubin, "Maximum Feasible Participation," *Poverty and Human Resources Abstracts* 2, no. 6 (Nov.-Dec. 1967), p. 5.
11. See Erving Goffman, "On Cooling the Mark Out," *Psychiatry* 15, no. 4 (Nov. 1952), pp. 450–63.
12. Max Weber, "Bureaucracy," in A. H. Rubenstein and C. J. Haberstroh, ed. *Some Theories of Organization* (Homewood, Ill.: Irwin, 1959), pp. 65–76.
13. Amitai Etzioni, *Modern Organizations* (Englewood Cliffs, N.J.: Prentice-Hall, Inc., 1964), p. 77.
14. Robert D. Vinter, "The Social Structure of Service," in *Behavioral Science for Social Workers,* ed. Edwin Thomas (New York: The Free Press, 1967), p. 193.
15. Harold L. Wilensky and Charles N. Lebeaux, *Industrial Society and Social Welfare* (New York: The Free Press, 1965), p. 319.
16. See George Homans, *The Human Group* (New York: Harcourt & Brace, 1950), and P. M. Blau, *Exchange and Power in Social Life* (New York: John Wiley & Sons, 1967).
17. See Uriel G. Foa, "Interpersonal and Economic Resources," *Science* 171 (Jan. 29, 1971), p. 320. Foa lists rewards as love, status, information, money, goods, and services; he discusses them in relation to exchange theory.
18. A. H. Maslow, *The Farther Reaches of Human Nature* (New York: Viking Press, 1971), p. 41.
19. Frederick Herzberg *et al., The Motivation to Work* (New York: John Wiley & Sons, 1961), pp. 113–119.
20. Malcolm S. Knowles, *The Modern Practice of Adult Education: Andragogy versus Pedagogy* (New York: Association Press, 1970).
21. Robert J. Lifton, "Psychological Man in Revolution," *Social Change in Human Behavior,* ed. George V. Cochle (Washington, D.C.: NIMH, 1972), p. 80.
22. Charles Hampden-Turner, *Radical Man* (Cambridge, Mass.: Schenkman Publishing Co., 1970), p. 55.
23. Quoted in Dedric Corney, *The Human Agenda* (New York: Bantam Books, 1972), p. 173.
24. Mary P. Follett, "Constructive Conflict," in *Dynamic Administration,* ed. Henry C. Metcalf and L. Urwick (New York: Harper and Row, 1940), p. 32.

25. Hampden-Turner, *Radical Man,* p. 55.
26. *Ibid.*

CHAPTER 2

1. Zilphia D. Smith, "Volunteer Visiting: The Organization Necessary to Make It Effective," *Proceedings of National Association of Charities and Corrections* (Washington, D.C.: 1885), p. 70.
2. *Ibid.*
3. Zilphia D. Smith, "The Education of the Friendly Visitor," *Proceedings of the National Conference of Charities and Corrections* (Denver, 1892), p. 447.
4. Zilphia D. Smith, "Friendly Visitors," *Charities* 7 (Aug. 24, 1901), pp. 159–160.
5. Quoted in Margaret E. Rich, *A Belief in People* (New York: Family Service Association of America, 1956), p. 32.
6. See Evelyn Stiles, "Supervision in Perspective," *Social Casework* 44, no. 1 (Jan. 1963), p. 22.
7. Virginia P. Robinson, *A Changing Psychology in Social Case Work,* (Chapel Hill: University of North Carolina Press, 1930).
8. Grace Marcus, "How Case Work Training May Be Adapted to Meet the Worker's Personal Problems," *Proceedings of the National Conference of Social Work* (Des Moines, 1927), p. 305.
9. Irving Miller, "Supervision in Social Work," *Encyclopedia of Social Work* (New York: NASW, 1971), p. 1494.
10. Marcus, "How Case Work Training May Be Adapted," p. 385.
11. *Ibid.,* p. 386.
12. Eisenberg, *Supervision in the Changing Field of Social Work,* p. 22.
13. Grace Marcus, "The Case Work of Supervision," *Survey* (Aug. 15, 1927), p. 558.
14. Marcus, "How Case Work Training May Be Adapted," p. 386.
15. Caroline Bedford, "An Analysis of the Problem of Case Supervision," *The Family* (Feb. 10, 1930), p. 309.
16. Miller, "Supervision in Social Work," p. 1495.
17. Hedley S. Dimock and Harleigh B. Trecker, *The Supervision of Group Work and Recreation* (New York: Association Press, 1949), p. 3.
18. Margaret Williamson, *Keeping the Vision in Supervision* (New York: The Women's Press, 1944), p. 3.
19. Virginia P. Robinson, *Supervision in Social Case Work* (Chapel Hill: The University of North Carolina Press, 1936), p. 53.
20. Bertha Reynolds, *Learning and Teaching in the Practice of Social Work* (New York: Russell & Russell, 1965), p. 21.

21. Arthur L. Swift, Jr., foreword to Sidney Lindenberg, *Supervision in Social Group Work* (New York: Association Press, 1939), p. viii.

22. Lindenberg, *Supervision in Social Group Work*, p. xii.

23. Charlotte Towle, *Common Human Needs* (Washington, D.C.: Social Security Board, 1945), p. 95.

24. Miller, "Supervision in Social Work," pp. 1495–96.

25. *Ibid.*, p. 1498.

26. Harriet M. Bartlett, "Consultation Regarding the Medical Social Program in a Hospital," in *Consultation: Two Papers* (Menasha, Wisconsin: George Banta Publishing Co., 1942), quoted in "Consultation: Some Guiding Principles," by Doris Siegel, in *Administrative Supervision and Consultation* (New York: Family Association of America, 1955), p. 99.

27. Mary Holmes Gilmore, "Consultation as a Social Work Activity," in *Consultation in Social Work Practice*, ed. Lydia Rappoport (New York: NASW, 1963), pp. 35–36.

28. See, for example, Gerald Caplan, *The Theory and Practice of Mental Health Consultation* (New York: Basic Books, 1970), p. 19.

29. Robert Blauner, reported in Timothy W. Costello and Sheldon S. Zalkind, *Psychology in Administration* (Englewood Cliffs, N.J.: Prentice-Hall, 1963), p. 79.

30. Herzberg, as reported in *ibid.*, p. 95.

31. *Ibid.*, p. 97.

32. Frederick Herzberg *et al.*, *Job Attitudes: Review of Research and Opinion* (Pittsburgh, 1957): adapted from figure 3, p. 44. In order of importance on the job, factors are (1) security; (2) interest (from intrinsic aspects of the job); (3) opportunity for advancement; (4) appreciation (from supervisor); (5) company and management; (6) intrinsic aspects of the job.

33. Frederick Herzberg, Bernard Mausner, and Barbara B. Syderman, *The Motivation to Work* (New York: John Wiley & Sons, 1962), pp. 113–19.

34. One attempt to do this appears in Paul Abels, "The Agency Trained Worker" (doctoral dissertation, University of Chicago, 1962).

35. Bernard Levenson, "Bureaucratic Succession," *Complex Organizations,* ed. Amitai Etzioni (New York: Holt, 1965), p. 369. In discussing the inability of a worker to move up the ladder, Levenson says, "Employees who do not have the economic leverage or the physical vitality to start anew may resign themselves to the fact that they have reached a point of no return. . . . Aware that they must remain on the job despite blocked mobility, they may

gradually lose interest in their work and settle down to a minimum level of performance," p. 369.

36. Robert D. Vinter discusses this in "Report of the Personnel Turnover Study," *The Round Table* (New York: National Federation of Settlements, May-June, 1957), p. 3. He points out that in order of frequency of reasons given, people left social work positions because of: (1) work content (2) staff relations, and (3) personal.

37. See, for example, Nancy Morse, *Satisfaction in the White-Collar Job* (Ann Arbor: University of Michigan Press, 1953); and Herzberg *et al.*, *Job Attitudes.*

38. Leonard I. Pearlin, "Alienation from Work: A Study of Nursing Personnel," *American Sociological Review* 27, no. 3 (June 1962), p. 320.

39. Barry Collins and Harold Guetzkow, *A Social Psychology of Group Process* (New York: John Wiley & Sons, 1964), p. 189.

40. Frank G. Goble, *The Third Force* (New York: Pocket Books, 1971), p. 38.

41. Quoted in Hampden-Turner, *Radical Man,* p. 55.

42. Warren G. Bennis and Philip E. Slater, *The Temporary Society* (New York: Harper Colophon Books, 1969), p. 98.

43. George R. Berkley, *The Administrative Revolution* (Englewood Cliffs, N.J.: Prentice-Hall, 1971), p. 171.

44. *Ibid.,* p. 172.

45. See, for example, Stanley Milgram, "Behavioral Studies of Obedience," *Journal of Abnormal and Social Psychology* 67, no. 4 (1963), p. 371.

46. See Charlotte Towle, "The Role of Supervision in the Union of Cause and Function in Social Work," *Social Service Review* 36, no. 4 (Dec. 1962), p. 404.

47. Paul Abels, "The Managers Are Coming! The Managers Are Coming!" *Public Welfare* 3, no. 4 (Fall 1973), pp. 13–15.

48. Samuel A. Richmond, Sonia Abels, and Paul Abels, "The Normative Model of Social Work," paper presented at NCSW, May 1975.

49. By the concept of primacy we mean that the manner in which one is first taught to do a thing is the way one will usually do it thereafter.

50. Laura Epstein, "Is Autonomous Practice Possible?" *Social Work* 18, no. 2 (Mar. 1973), pp. 5–12. A different arrangement of models in supervisory practice which uses basic education models is presented by Alex Gitterman, "Comparison of Education Models and Their Influences on Supervision," in *Issues in Human Serv-*

ices, ed. Florence Whiteman Kaslow (San Francisco: Jossey-Bass, 1972).

51. Epstein, "Autonomous Practice," p. 10.
52. *Ibid.*
53. *Ibid.*
54. *Ibid.,* p. 11.
55. *Ibid.,* p. 8.
56. *Ibid.,* p. 11.
57. For a comprehensive analysis, see Alfred Stanton and Morris B. Schwartz, *The Mental Hospital* (New York: Basic Books, 1954).
58. This material is adapted from Murray Gruber and Paul Abels, "Organizational Injustice and Domain Conflict," paper presented at NASW Symposium, New Orleans, La., Nov. 1972.
59. See, for example, M. Aiken and J. Hage, "Organizational Alienation: A Comparative Analysis," *American Sociological Review* 21 (Aug. 1966), pp. 497–507.
60. William Tollen, *Study of Staff Losses* (Washington, D.C.: Dept. of Health, Education and Welfare, Children's Bureau, 1960); quoted in Kaslow, *Issues in Human Services,* p. 117.
61. See, for example, Melvin Seeman, "On the Meaning of Alienation," *American Sociological Review* 24 (1959), pp. 783–791.
62. George Konrad *The Caseworker* (New York: Harcourt Brace, 1974), pp. 15–16.
63. Alfred Kadushin, "Games People Play in Supervision," *Social Work* 13, no. 3 (July 1968), p. 23.
64. Aaron Rosenblatt and John E. Mayer, "Objectionable Supervisory Styles: Students' Views," *Social Work* 20, no. 3 (May 1975), p. 184.
65. Charles S. Levy, "The Ethics of Supervision," *Social Work* 18, no. 2 (Mar. 1973), pp. 18–19.
66. Rosenblatt and Mayer, "Objectionable Supervisory Styles," p. 187.
67. *Ibid.*
68. Peter Blau and W. Richard Scott, *Formal Organizations* (San Francisco: Chandler Publishing Co., 1962), pp. 128–129.

CHAPTER 3

1. Kurt Baier, "What Is Value? An Analysis of the Concept," in *Values and the Future,* ed. Kurt Baier and Nicholas Rescher (New York: The Free Press, 1969).
2. Havelock and Havelock consider the principle of synergy to be the following: "When a number of inputs or stimuli from different sources converge on one point." Ronald G. and Mary C. Havelock,

Training for Change Agents (Ann Arbor: Institute for Social Research, 1973), p. 29.

3. Thomas Kuhn, *The Structure of Scientific Revolution* (Chicago: University of Chicago Press, 1962).

4. Charlotte Towle, "The Role of Supervision in the Union of Cause and Function in Social Work," *Social Service Review* 36, no. 4 (Dec. 1962), p. 405.

5. C. Wright Mills, "The Sociological Imagination" and "The Promise," *The Sociological Imagination* (New York: Oxford University Press, 1959), p. 8.

6. Chris Argyris, *On Organizations of the Future* (Beverly Hills: Sage Publications, 1973), p. 1.

7. Amitai Etzioni, *A Comparative Analysis of Complex Organizations* (Glencoe, Ill.: The Free Press, 1961), p. 113.

8. Leonard I. Pearlin, "Alienation from Work: A Study of Nursing Personnel," *American Sociological Review* 27, no. 3 (June 1962), p. 320.

9. William G. Scott, *The Management of Conflict* (Homewood, Ill.: Dorsey Press, 1965), p. 40.

10. Philip Selznick, "Critical Decisions in Organizational Development," in *Complex Organizations*, ed. Amitai Etzioni (New York: Holt, 1965), p. 357.

11. Mary Follet, quoted in Bertram Gross, *The Managing of Organizations* (New York: The Free Press, 1964). "In a true integration of conflicting views, a place is found for each desire and neither side sacrifices anything. In fact both sides gain" (p. 153).

12. E. Wight Bakke, *Bonds of Organization* (New York: Harper & Row, 1950), p. 20.

13. Virginia Robinson, *The Dynamics of Supervision Under Functional Control* (Philadelphia: University of Pennsylvania Press, 1949).

14. Abraham Maslow, *Eupsychian Management* (Homewood, Ill.: Dorsey Press 1965), p. 88.

15. R. Buckminster Fuller, *Synergetics* (New York: Macmillan, 1975).

16. Nena and George O'Neill, *Open Marriage* (New York: Avon Books, 1972), p. 258.

17. *Ibid.*, p. 259.

18. William J. Gordon, *Synectics* (New York: Collier Books, 1961), and George M. Prince, *The Practice of Creativity* (New York: Collier Books, 1970).

19. Gregory Bateson, "The Cybernetics of Self: A Theory of Alcoholism," in *Steps to an Ecology of Mind* (New York: Ballantine Books, 1972), pp. 309–37.

242   The New Practice of Supervision and Staff Development

20. *Ibid.*, p. 313.
21. Lester F. Ward, the sociologist, had defined *synergy* in 1903 as "The systematic and organic working together of the opposing forces of nature." *Pure Sociology* (New York: Macmillan, 1903), and *The Sociology of Lester F. Ward,* ed. Clement Wood (New York: Vanguard Press, 1930), p. 183.
22. Ruth Benedict, "Patterns of the Good Culture," *Psychology Today* 4, no. 1 (June 1970), p. 54.
23. *Ibid.*
24. See Alfred Kadushin, "Games People Play in Supervision," *Social Work* 13, no. 3 (July 1968), p. 23.
25. Benedict, "Patterns of the Good Culture," p. 55.
27. For further comments on this idea, see Maslow, *Eupsychian Management,* p. 15.
28. Mary E. Brassel, Student paper on synergy, School of Applied Social Sciences, Case Western Reserve University, Dec. 4, 1974, p. 5.
29. Carl R. Rogers, "The Person of Tomorrow," Sonoma State College, Commencement Address, June 7, 1969 (mimeo).
30. See the work of the Tavistock Clinic, particularly W. R. Bion, *Experiences in Groups* (New York: Ballantine Books, 1974).
31. Seymour Melman, "Industrial Efficiency Under Managerial vs. Cooperative Decision-Making: A Comparative Study of Manufacturer Enterprises in Israel," *The Review of Radical Political Economics* 2, no. 1 (Spring 1970), p. 9.
32. Ivan Illich, *Medical Nemesis,* Cuernavaca, Mexico (CIDOC, 1974).
33. Samuel A. Richmond, Sonia Leib Abels, and Paul Abels, "The Normative Model of Social Work," paper presented at NCSW, May 1975, p. 12.
34. See Gregory Bateson's analysis of complementary and symmetrical relationships as a basis for conflict, in "The Cybernetics of Self," p. 309.

CHAPTER 4

1. For various conceptions of "passage" as a theoretical and analytical tool, see Barney G. Glaser and Anselm L. Strauss, *Status Passage* (Chicago: Aldine, 1971).
2. Bertha Reynolds, *Learning and Teaching in the Practice of Social Work* (New York: Russell & Russell, 1965), p. 305.
3. Herbert Thelen, "Emotionality and Work in Groups," in *The State of the Social Sciences,* ed. L. D. White (Chicago: University of Chicago Press, 1956), p. 10.

4. Jerome S. Bruner, *Toward a Theory of Instruction* (Cambridge: Harvard University Press, 1966), p. 23.

5. Wilfred R. Bion, *Experience in Groups* (New York: Basic Books, 1961), p. 14.

6. Barney G. Glaser and Anselm L. Strauss, *Awareness of Dying* (Chicago: Aldine, 1965).

7. Kurt Lewin, "Group Decision and Social Change," in *Readings in Social Psychology,* ed. Eleanor Maccoby and Theodore Newcomb (New York: Henry Holt, 1952), p. 57.

8. Ernest Becker, in *Beyond Alienation,* interprets history as a struggle to find meaning with others (New York: George Braziller, 1967).

9. R. G. H. Siu, *The Tao of Science* (Cambridge: M.I.T. Press, 1957), p. 73.

10. Paul Abels, "Playing It Straight: The Social Work Contract," presentation, NASW, Cleveland chapter, 1967 (mimeo).

11. See, for example, Frank Riesman, "The Helper Therapy Principle," *Social Work* 10, no. 2 (Apr. 1965), p. 27.

12. By *contrived* we mean "created experiences which may reflect reality, but in fact never provide the 'for realness' that training through actual contact with the client permits."

13. Alan Wheelis, *How People Change* (New York: Harper & Row, 1974), p. 130.

14. Reynolds, *Learning and Teaching,* pp. 69–85.

15. George Braeger, "A First Conference with an Inexperienced Group Leader," *The Group* 16 (Dec. 3, 1953), p. 5.

16. See E. Fuller Torrey, *The Death of Psychiatry* (New York: Penguin Books, 1974), p. 115, and Ernest Becker, *Revolution in Psychiatry* (New York: The Free Press, 1974), p. 38.

17. Karl Deutsch, "What Do Our New Computers Tell Us About the Way Our Children Grow?" *Child Study* 36, no. 3 (Summer 1959), p. 25.

18. J. S. Bruner, *Theory of Instruction,* pp. 129–30.

19. Idries Shah, *The Sufis* (New York: Anchor Books, 1971), p. 85.

20. Hilda C. Arndt, "The Learner in Field Work," *Education for Social Work* (New York: Council on Social Work Education, Proceedings 1956), p. 40.

21. For a comprehensive view of relationship and individualization, see Charlotte Towle, *The Learner in Education for the Professions* (University of Chicago Press, 1954).

22. Margaret Mead, *Cultural Patterns and Technical Change* (New York: Mentor Books, 1955), p. 56.

23. The University Settlement in Cleveland, for example, had as its

origin the idea of a commune for women. For further reading of the settlement as a working-learning community, see *Readings in the Development of Settlement Work*, ed. Leone M. Paley (New York: Association Press, 1950).

24. Ronald Lippitt, Jeanne Watson and Bruce Westley, *The Dynamics of Planned Change* (New York: Harcourt Brace, 1958), p. 131.

25. Ronald G. Havelock, *Planning for Innovation* (Ann Arbor: Institute for Social Research, 1973), pp. 11–42.

26. Kurt Lewin, *Resolving Social Conflict* (New York: Harper, 1951), and Kurt Lewin, "Group Decision and Social Change," in *Readings in Social Psychology*.

27. Kurt Lewin, "Group Decision and Social Change," p. 57.

28. John D. Ingalls, *A Trainer's Guide to Andragogy* (Washington, D.C.: Superintendent of Documents, 1972), p. 39.

29. Sonia L. Abels, "Assignment on Method of Ethical Decisions," Department of Social Services, Cleveland State University, 1973 (mimeo).

30. *Ibid.*, p. 2.

31. Harold L. Wilensky and Charles N. Lebeaux, *Industrial Society and Social Welfare* (New York: The Free Press, 1965), pp. 241–242.

32. Mary Hester, "Educational Process in Supervision," *Social Casework* 32, no. 6 (June 1951), p. 246.

33. A comprehensive review of this material, as well as an assessment of paraprofessional performances, can be found in Alan Gartner, *Paraprofessionals and Their Performance* (New York: Praeger, 1971). Workers without MSW's were at one time (early sixties) considered paraprofessionals. Since the B.A. in Social Work became the first "professional" degree, the word *paraprofessional* refers to those with less than a formal B.A. education.

34. Arthur Pearl and Frank Riessman, *New Careers for the Poor* (New York: The Free Press, 1965), pp. 144, 167.

35. We see this in Nader's groups, anti- and pro-abortion groups, Common Cause, and political movements.

36. For a comprehensive view of evaluation, see Reynolds, *Learning and Teaching*, p. 267.

37. Muriel W. Pumphrey, *The Teaching of Values and Ethics in Social Work Education* (New York: Council on Social Work Education, 1959).

38. Robert L. Beck and John A. Orr, *Ethical Choice* (New York: The Free Press, 1970).

39. Charles S. Levy, "The Ethics of Supervision," *Social Work* 18, no. 2 (March 1973), p. 20.

40. *NASW Standards for Social Work Personnel Practices* (New York: NASW, 1971), p. 9.
41. *Ibid.*, p. 13.
42. *Ibid.*, pp. 13–15.
43. For a more comprehensive view, see Sonia Abels, Samuel Richmond, and Paul Abels, "Ethics Shock," *Journal of Sociology and Social Welfare* 2, no. 2 (Winter, 1972), p. 40.

CHAPTER 5

1. George Homans, *The Human Group* (New York: Harcourt Brace, 1950), pp. 1–3.
2. C. West Churchman, *The Systems Approach* (New York: Dell Publishing Co., 1968), p. 11.
3. James David Barber, *Power in Committees: An Experiment in the Governmental Process* (Chicago: Rand McNally, 1966), p. 11.
4. Richard Heslin and Dexter Dunphy, "Three Dimensions of Member Satisfaction in Small Groups," *Human Relations* 20 (1967), p. 101.
5. Herbert A. Thelen, *Dynamics of Groups at Work* (Chicago: University of Chicago Press, 1954), p. 222.
6. Donald Klein, *Community Dynamics and Mental Health* (New York: John Wiley & Sons, 1968), p. 35.
7. Erving Goffman, *Asylums* (New York: Doubleday Anchor Book, 1961), p. 175.
8. Wilfred R. Bion, *Experience in Groups* (New York: Basic Books, 1961), p. 81.
9. See, for example, Nelson B. Henry, *The Dynamics of Instructional Groups* (Chicago: University of Chicago Press, 1960); Herbert A. Thelen, *Dynamics of Groups at Work* (Chicago: University of Chicago Press, 1954); and Eileen Blackey, *Group Leadership in Staff Training* (Washington, D.C.: Department of Health, Education, and Welfare, 1957).
10. For discussion of self-actualization as the essential and basic drive, see Kurt Goldstein, *Human Nature in the Light of Psychopathology* (New York: Schocken Books, 1963), p. 25; and Robert W. White, *Psychological Review* 66, no. 5 (1969), p. 329.
11. Jack R. Gibb, "Socio-psychological Processes of Group Instruction," in *The Dynamics of Instructional Groups*, ed. Nelson B. Henry (Chicago: University of Chicago Press, 1960), p. 127.
12. The nature of the social work contract with both groups and individuals is discussed in Paul Abels, "The Social Work Contract: Playing It Straight" (1967; mimeo).

13. For discussion of the difficulties certain "content" may create for students, see Bernard Bandler, "Ego-Centered Teaching," *Smith College Studies in Social Work* 30, no. 2 (Feb. 1960), and the discussion by Jerome Bruner, "Perspective Metaphors," in *Toward a Theory of Instruction*, 1966, pp. 134–38.

14. Gisela Konopka, *Social Group Work* (Englewood, N.J.: Prentice-Hall, 1963), p. 109.

CHAPTER 6

1. Material for the Thelen model is from Professor Thelen's courses at the University of Chicago, from *Education and the Human Quest* (New York: Harper, 1960), and *Dynamics of Groups at Work* (Chicago: University of Chicago Press, 1954).

2. *Learning and Teaching in Public Welfare.* Vol. 1: *Report of the Cooperative Project on Public Welfare Staff Training* (Annandale, Virginia: Turnpike Press, 1963), p. 6.

3. *Building the Social Work Curriculum* (New York: CSWE, 1960).

4. Ralph W. Tyler, "In-Service Training Problems and Needs," *Planning In-Service Training Programs for Mental Health*, Region VI Conference, Omaha, Nebraska (Dec. 1963).

5. Malcolm S. Knowles, *The Modern Practice of Adult Education* (New York: Association Press, 1970), and John D. Ingalls, *A Trainer's Guide to Andragogy* (Washington, D.C.: Superintendent of Documents, 1972).

6. Ingalls, *Trainer's Guide*, p. 11.

7. Marshall McLuhan, *Understanding Media: The Extensions of Man* (New York: Signet Books, 1966), p. 36.

8. We will use *teacher* interchangeably with *trainer* or *supervisor* in support of the theme that a major task of the supervisor is teaching.

9. B. Othaniel Smith, "A Concept of Teaching," in B. Othaniel Smith and Robert H. Ennis, *Language and Concepts in Education* (Chicago: Rand McNally and Co., 1971), p. 88.

10. A comprehensive discussion of influences on teacher behavior patterns is presented by Norman E. Wallen and Robert M. W. Travers in "Analysis and Investigation of Teaching Methods" in *Handbook of Research on Teaching*, ed. N. L. Gage (New York: Rand McNally, 1963).

11. Charlotte Towle, "The Role of Supervision in the Union of Cause and Function in Social Work," *Social Service Review* 36, no. 4 (Dec. 1962), p. 390.

12. For a comprehensive analysis of the "organizer" role, see J.

Richard Suchman, "The Pursuit of Meaning: Models for the Study of Inquiry," in *Behavioral Science Frontiers in Education*, ed. Eli M. Bower and William G. Hollister (New York: John Wiley & Sons, 1967).

13. *Ibid.*, p. 487.
14. Karl Deutsch, "What Do Our New Computers Tell Us About the Way Children Grow?" *Child Study* 36, no. 3 (Summer, 1959), p. 25.
15. Jerome S. Bruner, *Toward a Theory of Instruction* (Cambridge: Harvard University Press, 1966), pp. 113–28.
16. Jerome S. Bruner, "On Cognitive Growth," in *Studies in Cognitive Growth* (New York: John Wiley & Sons, 1966), p. 6.
17. R. W. White, "Motivation Reconsidered: The Concept of Competence," *Psychological Review* 66 (1959), p. 329.
18. Suchman, "Pursuit of Meaning," p. 484.
19. *Ibid.*
20. J. S. Bruner, "The Act of Discovery," *Harvard Educational Review* 31 (1961), pp. 21–32.
21. J. Richard Suchman, "Building Skills for Autonomous Discovery," *Merrill-Parmer Quarterly* 7, no. 3 (July 1961), p. 148.
22. Carl C. Rogers, "Student-Centered Teaching," in his *Client-Centered Therapy* (Boston: Houghton Mifflin, 1965), p. 427.
23. Herbert A. Thelen, "Some Classroom Quiddities for People-Oriented Teachers," *Journal of Applied Behavioral Science* 10 (1974), p. 282.
24. Jerome S. Bruner, *The Process of Education* (New York: Vintage Books, 1960), pp. 81–82.
25. These are discussed in *Social Work Education Reporter* 16, no. 3 (Sept., 1968), p. 24.
26. Bruner, *Process of Education*, pp. 81–82.
27. See, for example, Alan F. Klein, *Role-Playing in Leadership Training and Group Problem Solving* (New York: Association Press, 1959), and Lila Swell, "Role-Playing in the Context of Learning Theory in Casework Teaching," *Journal of Education for Social Work* 4, no. 1 (Spring, 1968), p. 70.
28. Using persons designated as "alter egos," as is done by psychodramatists, is an example of this technique.
29. Adapted from Paul Abels, "Simulation: A Mini-Annotated Bibliography," Case Western Reserve University, School of Applied Social Sciences (Nov., 1968; mimeo).
30. Bruner, *Process of Education*, p. 72.
31. A number of articles dealing with the use of television and videotapes have appeared in the *Social Work Education Reporter*:

Reba Ann Beughoter, Charles Garetz, and Pringle Smith, "The Use of Closed T.V. and Video-Tape in the Training of Social Group Workers" 15, no. 1 (Mar., 1967); "Use of Open Circuit T.V. in Teaching Social Welfare" 16, no. 3 (Sept., 1968), p. 24.

32. "New Audio Tapes on Poverty," *Social Work Education Reporter* 16, no. 3 (Sept., 1968).

33. See, for example, Nelson B. Henry, ed., *The Dynamics of Instructional Groups* (Chicago: University of Chicago Press, 1960), p. 25. Herbert Thelen, "Group Interactional Factors in Learning"; W. J. McKeachie, "Research on Teaching at the College and University Level," in Nathaniel Less Gage, *Handbook of Research on Teaching* (Chicago: Rand McNally, 1962), pp. 1133–1139.

34. *Report of the Committee on the Student in Higher Education* (New Haven: The Hazen Foundation, Jan., 1968), p. 12.

35. Thelen, "Classroom Quiddities," p. 277.

36. For a further discussion on the use of group in supervision, see Paul Abels, "The Medium Is the Group" (Case Western Reserve University, School of Applied Social Sciences, 1967; mimeo).

37. James V. Clark, *Education for the Use of Behavioral Science* (Los Angeles: University of California, Institute of Industrial Relations, 1962), p. 61.

38. Kenneth Keniston, "Youth, Change and Violence," *American Scholar* 37, no. 2 (Spring, 1968), p. 234.

39. Bertha Reynolds, *Learning and Teaching in the Practice of Social Work* (New York: Russell & Russell, 1965), p. 120.

40. The material based on the role of the nurse group worker appears more fully in Paul Abels and Serapio Zalba, *Training the Nurse in Psychiatric Group Work* (Sagamore Hills Children's Psychiatric Hospital, Sagamore Hills, Ohio, 1970) mimeo. The evaluative materials were prepared by them for the program.

41. Wilfred R. Bion, *Experiences in Groups* (New York: Basic Books, 1959).

42. Eric Berne, *Games People Play* (New York: Grove Press, 1964).

43. R. G. H. Siu, *The Tao of Science* (Cambridge, Mass.: M.I.T. Press, 1957), p. 150.

CHAPTER 7

1. Charles A. Reich, *The Greening of America* (New York: Random House, 1970).

2. Marcus Raskin, *Being and Doing* (Boston: Beacon Press, 1973), p. 260.

3. Jules Henry, *Culture Against Man* (New York: Random House Vintage Book), p. 474.

4. Allen Wheelis, *How People Change* (New York: Harper & Row, 1974), p. 115.
5. R. G. H. Siu, *The Tao of Science* (Cambridge, Mass.: M.I.T. Press, 1957), p. 139.
6. Lao-tzu, *Tao-te-ching*, p. 33.
7. Confucius.
8. Morris Stambler and Chester Pearlman, "Supervision as Revelation of the Pattern: I Ching Comments on 'The Open Door,'" *Family Process* 13, no. 3 (Sept. 1974). They comment: "The I Ching (Book of Changes) is a three- to four-thousand-year-old classic of both Confucian and Taoist philosophy which was used as an oracle" (p. 371).
9. *The I Ching*, trans. Richard Wilhelm (Princeton: Princeton University Press, 1973), p. 48.
10. Stambler and Pearlman, p. 375.
11. Carl C. Jung, in his introduction to the I Ching, states: "He who is not pleased by it does not have to use it, and he who is against it is not obliged to find it true. Let it go forth into the world for the benefit of those who can discern its meaning" (p. xxxix).
12. Ivan Illich, *Tools for Conviviality* (New York: Harper & Row, 1973).
13. Catherine P. Pappell and Beulah Rothman, "Social Group Work Models: Possession and Heritage," *Education for Social Work* 2, no. 1 (Fall, 1966), p. 66.
14. Joseph W. Eaton, "Community Development Ideologies," *International Review of Community Development*, no. 11 (1963), p. 37.
15. The concepts of status versus contract were first discussed by Henry Maine, *Ancient Law* (Boston: Beacon Press, 1963; reprinted from 1861 edition). Its influence on Tonnies and Durkheim is discussed by Robert Redfield in *The Little Community* (Chicago: University of Chicago Press, 1961), pp. 132–48.
16. Robert Vinter, "Social Group Work," in *Encyclopedia of Social Work* (New York: National Association of Social Work, 1965), p. 720.
17. See, for example, Charles Silberman, *Crises in Black and White* (New York: Random House, 1964), p. 312; and Robert Perlman and David Jones, *Neighborhood Service Centers* (Washington, D.C.: U.S. Department of Health, Education, and Welfare, 1967), p. 5.
18. R. G. H. Siu, *The Tao of Science* (Cambridge, Mass.: M.I.T. Press, 1957), pp. 150–55.
19. John Mitchel, *The View Over Atlantis* (New York: Ballantine Books, 1972), p. 1.

20. See Donald T. Cambell, "On the Genetics of Altruism and the Counter-Hedonic Components in Human Culture," *Journal of Social Issues* 28, no. 3 (1972), p. 21.

21. Doris Lessing, "A Revolution," *New York Times,* August 22, 1975, p. 32. See also Idries Shah, *The Sufis* (New York: Anchor Books, 1971).

22. John Friedman, *Retracking America* (New York: Anchor Books, 1973).

23. Ivan Illich, *Medical Nemesis* (Mexico: CIDOC, 1973).

24. Adapted from the Richmond, Abels and Abels paper on normative social work practice (see chapter 2, note 48).

25. Kurt Baier and Nicholas Rescher, *Values and the Future* (New York: The Free Press, 1969), p. 33.

26. J. R. Pasteel and R. J. Stahl, *Value Clarification in the Classroom* (Palisades, California: Goodyear Publishing Co., Inc., 1975), p. 1.

27. *Ibid.,* p. 2.

28. Lawrence Kohlberg *et al., The Just Community Approach to Corrections: A Manual* (Cambridge, Mass.: Harvard University Press, 1970), pp. 1–2.

29. *Ibid.,* p. 6.

30. *Ibid.,* p. 7.

31. Samuel A. Richmond, Harry Butler, and Sonia Abels, "The Logic and Justice of Social Practice," paper presented at CSWE, Chicago, 1975 (mimeo).

32. Lawrence Kohlberg, "Stage and Sequence: The Cognitive Development Approach to Socialization," in *Handbook of Socialization Theory and Research,* ed. David A. Goslin (New York: Rand McNally, 1969), p. 375.

33. Jane Addams, *Twenty Years at Hull-House* (New York: New American Library, 1961), p. 234.

INDEX